The Fictional Father

The Fictional Father

Lacanian Readings of the Text

Edited by Robert Con Davis

The University of Massachusetts Press

Amherst, 1981

Copyright © 1981 by
The University of Massachusetts Press
All rights reserved
Printed in the United States of America
Library of Congress Cataloging in Publication Data
Main entry under title:
The Fictional father.
    Includes index.
    1. Fathers in literature—Addresses, essays,
lectures.   2. American fiction—History and criticism—
Addresses, essays, lectures.   3. English fiction—
History and criticism—Addresses, essays, lectures.
4. Psychoanalysis and literature—Addresses, essays,
lectures.   5. Lacan, Jacques, 1901–   Addresses,
essays, lectures.   I. Davis, Robert Con, 1948–
PS374.F35F5   813'.009'3520431   80-26222
ISBN 0-87023-111-1

Grateful acknowledgment is made for permission to reprint the following copyrighted material:

Excerpts from *The Dead Father*, by Donald Barthelme, copyright © 1975 by Donald Barthelme, reprinted by permission of Farrar, Straus and Giroux, Inc., and by permission of International Creative Management.

Excerpts from *The Sound and the Fury, Absalom, Absalom!*, and *Sartoris*, by William Faulkner, copyright by Random House, Inc., and reprinted by their permission.

Excerpts from *The Odyssey*, by Homer, translated by Robert Fitzgerald, copyright © 1961 by Robert Fitzgerald. Reprinted by permission of Doubleday and Company, Inc.

The selection from *Doubling and Incest/Repetition and Revenge*, by John T. Irwin, originally published by The Johns Hopkins University Press; copyright by The Johns Hopkins University Press and used by their permission.

"Post-Modern Paternity: Donald Barthelme's *The Dead Father*," by Robert Con Davis, was first published in *Delta*, Montpellier, France.

A shorter version of "Fathers in Faulkner," by André Bleikasten, was published in *Revue Française d'Etudes Américaines* 8 (October 1979), under the title, "Les maîtres Fantômes, paternité et filiation dans les romans de Faulkner."

The following essays are printed here for the first time, courtesy of their authors:

"Fathers in Faulkner," by permission of André Bleikasten.

" 'The Captive King': The Absent Father in Melville's Text," by permission of Régis Durand.

"Paternity and the Subject in *Bleak House*," by permission of Thomas A. Hanzo.

"A Clown's Inquest into Paternity: Fathers, Dead or Alive; in *Ulysses* and *Finnegans Wake*," by permission of Jean-Michel Rabaté.

Acknowledgments

The contributors to this volume deserve more than the credit contributors usually get, as they all helped me with my job as editor. John T. Irwin, for example, for some time has encouraged and supported the development of this book, for which I am very grateful. Also, Régis Durand, in particular, did much to shape the book at its inception, as he introduced me to the work of Jean-Michel Rabaté and André Bleikasten, and he generously helped me to learn through his knowledge of contemporary critical thought in France. I thank him heartily. I also thank Jean-Michel Rabaté and André Bleikasten for help beyond the writing of their good essays. To Thomas A. Hanzo I have heavy and welcome debts, indeed. From him I have learned and continue to learn about literary criticism and literature. My debt to him mounts constantly. The Department of English at the University of California at Davis supported me while this book was being prepared and then typed and retyped the manuscript. Also, the Office of Research Administration at the University of Oklahoma on short notice gave support for the final preparation of the book. I deeply appreciate the support and trust of these two universities.

Melanie Ruth Collins I thank for her careful reading of parts of this book and for her belief in me. To her, and to Thomas A. Hanzo, this book is dedicated.

Robert Con Davis

About the Contributors

THOMAS A. HANZO teaches English and American literature and critical theory at the University of California, Davis, where he is the department chair. His recent publications include essays on science fiction and fantasy.

RÉGIS DURAND teaches American literature at the Université des lettres et des sciences humaines de Lille III. He recently published, in France, *Melville, Signes et Métaphores* (Lausanne: L'Age d'Homme, 1980).

JEAN-MICHEL RABATÉ teaches English and American literature at the Université de Dijon. He has published on James Joyce before and is currently working on the poetry of Ezra Pound.

ANDRÉ BLEIKASTEN teaches American literature at the Université de Strasbourg. He has published on modern literature, and two of his books on Faulkner have come out in the U.S.

JOHN T. IRWIN is chair of The Writing Seminars at The Johns Hopkins University. Most recently he published *American Hieroglyphics: The Symbol of the Egyptian Hieroglyphics in the American Renaissance* (New Haven and London: Yale University Press, 1980).

ROBERT CON DAVIS teaches American literature and critical theory at the University of Oklahoma, Norman. He recently has published articles on the family and the father as aspects of narrative.

Contents

Paternity Suit(e)

1   It's a wise child that knows its own father. (*The Odyssey*)

2   I and the Father are one. (John 10:30)

3   I said to the almond tree: "Speak to me of God."
And the almond tree blossomed.

    God Speaks

Whoever seeks me finds me,
Whoever finds me knows me,
Whoever knows me loves me,
Whoever loves me, I love,
Whomever I love, I kill.

(Sidna Ali the Moslem, quoted in Nikos Kazantzakis'
The Fratricides)

4   Yea, but a man in the darke, if chaunces do wincke,
As soone he smites his father as any other man,
Because for lacke of light discerne him he ne can.
(*Gammer Gurton's Needle*)

5   Thus when I shun Scylla, your father, I
fall into Charybdis, your mother.
(*Merchant of Venice*)

6   Love cools, friendship
falls off, brothers divide: in cities, mutinies;.in countries,
discord; in palaces, treason; and the bond crack'd
'twixt son and father. (*King Lear*)

7   Thus did the Will, the emancipator, become a torturer; and
on all that is capable of suffering it taketh revenge, because it
cannot go backward.

This, yea this alone is *revenge* itself: the Will's antipathy
to time, and its "It was."

"And this itself is justice, the law of time—that he must
devour his children": thus did madness preach.
(*Thus Spake Zarathustra*)

8   Many of the historical proverbs have a doubtful paternity.
(*Letters and Social Aims*, Emerson)

9   Fatherhood, in the sense of conscious begetting, is unknown
to man. It is a mystical estate, an apostolic succession, from
only begetter to only begotten. On that mystery and not on
the madonna which the cunning Italian intellect flung to the
mob of Europe the church is founded and founded irremov-
ably because founded, like the world, macro- and microcosm, upon the void. Upon incertitude, upon unlikelihood.
Amor matris, subjective and objective genitive, may be the
only true thing in life. Paternity may be a legal fiction. Who
is the father of any son that any son should love him or he
any son? (*Ulysses*)

10   I had dug up the truth and the truth always kills the father,
the good and weak one or the bad and strong one, and you
are left alone with yourself and the truth, and can never ask
Dad, who didn't know anyway and who is deader than
mackerel. (*All the King's Men*)

11   . . . not out of vengeance have I accomplished all my sins but because something has always been close to dying in my soul, and I've sinned only in order to lie down in darkness and find, somewhere in the net of dreams, a new father, a new home. (*Lie Down in Darkness*)

12   The father is a motherfucker. (*The Dead Father*)

The Fictional Father

Critical Introduction:

The Discourse of the Father

ROBERT CON DAVIS

Critical movements, like people, develop in a pattern of youth, maturity, and decline. The good ones, also like people, often leave healthy offspring behind and then pass away spent but well used. Russian formalism, for example, can claim a measure of parental influence on the diverse movement that is called structuralism in literature. Russian formalism contributed characteristics to its progeny, suggestions about the differences between diachronic and synchronic analyses, but the result is a critical entity not identical to the parent. What does not happen very often is the virtual rebirth of a movement that has died. Most notably, one thinks of the reappearance of classicism in its many guises, from the early Renaissance Aristotelians through the early twentieth century and the new humanists. But even that example does not quite fit, as a few strong relatives always thrived while the next generation of neo-classicists were being conceived. More the special case is psychoanalytic criticism, with which the situation is not clear-cut either, but in which something very like a rebirth has occurred since the late 1960s. A first generation of Freudian interpretation in America continued until that time and included some of the better critical minds of the twentieth century, such as Edmund Wilson, Lionel Trilling, Simon O. Lesser, Frederick Crews, and Norman Holland, among others. This movement began to flounder at middle century, as did Jungian criticism and "new criticism," largely because of an inability to go beyond thematic comment and to confront literary structure. Then, a reborn literary Freudianism, based initially on the suggestions of Jacques Lacan's seminar papers, started in France in the late 1960s. Bearing little similarity to the earlier Freudianism, this offspring seemed not to be an offspring at all but a direct descendant from the parent's origin—like a child who takes characteristics nearly directly from its grandfather.

The maturity of the new Freudian criticism in America can be gauged according to its usefulness as practical criticism—as interpretation. For example, Anthony Wilden published an English translation and study of Jacques Lacan's *Discours de Rome* in 1968,[1] but it was not until John T. Irwin's study in 1975 of several novels by William Faulkner[2] that a new Freudian criticism was clearly alive in America. Since the publication of Irwin's book, a great many have seen that a symbolic triadic relationship—the family—stands at the center of French Freud's paradigm for defining the literary text, and that the allegorizing tendency of an older Freudian paradigm (one that would say, "this character's greed is the surface of what at another level is anal retentiveness") has little import for the new thought.

The Fictional Father is directed to what is likely the ideal subject of the new criticism—the father in fiction—for central to Lacanian thought is the concept of the "symbolic father," the agency of law. In the course of my work on the symbolic father, as I pursued French Freud through Jacques Lacan, Jean Laplanche, Anika Lemaire, Anthony Wilden, John T. Irwin, and many others, and after I made my own cautious and tentative gestures toward Lacan's influence,[3] I realized that the best theoretical criticism on the subject of the father, while much discussed in France, was largely alien to an American readership. Curious to see if a larger channel to French thought could be opened, I sought prominent French Freudians and asked if they would write for an American audience. I found willing critical emissaries in Régis Durand (on Herman Melville), André Bleikasten (on William Faulkner), and Jean-Michel Rabaté (on James Joyce), each capable of explaining Lacanian Freudianism in practical criticism of well-known writers. Next, I approached Thomas A. Hanzo, who I knew was deeply engaged in applying Lacanian and Derridian hermeneutics to the fiction of Charles Dickens, and found another willing interpreter. To the four statements of these critics, I added my essay on Donald Barthelme (previously published only in France) and an illuminating section from John T. Irwin's study of Faulkner. These six essays—all focused on a theory of the father in narrative—make a coherent and searching appraisal both of the fictional father and of the literary criticism derived mainly from Jacques Lacan's work. The result is a book that defines the fictional father according to the operations of the symbolic father in a radical psychoanalysis.

The major theoretical premise underlying these six essays can be called a *psychoanalytic anthropomorphism of the text*. I will demonstrate what this statement means in a discussion of *The Odyssey*'s narrative structure. In short, the pronouncement says that a Freudian theory of certain laws of transformation suggests a paradigm for textuality—for the structural relations within a text. Since the operations of the psychoanalytic subject and the text are synonymous—rather, since textuality is an inscription of the subject—many of the same laws govern both. So, a literary narrative shows aspects of such unconscious processes as seduction, primal scene, and castration—the operations of repression—and these operations (as corresponding functions in narrative) constitute the fictional substance of a text, what the Russian formalists called the text's "literariness." At base, the six essays in this book require one to grapple with the "literariness" of the father as a fictional concept in relation to three closely linked axioms of Lacanian thought: (1) that the question of the father in fiction, in whatever guise, is essentially one of father absence; (2) that each manifestation of the father in a text is a refinding of an absent father; (3) and that the father's origin is to be found in the trace of his absence. I will take up these cryptic pronouncements, one at a time, in my consideration of *The Odyssey* in order to show one version of how they fit together in a theory of the fictional father and to clear the way for the essays that follow. While I cannot pretend to speak for the critics in this book and do not presume to explain them, I can show how a complex narrative manifests structural absence and the symbolic authority of the father—concepts important to all six critics—and, further, what a Lacanian theory of the father implies about the nature of narrative.

II

"Through the word—already a presence made of absence—
absence itself comes to giving itself a name in that moment of origin."
(Jacques Lacan, "The Function of Language in Psychoanalysis")

We can look to the beginning of *The Odyssey* for the staging of a Lacanian scene. Here we find a "problem" to be solved in the same sense that Vladimir Propp speaks of a narrative's problematic beginning; it is the problem for which the completed narrative will be the solution. Very early in the epic, Athena introduces the epic's central dilemma—thematic and structural—when she asks Telémakhos, "Who is your father?" The boy, having grown up without a father, cannot at once answer her question with any certainty. Yet, the asking of the question coincides with other significant occurrences, with Odysseus' release from Kalypso's island and with Penélopê's rekindled interest in her husband's return. In other words, a process concerning paternity is set in motion. Shortly thereafter, with the help of Zeus, Father of Men, Odysseus arrives in Ithaka where he reenters his kingdom with the support of Telémakhos. Then, after killing Penélopê's suitors, rejoining his wife, doing obeisance to his own father, and making peace with the suitors' relatives, Odysseus rules once again, father and king home from a ten-year adventure after the Trojan Wars. Therefore, what begins in the epic with father absence, and with Telémakhos' predicament of powerlessness and frustration as he watches his home besieged by his mother's suitors, moves through a transforamtion that ultimately reinstates Odysseus as the representative of paternal authority.

But why, one may wonder, should there be so much initial emphasis in *The Odyssey* on the son? The first four books are devoted to Telémakhos and his domestic troubles. And since the twenty-four books of the epic, as Robert Fitzgerald notes, divide into six "waves of action" (four books each), one full portion of the epic (one sixth of the whole) shows Telémakhos struggling with the suitors.[4] As we consider that the action of the twenty-four books will mount until Odysseus acts decisively to regain his family and throne in books 21 through 24, it is puzzling that considerable space is given to develop many aspects of Telémakhos' frustration at home that do not contribute directly to the major action, Odysseus' return, because in book 5 attention shifts abruptly away from Telémakhos and toward Odysseus, never fully returning to the son. What is the relationship of the Telemakhiad to what follows it?

Telémakhos' home and land are violated by his mother's suitors who, like competitive brothers, conspire to ravage the estate and to destroy Telémakhos as its defender. Thus, Telémakhos is a son in trouble whose foremost responsibility is to seek his father's help. In order to survive, he needs to assert his claim as Odysseus' true heir; yet he cannot find the strength he needs to act effectively. His attempts to inquire after his father and to hasten his return are ineffectual. He cannot recognize his father even when they do meet, although reunion is an occasion to satisfy his deepest needs. And when father and son dispatch the suitors, Telémakhos mainly assists Odysseus' efforts instead of measurably extending his own. It is especially clear in the first four books that, deprived of power in the absence of his father, Telémakhos is rendered immobile in the face of hostile events. A young man able to recognize his need, or lack of power, yet unable to act, he keeps a melancholy watch at his father's empty place and yearns for the power to fill it.

The source of his paralysis is explained in part by his reply to Athena's question—"Who is your father?" Seeming to address the ultimate reference of the question, the boy replies to her: "I know not / surely. Who has known his own engendering?"[5] In the traditional and better known translation, he replies to the question in an aphorism as old as it is familiar: "for myself I cannot tell. It's a wise child that knows its own father."[6] In both versions, his emphasis is clear: he highlights his own predicament in confronting his father's absence and claims that though he cannot know his origin absolutely, yet he believes that wisdom resides in possessing the knowledge of origins connected with fatherhood. Answering as he does, he establishes the terms of a dilemma in which one is a "wise child" by virtue of knowing one's father, a task that he defines as problematical. Above all, the logic of his answer asserts that the father's absence creates a predicament wherein a son must discover wisdom within the limitations of his own efforts.

The epic associates sonship, then, with restricted action. Nevertheless, as soon as we try to contrast Telémakhos' status with Odysseus' in any simple way, say, in the opposition of weak (the powerless son) and powerful (the potent father), contradictions are apparent. Odysseus, who eventually does act to take back his home, is in most respects as restricted in his power to act as is his son. As a leader in exile,

Odysseus' first responsibility is to find the way back home to the civilized community of subjects and family he ventured from when he reluctantly went to war, and it is precisely this task that he is long delayed in accomplishing. As a result of blinding the Kyklopês and earning the vengeful harassment of the Kyklopês' father, the god (Poseidon) who continually tosses Odysseus into the sea, Odysseus is stranded outside of his home, much as his son is imprisoned within it. Odysseus escapes the sea and proceeds home only when Athena, who favors him, asks Zeus to restrain Poseidon. But while Athena does eventually help Odysseus, she could have intervened earlier, a situation suggesting ambivalence in her attitude toward him.

Greek tradition explains—though *The Odyssey* does not elaborate this point—that Athena is angry with the Greeks and scatters their ships to block, temporarily, their return home. She scatters the Greek ships in the first place because, as Goddess of the City, she becomes angry at the Greeks when Odysseus, Sacker of Cities, steals the Palladion, "the fatal image of Pallas Athena on the possession of which the luck of the city [Troy] depended."[7] Although subsequently the Greeks win the war when Troy is weakened, Odysseus, in Athena's eyes, apparently goes too far to secure victory, and so she detains him the longest. Thus, although stranded partly by his own arrogance in announcing his name to the Kyklopês he has just blinded, Odysseus moves toward home according to Athena's favor and the aid she chooses to withhold or to give. By tampering with the gods' sanction of Troy, Odysseus violates the gods' sanction of a culture and, indirectly, the base of all culture; he then becomes a cultural outlaw who must earn his way back into civilization. Even in war's destruction there are rules, and, so Athena seems to say, crimes against civilization cannot go unpunished. Odysseus must then wander through the encyclopedic possibilities of human community—the odyssey—and into the fringes of civilization to expiate himself by discovering the essence of what binds humans together in a community; that is, since his crime was to stray from and to deny the meaning of culture, thereby plundering culture (disastrous for a king or a father), retribution entails wandering through the world to relearn the forgotten basis on which culture rests.

Therefore, the simple contrast between father and son breaks down, and it is for good reason that Odysseus' dilemma is not essentially different from his son's. Just as Telémakhos waits on Odysseus' will to return, Odysseus waits on Zeus' will to punish and to educate (through Athena's commands). Accordingly, as the epic first opens on Odysseus in book 5, Odysseus sits a prisoner on Kalypso's island and waits for Zeus to decide when he may proceed to the next step of his education and, ultimately, to return home. Strongly reminiscent of Telémakhos in the first four books, Odysseus sits "with eyes wet / scanning the bare horizon of the sea" (97), waiting passively for a father whose presence he cannot command. And since restricted action identifies sons, Odysseus must be included with Telémakhos as a son. Even though this inclusion undermines the stature of one who is pre-eminently a king and father, the awkwardness must be allowed for the moment while we see what it reveals, as there can be no doubt that the first view of Odysseus in book 5 shows a man forced into passivity as clearly as books 1 through 4 show the same of Telémakhos.

Although we have gotten only as far as book 5 of the epic, it is apparent that Telémakhos' frustration is the same as Odysseus', and the seeming leisure of the Telemakhiad's development is a narrative means of concentrating attention where it belongs. That is, in one sense what we are calling the "problem" at the epic's beginning is a simple case of a missing family member; when Odysseus comes home and is "found" by his son, the problem will be solved. But in terms of narrative function, it is also clear that Odysseus' absence and Telémakhos' awareness of that absence satisfy what Lacanian theory shows to be a need for the inauguration of discourse. This absence—what Lacan calls the *manque-á-être,* a primordial want-to-be—is pre-ontological and, as such, is a theoretical precondition of all structure.[8] Just as in Lacanian theory where the initial absence of the father inaugurates a desire for the father's function, and the child thereby becomes the embodiment of knowledge about the father (and the absence associated with him), the odyssean son begins the epic as he gazes toward a fatherless horizon and answers Athena's question about what it is to know a father. The paternal absence at the beginning of *The Odyssey*, then, has a necessary structural function in the evocation of a lack, but this lack is not irrevocably bound to father figures. Absence can also be indicated in complex and indirect ways—there is no limit—such as in the loss of power and authority that Odysseus must contend with while in exile. And the passivity that Telémakhos and Odysseus are forced into by the fact of paternal absence tells something further about narrative structure: just as they are passive in relation to an absent father, the development of narrative, likewise, is fully dependent on the structural absence that initiates it. Thus, at the beginning of *The Odyssey* we see the emergence of a set of relationships out of a primary evocation of lack. The theoretical implications of this structural lack extend, of course, far beyond an interpretation of Homer's epic, and this lack—an aspect of the father's discourse—is an originary feature of every narrative.

As the concept of sonship expands to include Odysseus, traditionally the heroic actor par excellence, we can wonder whether passivity as a state may not be a prerequisite of action. Using the term "passivity" in this way, we draw on its original meaning, "being capable of suffering" (*passivus* in Latin), the sense in which Christ undergoes the "passion" of crucifixion. In this sense, Odysseus, who was initially incapable of suffering the discipline of restraint in Troy, and who could not then guide his own way home, undergoes an education by suffering exile—one like Christ's exile on earth—as he waits for Zeus' intervention. Once he can properly sustain the son's passion, he has been educated and can proceed toward home. Passivity in *The Odyssey*, then, is a total surrender, a suffering in a relationship with the father, "so that," as John T. Irwin notes for the Christian context, "the Son's will becomes one with, is wed to, that of the Father"[9]—suffering being an avenue to knowledge about the father.

The Freudian analysis goes even further in suggesting that passivity, as a conceptual corollary of activity, applies as a term in rather important ways to subjects in all relationships. Especially in response to the inauguration of relationship—as is the concern here with Telémakhos and Odysseus—passivity is a particularly important conception. That is, the castration threat, the central event of the Oedipal crisis, must be resolved in an acceptance of passivity in regard to the father's authority for the crisis to be ended. So while it is true that, according to psychoanalysis, all desires originate in active drives and in aggression (in "demands," as Lacan shows), "it is in a purely passive, non-drive way" that essential links—essential even to pure activity—are established between a subject and the "external world."[10]

We have already noted that passivity describes how Telémakhos depends on Odysseus and cannot act without his help, and how Odysseus cannot act without Zeus' aid. In the Freudian view, this dependence is expressed as a fantasy "seduction" that has important implications for a theory of the father in narrative. This attachment to the father comes by way of dependence on the mother and the satisfaction of specific needs. When needs inevitably go wanting (as they must in the post-uterine world), the child must regard a body of unanswered demands for satisfaction. Thereafter, having been seduced into dependence by a fantasy of absolute satisfaction with (or in) the mother, the child is left to face the gaps of a pervasive absence. This absence becomes functional as it, henceforward, by its very existence, prohibits direct and "natural" satisfactions. Further on in development the son's insertion in relationship is confirmed in a passive relation to the father's authority, wherein by accepting his own passivity in relation to the father's "absence," the son "acts" decisively to affirm the possibility of relationship. The content of seduction as a fantasy, in short, is an attachment to an empty paternal position and to the potential of relationship such an emptiness makes possible. Knowledge of the father's empty place, subsequently, constitutes desire itself. So, as Freudian theory and *The Odyssey* show, while desire for the father belongs to the son, the desire paradoxically—as it is constituted by prohibition (law)—"is entirely organized by something which comes to [the child], as it were, from the outside," from the father himself.[11]

This seduction of the son into relationship, part of a triadic process in existence even before the Oedipal situation, should be treated not as a mere motif within narrative, but as a "primal datum," a "primal phantasy," as Freud calls it, that expresses an elemental structure of the subject and of narrative. Instituted by the discovery of absence, the desire for the father will be articulated in what is essentially a narrative, one with correspondences to elaborated evocations of the father in the offices of mass and of prayer. In the next step of that articulation, the son faces a crisis, for subsequent to this primal seduction is an inevitable betrayal in the staging of a primal scene. Here, without warning, what was a surrender to the father (in passivity) is turned around and becomes an act of aggression by the father (directed, perhaps, in fantasy toward the mother), one that prohibits desire out of relation to the father and the seeking of narcissistic, pre-paternal (maternal) satisfactions: that is, having found the father as the route to the satisfaction the mother represents, the son may not abandon him. In this way, seduction into relationship "forms an indissoluble link between [the son's] wish and [the father's] law" that makes of the father a beginning and a destiny for the son.[12] This state of affairs will be formalized in the resolution to the Oedipal crisis. In addition to seduction and primal scene, there is a third Oedipal fantasy, castration. Castration is the visible trace left by the success of the other two fantasies, and it, as a kind of sign or inscription, "sets the seal" on the tie with the father; in other words, the successful castration celebrates the institution of relationship. In terms of the narrative theory we are evolving, the wish is precisely the evocation of lack in narration, and the law is the principle by which that lack is articulated. Accordingly, Telémakhos' desire for his father contains its own direction toward a goal and even the means for attaining the goal. The fact of an accomplished narration—not unlike the father's mark of circumcision or the child's abandonment of the pre-Oedipal mother—expresses the fantasy of castration, so that what we first saw as the relation of son and father is here a relation of a text clearly bound to its paternal origin.

In using these psychoanalytic terms to describe relations within narrative, I am demonstrating certain very selective correspondences between a theory of narrative and a theory of the (Freudian) subject. An analysis of narrative based on such a correspondence necessarily is vulnerable to Edmund Husserl's charge that it merely "psychologizes" —that is, it translates concepts into privileged psychological terms without any gain in precision or understanding. In this discussion, however, we are not translating existing concepts, but radically interpreting various aspects of narrative function. This examination moves beyond the usual thematic references to father and son and into a system of narrative functions. For example, psychoanalysis begins with the structure of the family and focuses intensely on the transformations of sexuality within that structure—transformations governed at crucial stages by the function of paternity. In this Freudian view the son is one who moves through the process consisting of seduction, primal scene, and castration. And with these phases of transformation in mind, we can see more clearly than before that Telémakhos and

Odysseus can be classed together as sons: both are restrained in their spheres of action (castration) and manifest the desire for the father that—thematically and functionally—is at the heart of *The Odyssey*'s structure. Likewise, in Freudian terms, and in response to Husserl's charge, we can be more specific than we were before about the nature of what keeps Odysseus from going home. As Lacan says, "the order of the law [which the father represents] can be conceived only on the basis of something more primordial, a crime."[13] Accordingly, by violating the sanction Zeus had given Troy, Odysseus commits a crime as he denies the father and his law, "the primordial law . . . that . . . superimposes the kingdom of culture on that of nature":[14] the father's law is what binds people together in culture. Odysseus breaks that law and commits a crime against culture, and so it is that law Odysseus must find for himself before he can rejoin the human community: Odysseus' failure to find the father commits him to living in a narcissistic world outside of family and culture.

Also, from the Freudian viewpoint we can see that there are characters in this epic who have no desire to know the father: Penélopê's suitors. Whereas Telémakhos and Odysseus surrender to a relationship with the father, the suitors try to blot out any link with their lost king. With Odysseus gone, the suitors could choose to participate in the reaffirmation of culture that Odysseus' return, or even his failure to return, brings. To undergo this process, they would have to acknowledge the significance of absence by protecting the father's empty place at home until it can be filled by the rightful heir in the father's line. But instead of respecting his home, they pillage it, and instead of respecting his heir, they try to kill him; and they shamelessly pursue Penélopê to take Odysseus' place in bed, in each case trying to obliterate any knowledge of Odysseus' absence—and of structural absence—by filling it themselves. In being unable to bear their ruler's absence, they deny any connection with an authority beyond themselves and deny (structurally) the father and membership in his dynastic line.

Thus far, insights for a theory of the father still have come from our investigation of the "absence" that pervades *The Odyssey* through book 5, much of the discussion suggesting a theory of sonship. Now turning to Zeus, we can examine absence from the standpoint of the paternal function, what Lacan calls "the Name-of-the Father." What

makes Zeus a father is quite simple: alone of all gods and humans, he
bows to no greater power—he alone holds the Greek world together.
True, his authority does come originally from Kronos (the all-father
who pre-dates and is the origin of time), who ate Zeus' brothers and
sisters, Hestia, Demeter, Hera, Hades, and Poseidon, and who had
earlier castrated his own father, Uranus (who, likewise, had castrated
his father). Needing to overthrow Kronos or be eaten, Zeus survives
through a conspiracy with his mother, Rhea, and eventually topples
his father, thereafter forcing the old god to vomit up the brothers and
sisters. In his victory, however, Zeus does not take his father's empty
place as those before had done and thus desiccate the old order; on the
contrary, his revolt is unique in that in his triumph Zeus effects a retrograde reordering of the relationship between old and new that saves
his own life and renews Kronos' fatherhood. To begin with, Zeus' victory could not destroy his father's authority, since by killing his children, Kronos was already destroying fatherhood. Faced with the
threat of filicide, which by extension is also the patricidal threat
(because fathers are created by having children), Zeus saves his own
life as he simultaneously reinstates Kronos' fatherhood; in so doing,
Zeus actually undoes the ravage of the past. Zeus simultaneously
transforms and institutes Time's reign by bringing back his brothers
and sisters and, further, by guaranteeing that children will have an existence in relation to Time (to Kronos). In short, Zeus legislates a new
law of relationship in one fell swoop as he breaks the tyranny of
Kronos and, simultaneously, protects Kronos' domain (fatherhood in
time) by forbidding the eating of children. Therefore, the paternal
identity that Zeus fashions as protector of fathers and children institutes the law by which parents and children can coexist in a family.

Little about Zeus' origin and that of the law are explained in so
many words in *The Odyssey*. Yet such paternal authority permeates
the epic as the cultural backdrop, the code within which the epic is articulated. Zeus' authority in the strict sense must be situated at the
origin of the text as a principle according to which the narrative un-
folds, his authority constituting a structural pre-text. In that his extra-
textual "pre-existence," paternity itself, is the source of first distinctions in narrative, his law is invoked predictably at the epic's
beginning as Telémakhos' desire for reunion with his father and
Odysseus' wish to go home. Zeus as a figure does appear in the narra-

tive at crucial points, as when Athena pleads to let Odysseus go home, and when she asks Zeus to stop the fighting in Ithaka, but even without these appearances his authority is omnipresent from beginning to end (structurally) as a paternal inheritance that links present and past in a narrative line. Although the character of Zeus is not important to narrative structure, his paternal function is.

We now have some of the essential concepts for a theory of the father in narrative. First, in the predicaments of Telémakhos and Odysseus there are the awareness of absence and the expression of desire; and in Zeus' function in narrative, the implementation of prohibition, is the law. Second, in the binding of desire to the law is the essence of the father's discourse and the structure of all narratives. In short, the father is a "no" that initiates narrative development by enfranchising one line of continuity over other possibilities; the son's desire is a "yes" that leaves behind maternal demands, gets bound to the father's law, and proceeds in a narrative advance that plays out the father's meaning in time. Suggested here is a dynamic model of narrative, as Peter Brooks describes it, "which effectively structures ends . . . against beginnings . . . in a manner that necessitates the middle as *détour,* as a struggle toward the end under the compulsion of the imposed delay, as arabesque in the dilatory space of the text."[15] But while it is evident that law and desire unite in the Oedipal seduction of the son, still needed is a conceptual grasp of what that meeting—the *détour*—and the mediation of conflict lead to. Narratives begin with the binding of the son's desire to the father, but whereas the father is a "pre-existent" first term of relationship from which the son's desire is distinguished as a second term, there is a third (like spirit or soul in Trinitarian thought) that expresses the binding of the first two as well as restates the principle of the binding. This third term will express the father's law through the various stages of sonship, seduction, primal scene, and castration.

"The finding of an object is in fact a refinding of it."
(Freud, *Three Essays on the Theory of Sexuality*)

The epic's major action, of course, is Odysseus' return from the Trojan Wars, and it is clear that his difficulties in returning to Ithaka derive from his transgression of the gods' will. For punishment he must proceed home in a manner that will make him suffer passively in a relationship with the father (as Christ does) in order to be enlightened about what links culture and the gods. Athena's first lesson teaches Odysseus what culture is not, as she forces him to wander through communal possibilities (and impossibilities) as an outsider, as one who has membership in nothing. Then follows the major portion of Odysseus' education in the manner in which he reenters his kingdom and once again assumes the kingship. In reentering, because long absent and nearly given up by many as dead, he has to find a way of reclaiming both familial and regal powers. This last task is great because his wife and child and father do not immediately recognize him, and because Penélopê's suitors are prepared to guard their own fortunes against the returning monarch. To regain the throne Odysseus must reveal himself to his family, but in a manner that will not make him vulnerable to the suitors. And, above all, his manner of return must assert the father's law, the loss of which excludes him from community.

The precise arrangement of events in Ithaka is crucial for understanding the significance of the return and the refinding of paternity. First, Odysseus meets Telémakhos and gradually reveals his identity. Next, disguised as a beggar, Odysseus comes with his son into his own hall and fools the suitors for some time, then reveals himself at the moment when he attacks them. Assisted by his son, he kills all of the suitors and turns to purge his household of women who consorted with them. Then, reunited with his son and rid of the suitors, Odysseus approaches Penélôpe, shows the secret of their marriage bed (it was constructed on a living olive tree, an ever-green symbol of the father's return), to prove who he is; thereafter, they too, are reunited. After this reunion, he goes to visit his old father, Laërtês, while the suitors' angry relatives band together and swear to take revenge on Odysseus, saying "we'd be disgraced forever! Mocked for generations / if we cannot avenge our sons' blood, and our brothers!" (470). Upon Odysseus' return a new battle seems imminent, so Athena implores Zeus to "impose a pact on both" Odysseus and the suitors' relatives to end the fighting and to bring a lasting peace (471). Zeus subsequently answers in a definitive verdict on the struggle:

Odysseus' honor being satisfied,
let him be king by a sworn pact forever,
and we, for our part, will blot out the memory
of sons and daughters slain. . . . (471)

The fighting barely starts, when Zeus, dropping a thunderbolt between the contestants, suddenly halts the dispute. At long last, pro-
claimed "king in a sworn pact forever," and with the fighting ended,
Odysseus comes home from his odyssey.

The first striking aspect of Odysseus' return is that as father and son
unite and enter the hall of suitors together, Odysseus takes over a
rivalry previously belonging to Telémakhos. Before Odysseus' return,
with the father absent, son and suitors were rivals for dominance in a
relationship with Penélopê: each suitor wanted her hand and her estate, while Telémakhos wanted to make her wait for his father's return. Without someone to enforce a familial hierarchy, there was only
strife in Ithaka. Odysseus returns and takes up the conflict not as another rival among many, but as a dominant figure who says "no" to all
competitors in order to reassert a right of priority: he came to
Penélopê first, and others must approach her through him. By killing
the suitors, who as subjects have a filial relationship with him, Odysseus expresses the father's interdiction that will make "sons" sub-
ordinate to him as a father. Without the paternal "no," which is essentially aggressive, there is no law in the Ithakan community: the "no"
directs sons into a relationship with the father.

In having made the aggressive paternal gesture, Odysseus represents
the father's authority. And further, when the suitors' relatives come
for another battle, they threaten more than additional bloodshed, because after the relatives' deaths more attempts at revenge will follow,
and more after that. If Odysseus continues to kill his subjects, as
Kronos ate his children, then he destroys kingdom and kingship alike.
On the other hand, if the relatives kill their king, then the ransacked
Ithaka will not be restored, and its inhabitants will perish. Athena sees
both dangers, and she also sees how continual dispute would spread
into chaos and, contrary to what Odysseus' return should mean, an
undermining of community. Therefore, determined to avoid disaster
and to complete Odysseus' education, she requests Zeus to give a new
testament of men's relations to each other and to the gods to replace

the old order of unlimited aggression that, as a mode of action, made Odysseus an outlaw and left his kingdom in shambles. Zeus decrees that, since Odysseus has asserted the father's law, he now should allow his subjects to exist within it; that is, having killed "sons" to assert the law, "the father . . . too, must submit to the bar [the law]";[16] Odysseus must forbear from killing sons. Zeus' interdiction ends the fighting by making king and subjects accountable in a common pact, as the gods, according to Zeus' pronouncement, take the sins and guilt of the past into themselves. Odysseus and his people are then free from the burden of the past at the moment they are bound to the law.

Although Odysseus' manner of coming home expresses the principle of the father, by acquiescing to Zeus and by ending the fighting, he symbolically affirms himself as a son—one dependent on Zeus' transcendent authority. That is, Odysseus/son takes up arms against the suitors and then lays them down as signal of obeisance to the father. In relation to the suitors, Odysseus/father kills son figures and then refrains from doing so as a means of fully implementing law. With Zeus and again with the suitors, Odysseus embodies the same principle of subordination through difference; in so doing, he signifies the father's function by expressing the relationship of aggression and forbearance (activity and passivity), ultimately deriving his power to act from the law expressed in a "sworn pact forever." So fundamental is this law that even Zeus, who knows no power or authority higher than his own, binds himself to humans through the principle Odysseus embodies, the law that he created in the revolt against Kronos. The law exists prior to Odysseus' return, or else it could not be "found," and it must be "refound" in the other scene of Odysseus' return, or else the law breaks the law as it fails to express difference.

"The discovery of One—the discovery of difference—is to be
condemned to an eternal desire for the nonrelationship of zero,
where identity is meaningless."
(Anthony Wilden, *The Language of the Self*)

The complexity of Odysseus' function in the epic is considerable. He is a son in relation to Zeus, a father in relation to Telémakhos and the suitors, a husband to Penélopê, and a mediator between Telémakhos/

suitors (desire) and Zeus (law). He mediates in this fashion between father and son, his character building on elements drawn from both. In this reconciliatory role as incarnation of the father in the substance of the son, he takes a central place in the epic as the special case of the son who participates in articulating the connection between the first and second terms (law and desire), and, by extension, the rule on which the connection is based. Odysseus represents the third term we are seeking. Telémakhos, as quester for the father, early in the epic gives a name for this special son, this third term, when he answers Athena's question about his paternity with the explanation, "It's a wise child that knows its own father." He cautions, we will remember, that he himself is not the wise child, the one who knows what the father means. The wise child, it turns out, is Odysseus, son/father who functions as the third term (which can be called "mediation," or simply "narration") in the discourse of law and desire. Odysseus/wise child knows his own father in that he articulates Zeus' authority, Odysseus' character bridging law and desire by showing the father-son relationship to be more than a mere conflict: it is a significant opposition that signifies the father's law.

Here we can examine the structural significance of opposition (and of mediation) by looking for a moment at an analogue of Homer's tri-une relationship in the Catholic theory of the Trinity, a conception also founded on formal opposition. For example, in Trinitarian theory the Son, above all else, like Odysseus, is knowledge of the Father, knowledge beginning with the awareness of difference and exclusion. That is, to know the Father, Trinitarian theory shows that the Son must be excluded from the Father's immediate presence—from sharing the Father's being—in order to be the Mind (Augustine's term) that has an object of awareness outside of itself; the Son, thus, must be opposed to (in a sense, in conflict with) the Father, much as Odysseus is in conflict with Zeus. John Burnaby explains the relationship of the Father as an original One and the Son as Mind and shows that Augustine, following Plotinus, distinguishes "within the external world of spiritual reality a 'trinity' of the One, Mind, and Soul or Life, in which Soul forms the link between spirit and matter, eternal and temporal. Soul is both one and many, and is itself product of the activity of self-conscious Mind—mind thinking itself; whereas Mind in turn derives from the ultimate and absolute Unity in which there is no distinction of subject and object."[17] In one sense, then, the Trinity is an outgrowth of the "ultimate and absolute Unity" of the Father, except that by himself, if such a state can be imagined, the Father is a kind of nothingness. Even to say that the One-ness of the Father *is,* as Burnaby points out, "would be to give it a second attribute in addition to its one-ness."[18] Like the Jungian Great Mother, the Father is the One out of whom everything derives, but as a person in the Trinity the Father is in a subject-object relationship with the Son, in that the Father is the One who is known by the Son. But it is not clear what it means to say that the Father is known by the Son, if the Father is "nothing" to begin with. What can the Son know?

The Father's name is simply "he that is" (Jehovah), because he is primary, without contingency, and irreducible to a prior state of being. The Father in his primary state cannot be articulated because, as is evident, without contingency he is without difference, and without difference he cannot have an identity. The integer "one" is used by theologians to designate God because it expresses the solitary state of something unaccompanied by anything else. There is a contradiction, however, expressed in the metaphor of "one" for solitariness, because, strictly speaking, there is no such thing as a solitary "one." If we treat "one" as in integer, we see that it implies an arithmetic principle of sequence and only has a meaning in relationship to other integers. That is, a single integer is meaningless because "one" as a cipher only has a meaning insofar as it holds an exclusive position in relation to the "two" that it is not. As we grant a difference between "one" and "two," a third thing as well has come into being, the relationship between one and two, the principle of relationship through exclusion. Further, "zero," because it is not an integer—though it holds an integer's place—stands for the principle of difference that connects integers.[19] In the same way, the meaning of the Father as One is only to be grasped within relationship, namely, within the sequential relationship of One, Mind, and Life. It follows that the Father as a solitary One is unknowable, except as he is found in a relationship with the Son. The Father and Son are separate, as integers, and rising from their separateness is a principle of relationship expressible in a third term, one which unites them through the fact of separation.

Still, it is not quite clear what the Son knows, if the Father by himself is nothing. Behind most theories of ritual sacrifice is a narrative about a god's re-creation of himself in a double (an offspring), an act that creates the world of things out of nothing. Likewise, the double (of Mind) in Christian terms is nothing except an awareness of the Father that brings the world into being. Yet if nothing exists before knowledge of the father, it must follow that the Son is Mind thinking of itself *as nothing*. But then, how can an awareness of nothing be an awareness? It is helpful here to reify the relationship of Father and Son so that the Father appears as an infinite black surface, one without the distinction of subject and object, top or bottom, and the Son comes out of the Father somewhat as a disk that is cut from the blackness. It is obvious that before the disk is cut out, there is nothing because the Father fills everything with himself (with his nothingness). Then, the disk, by being cut out, is excluded from the nothingness of the Father, and the Father's unity is broken. Thereafter, the Father, just as he dies in the primordial sacrifice made for the creation of the world, dies in the Trinity as his own absolute unity is sundered by the emergence of the Son out of himself. Furthermore, removal of the disk creates a relationship between the disk (as Mind) and the absence of the Father that the removal creates. Moreover, the disk cannot be in relation to the total black surface of the Father, which is without distinction and unknowable, but only to the absence left by the disk. In short, as the disk breaks off from the blackness, there is suddenly something to know in the absence (different from a nothingness) that is left. In this way, absence necessarily creates the knowledge of absence as a relationship, and, thus, this relationship of disk and absence is a primary object of awareness—the creation of a world of things. And with the introduction of relationship as a primary object the theory of Mind is also an epistemology and an ontology, a fact that emphasizes the Father as a structural principle of meaning. What Trinitarian theory provides is an organization of the father's relations, one that places him within a specific theory of narrative: in the mediation of Father and Son is a discourse between "one" and "many" (like law and desire) that takes place in the relationship of all texts.

Now, in important ways Homer's triadic relationship of father, son, and wise child parallels that of the Trinity. Just as the Catholic Soul, in

Augustinian terms, mediates a worldly conflict connected with the Son (Mind), which in turn derives from the lack of conflict in the Father (One), the wise child mediates the difference between father and son, a difference that in turn derives from a previous lack of conflict. The previous unity in Homer's epic has left a trace in the continuing existence of Kronos, who, as a kind of Father Time existing before human time, permits none to live within his narcissistic realm or to introduce any disharmony. Thus, Zeus' revolt against Kronos in a version of the primal scene, a veritable birth of Mind (in the Catholic sense), gives rise to productive conflicts that allow children to survive, and, in this way, knowledge of the father and of the world comes into being. Odysseus, as wise child, mediates the conflicts of *The Odyssey* by signifying a binding of conflict and unity (son and father), desire and law, in narrative time. It is important to see here that unity is not being imposed on conflict (such an imposition Lacan calls a "scandalous lie"),[20] but is structurally part and parcel of conflict.

Further, Odysseus himself bears a visible trace of the paternal state wherein, like Kronos, he knew a unity that was sundered. His scar, a reminder of a childhood event that shapes Odysseus' identity, is first revealed when, disguised as a beggar on the return to Ithaka, he sits in his own hall as his old nurse, Eurýkeia, washes his feet. Following her startled recognition of her master's identifying mark comes a narrative interjection explaining the scar's origin at Odysseus' first wild boar hunt. The scene is set at the home of Autólykos, Odysseus' grandfather, where Odysseus and the boar lock together in combat and pierce each other's bodies; and, for a moment, the two are united like lovers, their embrace breaking only as Odysseus' spear penetrates further and the beast dies. This scene is a highly concentrated tableau in which two figures first merge in a moment of unity that dissolves subsequently when the spear cuts their bond and separates them with death. Implicit in the thrusting of the spear into the boar and in the lodging of the boar's tusk in Odysseus' leg is the complementarity of a "yes" and a "no," a clear expression of ambivalence. Simultaneously, the opposition of sticking and being stuck denotes activity and passivity, essential "modalities of instinctual life" to which all relationships anchor.[21] Also, the movement of spear and tusk represents that phase of the Oedipal situation in which the father's law is asserted as a principle of opposition and difference. That is, the boar's resistance to Odysseus creates a structure wherein Odysseus can act only in relation to opposition; within that structure an absence opens, and the father's trace becomes visible. Moreover, in that Odysseus first encounters the father's law in the hunt incident, his assertion of that law in the return to Ithaka is a refinding of a latent meaning in experience. His killing of suitors and his refraining from killing their relatives manifest the same aggression/forbearance relationship that, in the hunt scene, sticking and being stuck convey in a highly cryptic fashion. By interjecting the boar hunt incident when Odysseus returns to Ithaka, the narrative provides its own commentary and a perspective on a structurally continuous experience—the past and its repetition in the present.

If we look back for a moment to Zeus' role in Odysseus' return home, we see that by legislating "a sworn pact forever" to stop the fighting in Ithaka, Zeus restates the significance of his own overthrow of Kronos, an action that limits as well as confirms the existence of Father Time: in effect, Zeus, the bringer of the law, also begins his life in passivity—he also simultaneously sticks and is stuck—and he repeats his own past when he rules on the battles in Ithaka, the law in this case being, as in that of Odysseus, a repetition of itself. The past and present dimensions of both Zeus' and Odysseus' experiences are, then, phases of an overarching narrative structure that expresses the father's law. The traces of this structure, shown in Kronos' continuing existence and in Odysseus' scar, signify outwardly, like an inscription, a rule that is incorporated in narrative progression. The wise child mediates the father's absence (desire) and his function (law); and Odysseus' identity, like Zeus', shapes this symbolic structure on all levels of the text. Odysseus and Zeus, like Oedipus with scarred ankles, are marked by the signs of their narrative function. That Laërtês believes his son has come home only when he sees the scar on Odysseus' leg emblematically suggests the centrality of the father's law in all narrative development.

The Odyssey goes one step further to an even sharper focus on the discourse of law and desire. For, even though the epic clearly is a meditation on the binding of law and desire, the epic does present a view of desire in which desire unbound to law—in a fashion—may be glimpsed briefly. This view of desire, expanding that shown in the

Telemakhiad, is presented when Odysseus, about to embark on the principal effort that brings him home, receives crucial sailing instructions from Kirkê. The most detailed of her instructions concern the strait of Skylla and Kharybdis, which Odysseus must navigate in order to reach home. Kirkê explains that to survive the strait, Odysseus must take note that on the Skylla side

> is a sharp mountain
> piercing the sky, with stormcloud round the peak
> dissolving never, not in the brightest summer,
> to show heaven's azure there, nor in the fall.
> No mortal man could scale it, nor so much
> as land there, not with twenty hands and feet,
> so sheer the cliffs are—as of polished stone. . . . (223–24)

The Skylla cliff, a protrusion insuperable and adamantine, makes demands on those who pass it by prohibiting any encroachment on its domain. Humans may sail close to the rock by cautiously maneuvering in relation to it, but they can never directly grasp its secrets or know it directly: at the top of its forbidding mass is a "stormcloud" that blocks the horizon Skylla stands against, so that heaven above the rock can never be viewed by "mortal man." An image of an irresistible demand, Skylla incorporates several aspects of the rigidity and the authority of paternal prohibition. Kirkê's depiction of the rock, in fact, is an accurate paradigm for the prohibition that Odysseus encounters in the childhood boar hunt and in the return to Ithaka. The image of the rock organizes many of Zeus' paternal characteristics—supremacy, invincibility, and inscrutability—to which Odysseus learns to surrender on the odyssey. Odysseus here again confronts a specialized version of the father's law, and this time, as always, the law must be recognized freshly, as if for the first time.

On the other side of the strait, Kirkê continues, Kharybdis

> lurks below
> to swallow down the dark sea tide. Three times
> from dawn to dusk she spews it up
> and sucks it down again three times, a whirling
> maelstrom; if you come upon her then
> the god who makes earth tremble could not save you. . . . (224)

Her description of the maelstrom provides an antithesis for that of the rock. Completely lacking in rigidity, the maelstrom has moments of relative stability that mask an incessant cycle of sucking and spewing, the inevitability of change being the only fixity in its nature. That is, without discrimination, the maelstrom takes in everything to satisfy its insatiable need. Where the rock expresses a prohibition, a "no," to all who sail by, the maelstrom gives a resounding and unqualified "yes" to all who would enter it. Its appetite, like its own dimensions, is without fixed bounds, the maelstrom constrained by no limits in its need to consume. Further, in never being satisfied, the maelstrom is unreconciled to the prohibitive rock that faces it across the strait, the two being unconnected.

What *The Odyssey* shows in Kirkê's descriptions is, in part, an archaic, nearly pre-human version of what exists before the father's discourse. Kirkê's vision is archaic in that the binding of law and desire, everywhere else in the epic manifested as a repetition, here has left no mark. Through this gap that opens just prior to Odysseus' final turn toward home, it is possible to peer briefly to see what exists when there is no mediation of the two sides. For instance, in the inert form of the rock is the familiar image of paternal opposition that we have been calling the law. But a measure of clarity can be gained by recognizing the rock as only a precursor of the law, which by definition governs desire. In the image of the maelstrom on the other side is a limitless and omnivorous appetite that, because not bound to a law of prohibition, is not a desire, in that the maelstrom takes in particular objects but does not discriminate between them and, therefore, cannot desire them, not in the sense that the law creates the potential for "bound" desire. On the two sides of the strait, then, is a radically different formulation for desire and law. In Kharybdis is an unbounded need (corresponding to the biological needs of the body)—insatiable in themselves and situated always outside of articulation.[22] In Skylla is an absolute demand, unfillable in its inscrutability, which is nonetheless a precursor of the law. Only in the possibility of traversing the passage between need and demand does desire (whose object is the father's law) come into being as a mediation of the two sides.

Kirkê's advice on how Odysseus must navigate the strait is central for an understanding of desire in narrative. Odysseus, she explains, can be destroyed by going too far toward either side, smashed by the hard rock or swallowed by the maelstrom. But, she goes on, neither is there any perfect middle course by which both threats can be cleared. Odysseus must be willing to venture near one of the sides and to suffer the loss entailed by that choice. Her sailing instructions are unequivocal: "hug the cliff of Skylla" (224). In these words, she tells Odysseus to commit himself to the law even though he will lose six men to the hydra who dwells on the rock: "Better to mourn / six men," Kirkê notes, "than lose them all, and the ship, too" (224). By hugging the cliff, Odysseus finds himself situated between need and demand in the field of desire, and thus binds desire to the rock. It is the process of binding itself that signifies the symbolic father. Odysseus' initial response prior to sailing, however, is to ask how he may fight and overcome Skylla and Kharybdis as he goes through the strait. Kirkê's response to this question, in some of the most poignant verses of the epic, admonishes, "Must you have battle in your heart forever? / The bloody toil of combat? Old contender, / will you not yield to the immortal gods?" (225). Here Odysseus is taught, as he is destined to learn elsewhere and later to teach others, that he must yield passively to his destiny and in so doing take up (with humility) the terms of sonship.

The Skylla/Kharybdis episode illustrates the father's discourse at a primoridal stage in which desire and law do not yet exist. Even so, this archaic confrontation with rock and maelstrom (essentially maternal), like the struggle of the boar hunt scene, inscribes a hieroglyph of the father's law. And that Odysseus' character cannot be separated from the aggression/forbearance opposition inherent in the strait episode is a reminder that the father's law constitutes the narrative structure of the text. However, in the moment we identify the strait episode as archaic (or as having connections with the maternal realm that precedes the law), we also categorize various other moments in *The Odyssey*. For example, in such scenes as Telémakhos' investigation into the meaning of his father's absence, Odysseus' servitude on Kalypso's island, Odysseus' boar hunt experience, and the manner of Odysseus' return to Ithaka, among others, are signs of connection that show the binding of law and desire—and the castration debt that is paid for this binding—as if projected visibly on the upper surface of narration, like insignia. Each of these nodal incidents advances narrative only as it suppresses, in obeisance to narrative law, a plenitude of pre-paternal or illicit meaning; the suppressed meanings are illicit in the same sense that the maelstrom's unbounded appetite lies outside of Skylla's and the law's domain. Each such "insignia," as Lacan explains, "represents" what cannot "enter the domain of the signifier [of narrative] without being *barred* from it, that is to say, covered over by castration."[23] In this way, each incident we have examined confirms the law—without being equivalent to the totality of the father's law— by contributing to an unbroken narrative line; and so each narrative incident navigates the waters of desire and law and in so doing advances narrative much as Odysseus' submission advances his journey between the maelstrom and the rock. Thus, this dimension of experience figured in the strait episode is a realm of archaic reference latent within the discourse of desire and law, within narration itself. When the epic comes to the last manifestation of the discourse as the fighting between Odysseus and the relatives stops, which the outcome of the strait episode adumbrates, Odysseus yields fully to paternal will at last with "his heart . . . glad" (474) and brings *The Odyssey*'s discourse to a close.

The symbolic father of *The Odyssey*'s narrative, or of any narrative, is a principle of function that stands behind the mechanisms (the primal fantasies) of seduction, primal scene, and castration. All of these functions are "unconscious" in that they are inherent to narrative structure. First among them, however, is the single principle of meaning that precedes the plurality of narrative meanings and stands behind all narrative developments, much as Kronos' paternal rebellion (from its beginning already in a line of paternal rebellions—therefore, already a repetition) stands behind *The Odyssey*. This narrative authority, the symbolic father, whose operations we have identified in the discourse of desire and law, is the centerpiece of theory in *The Fictional Father*, as each of the critics in this book looks to this concept as a theoretical guide for an understanding of the father in fiction. For, within this symbolic constellation lies the lack at the origin that authorizes narrative and intelligibility: that lack is the primal trace of paternal authority.

III

The six essays that follow cover a broad range of what usually is considered the "modern" Anglo-American novel. The essays discuss major novels by Charles Dickens, Herman Melville, James Joyce, William Faulkner, and Donald Barthelme. Each of the essays stages a closely watched encounter between a critical method and a fictional subject, the encounter between Lacanian interpretation and the subject of the fictional father. However, in addition to staging this convergence, this book's essays examine the modern novel (and modernism) in the context of nineteenth- and twentieth-century fiction. In the widest sense, then, this is a book about the father and also about the modern novel and its structure.

It will become apparent that each critic draws from the complex structure of the symbolic father in order to examine narrative as it constitutes that structure. In his study of *Bleak House* Thomas A. Hanzo views paternity as the function of interpretation and as what authorizes the narrative "subject," the structural site wherein meaning is given in a text. Régis Durand shows the complex link between structural and thematic "absence" in Melville's fiction. Jean-Michel Rabaté shows how paternal authority is manifested on many levels in Joyce's experimental narratives. André Bleikasten analyzes paternal failure (and symbolization) in the Southern tradition as a text, a text wherein Faulkner's novels are situated. John T. Irwin focuses on the dead father in Faulkner's fiction as an expression of temporal priority and authority. Then, in my essay on Donald Barthelme's *The Dead Father*, I examine the fragmentation of paternal authority in a postmodern fiction. Finally, in the critical epilogue, I discuss some of the controversial issues that surround Lacanian thought, especially with regard to feminism and Marxism.

1 Paternity and the Subject in

Bleak House

THOMAS A. HANZO

"Daddy's girl" is the American image of that favored and no doubt pampered young woman who must, if she is to mature, refuse her father's seductive gestures. In most families, barriers of law, moral principle, and other judgments contain and deflect the incestuous desire, so that to his dismay the father eventually is compelled to "give his daughter away" in marriage. *Bleak House*, like all of Dickens' novels, allows the barrier against incest to be breached: contrary to her deepest feelings, the heroine of Dickens' great novel agrees to marry the parental figure.

I exaggerate, of course, but not in presenting that natural state of sexual chaos which cultural order must revise. If myth and the imaginative power that creates it are to be credited with their full authority, they will always place us, historically and eternally, at that moment when and where a human destiny transforms the universal fate. I read the domestic conditions of the original *Bleak House* for a metaphoric precision that emphasizes the structural importance of the Oedipal situation and the daughter's desire for the father's love. These emotional reciprocities are remarkably displaced by Dickens, for how else could that house on the hill near St. Albans, that retreat from Chancery injustice and the poverty of Tom-All-Alone's, harbor an affront to the fundamental prohibition that brings human society into existence? It can, and does, and in so doing creates the thematic and formal means by which the novel's study of the unspeakable crime is conducted. For Dickens and his readers, incest, particularly in its primary form as a sexual alliance between parent and child, lies beyond the reach of serious fiction. Yet every novel he writes, every story he tells, reiterates the central failure of parental responsibility that he found everywhere in life. Mothers and fathers are equally guilty, Dickens believes, of this betrayal, and if not mothers and fathers, then their surrogates, familial replacements for the mother (like Pip's sister in *Great Expectations*) or legal guardians supplied by the social order, like John Jarndyce (or Jaggers of *Great Expectations*).

The failure of paternity is complex, and *Bleak House* stands in monumental indictment of that failure in an entire society. At the same time, the novel proliferates with a certain joyful abandonment. The accusation cannot be repeated often enough, as the forms of institutional, familial, and personal hostility toward children, in Dickens' novels, as well as their seduction by parental figures, grow in Dickens' imagination with all the perverted energy that in his case at least, if we dare to make such an assumption, must itself declare to us that he condemned his own mother out of an overwhelming sense of loss. Only psychoanalytic theory, of course, has evaluated the sexual content of the familial triangle with full attention to its determining influence in the life of the individual, but it is not only the Oedipal structure proper that Freud discovered. Early in his career, and momentously for psychoanalytic theory as a whole, he came upon another and more primordial feature of the emotional life of children and parents. When his hysterical patients elaborated their stories of seduction by adults, he first accepted the truth of these accounts; later, in an illuminating and celebrated insight that was to transform his psychology, Freud accepted the fact that the stories were fantasies. They expressed the woman's anxious desire to be seduced, her love and not her fear of her father. The fantasies created a monstrous aggressor out of the object of desire. The reinterpretation led Freud to the mechanisms of the unconscious, to infantile sexuality, to the Oedipus situation itself. In spite of this willingness to grant the phantasmal nature of the oft-repeated scene of seduction, Freud also continued to insist on the real fact that the parents often—or did he mean always?—in the very act of touching, cleaning, and feeding children accomplished their seduction. The as yet unspecialized sexuality of the child responds through every sensory experience, and such pleasures establish a pattern that the mature imagination will remember. In very early life, the proto-sexuality of the child is aroused when the mother, as well as the father, nurtures the child.

Two features of the psychoanalytic view of these events may be obscured by their more dramatic psychological themes. Infantile sexuality, for example, constitutes a major step forward in theory, but for their literary implications, the historical continuity of the psyche and the structure of change it implies suggest a fertile principle of interpretation. Just as the hysterical patient reversed roles and made of the loved object an aggressor, so, in the history of the affects that remain when their ideas are repressed, further conversions, substitutions, and exchanges of roles can and will occur.

The possibilities of conversion for the fictional imagination are limitless. In the fantasy of the woman who heard a child being beaten, Freud detected a series of transformations in which the objectification "she is being beaten" becomes "I am being beaten," and, finally, father loves me; I want father. With the guardian/ward relationship of *Bleak House,* Dickens isolated a peculiarly intense version of the history of fathers and daughters. He makes of the paternal figure a deposed authority, a self-exiled ruler, a father who has been weakened by the power of a corrupt society. What he should save and what he should rectify have overcome him; he lives on the remote fringe of society and confines his fatherly attention and his loving concern, often whimsically, to those who have suffered injustice or who, as with Skimpole, give the lie to oppressive institutional order. Skimpole is, in effect, Jarndyce's own rebellious and anarchic response to the law of Chancery. The father breaks his law by supporting one who in his irresponsible and fetching manner disclaims its power over him.

Weak—powerless, defeated, supplicating, appealing—fathers abound in fiction as structural complements to vigorous daughters full of promise (*Emma* is Jane Austen's definitive portrait of the relation). They express with extraordinary clarity that element of this familial history which binds the daughter in confusing attachment to the male parent. The father's approach to the daughter contradicts that aggressive attitude that haunted Freud's patients; he comes not as the conqueror but as the deposed king; it is his helplessness that attracts: "I need you because you will make me safe and whole," he says to one who cannot refuse him. This appeal, so the structure suggests, is absolutely successful. It can only be thwarted, not denied. In turn, the daughter is dangerously, catastrophically close to a gratification of the absolutely interdicted wish. And this possibility is enhanced by the rigorous demand of the structure that the mother is absent—generally, by her convenient death.

John Jarndyce makes his approach to Esther Summerson a lengthy and indirect one. Long ago he had brought the little girl (as though to camouflage his intentions) to his house along with two more wards, the heirs in Jarndyce vs. Jarndyce. Bleak House is a curious place, a warren, a hive, a structure built without plan, where a little, unexpected room opens to this narrow hall that leads surprisingly to that small, sunlit bedroom. The house is a universe of quaintness and coziness harboring a man given to extremes, a man of moods, who withdraws in the face of the "East Wind" of disappointment into a closet of self-pity. When the house finally duplicates itself at the conclusion of the novel, we shall see why it must be "bleak."

Esther becomes the mistress of the architectural oddity and carries her role as a ring of keys that open to her touch all the mysteries of the house. Guided by this metallic token of the wifely function, she becomes Dame Durden—and all the rest—lovingly regarded and incongruously named the mother. Young women must and will aspire to that position and seek to be the mother. The father is always wrong to capitalize on that aspiration and more mistaken still, more terribly destructive, when he plays his game of hide-and-seek with the daughter, presenting himself and then withdrawing. "See," he says, "what you are close to having," in a perfect expression of the ambivalent attitude of the daughter herself. Jarndyce's epistolary proposal is a variation of this indirection: *Here I am, I want you, take me, save me; be not afraid, I do not seek you.* Esther collapses when the proposal is made, in spite of her apparent calmness. Only the proposal's profound roots in Oedipal longings explain what is for her the most aberrant piece of behavior Dickens invents for her in a scene so strange that readers may simply regard it as Victorian excess of feeling. At the height of her agitation—at the moment she acknowledges that she will have the guardian—Esther steals into Ada's room and presses her one memento of Allan Woodcourt onto Ada's lips. Esther is perhaps the purest example in the English novel of the fundamental process of the psychic life, of the power of identification, the reaching out to appropriate the image of the other as oneself. To take a census of Esther's images would be to write her inner history, the tale of those people, almost always young women, for whom she cares and whom so obviously she adopts as she herself would be adopted. Ada becomes the central image in this array of mirrors, so that what Esther dares not do out of her love for Allan, the unconscious Ada must perform. It is a distressing piece of neurotic behavior rendered with absolute conviction. Dickens knows it is right even as he conveys it with his usual protective language. With maidens, like most of his fellows in the trade of fiction, Dickens must be spiritual; the intact virgin can be saved from lust only by providing her with angelic inaccessibility. Then, at that height, she may be desired in worship.

The plot of *Bleak House* creates the conditions of surprise only to disappoint its readers. Esther's discovery of her mother's identity serves no concluding function in the novel, and the end of Jarndyce vs. Jarndyce is a puzzling denouement: the money is gone as is what expectation the reader may have had of a just distribution of rewards. Richard Carstone cannot be granted money, we know, but could not John Jarndyce's suffering be compensated for or Esther become another Tom Jones? Dickens enjoys and is an expert in the blasting of false hope. *Bleak House* plots the exposure of plotting. At the end of this novel lies no parentage to be discovered or fortune to be won. Detective Bucket tracks down Lady Dedlock, exposes the Chadband circle as well as Smallweed, and triumphantly brings in the French murderess, saving George Rouncewell without redeeming Tulkingham, but it is all in Dickensian high spirits, the finest example we have of Dickens' gift for making novelistic coincidence an instrument of moral and social judgment. The novel's structure, the support for this large-scaled indictment of the social order, requires no plot or coincidence to sustain it and, in effect, disclaims these lesser devices of fiction. Behind coincidence lies the Oedipal seduction of the daughter in the professed weakness of the father; there is also, at last, for Esther, a timely escape.

It is possible to cast the private history of Esther Summerson in terms that may situate it in the public world of Chesney Wold and Chancery. These provisions I shall recover from a reading of Jacques Lacan, not in that heuristic principle can be vigorously applied to literary texts, but in the conviction that when a truth regarding the fundamental processes of psychic life has been approached, even a ten-

tative reappropriation of that truth in criticism might be worth attempting. Lacan's work, in my view, is a legitimate extension or
revision from within of Freud's discoveries; for literary criticism it has
a particular—it may be even decisive—relevance in permitting us to
rethink literariness itself, the figural mode of language, and to restore
to the literary language its truth as language, not as a kind of language
or a special use of language, but as the truth that language speaks,
the truth which, to the Lacanian ear, is spoken by the Other. The most
certain evidence we have in *Bleak House* of that intimidating capital-
ization (of the Other) confronts us in the scene I have mentioned,
Ada's sleeping farewell kiss to Esther's true love, and in the final
turn of the plot, to which I have just alluded. For with an effect of
greater astonishment than that which attends Esther's behavior upon
the loss of Allan Woodcourt, Esther regains him in a remarkable
sequence of events which brings her to her new—her very own—Bleak
House. Viewed within the context of the novel merely as the act of
a character no more harmful than most of Dickens' caricatures, John
Jarndyce's deception may seem merely extravagant, at most awkward, certainly not vicious. What he does is to pretend to hold Esther
to her promise to him, to arrange secretly a marriage to the man he
knows she loves, and to trick her into overseeing the preparation of
Allan's house. The act, in itself, is intolerable, too cruel to permit
its being seen as an expression of anything but John Jarndyce's odd,
if paternal, care.

The consequence of Jarndyce's deception is the building of another
Bleak House. "Bleak" is the word that ought to interrupt our smug
consciousness that the installation of Esther in the new home is another of Dickens' unashamed sentimentalities. "Bleak" gives us, in
its first use, a sense that contradicts the curious domesticity of Esther's
domain: far from the homely comforts the house affords, its name
suggests emptiness, a wasted, inhospitable structure where human
feeling is avoided and human life depressed. As for the second house,
what can it repeat, since it is described as the sunny residence of
marital and familial bliss, of that first set of meanings? At the risk of
dwelling too much on what Dickens never could have intended, I raise
the image of bleakness in connection with Esther's two dwellings in
order to focus through this lens upon another emptiness that stretches

before Esther. In the place of the father, she had seen installed the owner of the first house, a man of property and of history, but of a blighted history and of a property rescued from a much larger position of wealth now and for long contested. "Who owns the Jarndyce fortune?" is a question analogous to the one Esther's history asks, "Who is the father?" The occupant of the paternal role, so prominent in Esther's private story, is wholly absent from the public; the Jarndyce fortune has no caretaker, and John has retired from any interest in it. Then, as we have seen, he betrays the private aspect of his position by the proposal to Esther, abandoning as the weak father his guardianship as well as his public responsibilities. Two sets of discriminations are required to cope with this setting. The father has not one but a range of responsibilities, each relying on the other. These functions constitute a position that looks both toward the personal and toward the public dimensions of life. In the long view, it is this conjunction of the familial and social realms in the position of the father that gives his behavior such prominence in the life of the individual, though it does not seem a necessary condition of human existence that the access to the social order (to the transpersonal signifying systems) be left to this position. The father, furthermore and most importantly, has the function of displaying his position *as a position,* that is, of introducing the child to positionality itself, to relationality, to the institutional orders that will constitute the child as a subject. He must therefore vacate, in prospect, his position, though it would seem, if *Bleak House, Emma,* and other novels are to be trusted, that he finds this task, as it respects his daughter, nearly impossible. A law enjoins the father to reveal paternity as a relational principle. In so doing, the father dies, gives way, is (in another context) murdered: he becomes the symbolic father.

The symbolic father is neither real nor present. For Jacques Lacan[1] this metaphor of paternity founds and sustains the cultural orders into which the individual is born; he is the dead father of Freud's myth, whose murder is the beginning of human society. To this mythical founder, whose sons were compelled to patricide, we owe a debt so grievous that it can never be repaid: our very subjectivity, or the totality of our engagement in the exchanges and discourses that make

up the social structure. These systems of exchange—language, marriage customs, and so on—are the inherited laws of a culture given by
that mythical founder and condensed in his name, by which we are
signed and which we speak often only in trembling, if at all. The name
signifies culture itself, what essentially cannot be named, the system of
signifiers. And it signifies too the fact that the system is independent of
reality, an autonomous construct that cannot be bound in a natural
way to reality and that, as the symbolic order, therefore floats free—
except for certain critical events in the psychic history of individuals—
of reality and meaning. The name-of-the-father symbolizes this freedom, this absence of a present reality and this difference from the real
father; the name asserts that reality will be restored through the possibility of order implicit in the signifying system.

Governed according to syntagmatic and paradigmatic laws that
operate much like the audible signifiers of a language, social systems
create roles and positions, values and rituals, myths and religions.
Into this matrix, this system of systems, the person is introduced in the
first movements toward individuality, and it is by the father's word
that the child begins to acquire the signifying systems. Before the
father's word was uttered, the child yearned to be what the mother
desired; in her love, the child discovered desire and, in keeping
with this stage, knew no limits either to need or to satisfaction; the
child sought to be that which the mother's desire named, that is, in
psychoanalytic terms, the phallus. This yearning, anticipating and
informing a later, more conscious love of the mother, is forbidden
by her when she turns toward the father, at the point at which the
child learns that she or he fills that emptiness that the phallus names.
The interdiction is the father's finally to utter: you may not have the
mother. Desire to be the object of desire becomes desire to have the
object, and that desire encounters an obstacle. The progression is
natural and necessary; it is also terrible—for the boy the threat and
for the girl a realization of castration, the recognition of the absence
at the heart of one's own desire.

Castration is the moment of desire's emergence—not of need (that
unexpressible movement), nor of demand (the articulation of want)
but of the signification by which the object chosen refers to the chain
of signifiers that links it to the history of the subject's desire. Desire in

Lacanian terms is systematic and signifying, andwhat is spoken in language must be interpreted; who speaks here is of equal interest to and not to be identifed with the subject of the enunciation: the other of the unconscious. Castration is related to desire as the moment at which this language is spoken, the atemporal occasion continually repeated in the speech of desire. Because the father's interdiction compels the son to delay satisfaction as he overcomes infantile need, there appear now in the familial orbit not merely images and objects but relations and their positions. Before the child was, there was mother-and-father; where the father or mother are, the child shall be. The relational world as the area and horizon of desire congeals before the child's eyes. In this world a subject is manifested in predetermined relational terms that are not identified as persons. The child conceives the possibility of being—a father or a mother. The child is subjected to a system in which, such is the condition of the human, he is forever alienated.

For to be signified is to be absent, and kinship systems mark absences. If I am to be a father, I am not yet a father; if I am a father, my child will replace me. In addition to the splitting by which disappointed need (as opposed to demand) established the chain of desired objects in the unconscious according to the laws of the primary process, the individual is alienated again from her or his own subjectivity.

The symbolic father who presides over the process by which the subject is created, who exists from all time, who can never die (all these theological attributions are from the point of view of the subject only too true), this symbolic father who bears the signifier of signifiers, the phallus, authorizes language too. In its earliest use, the linguistic apparatus (which is not the beginning of communication as such) was applied to the alternation of presence and absence. The famous "fort-da" of Freud's nephew coincided with the effort that mastered desire and controlled absence in the fantasy of the game. The child's spool came and went in the phantasmal re-creation of the mother's presence which prefigures all presence as founded upon irreducible absence. The need which craves this presence is ambiguous and historically variable, particularly in the change which the father initiates. When the parental relation appears, "having" as a relation to an object also appears, and the infant wish for the incorporated other must be modified. This development is visible in the articulated need, the variations of "I want" that the child utters. Language not only calls up absences, it re-creates through the absence of the original object of satisfaction the fantasy of that satisfaction and disposes the subject in relation to an object in the linguistic structure itself. Language in Lacanian terms is the occasion, the condition, for the constitution of the unconscious. In this view, the unconscious is never the dark repository of myth or the realm of the wild instincts. It contains nothing that belongs to the romantic imagination and can be likened to a signifying system, such as language, deploying available "ideas" (remnants of conscious experience) in chains of association linked and cross-linked by reference to desired objects and by the deflections introduced by repression.

At this point the relation of the symbolic father to the literary language seems to me accessible. As language is acquired, as the play of absence-presence becomes the statement that "I want," the father who limits these statements of want by his interdiction reveals that language, too, like the order of relationality, is a relation of positions, for the "I have you" that concludes "I want" has been assumed by the father in relation to the mother. "I" is a linguistic shifter, a position occupied by others, and the fundamental structures of language, which precede the individual, belong not to her or him, but to that one who is absolutely the Other, forever absent and unachievable. To take up a pen, to submit to the institution of the written word, and to be enticed into textuality is to acknowledge this absence and accept the fundamental alienations it implies, not the least of which is the re-creation of the moment (not the time) of the constitution of the unconscious. To read the literary text, in all its conscious modes and operations, is to produce again that process by which an affective charge—a cathexis—is released from what it was attached to; to write/read directs this charge and provides it with the elements, phantasmally reproduced, that will attract it. The literary language has this creative power, the power of the beginning, and the power of linking, through the fantasy, the unconscious and conscious systems.

Just as language evokes the absent father who instituted it and its relation to the processes of desire, so it also arranges before us the promise of fulfillment, of meaning, which cannot be hoped for but always is there to be sought. The literary language refers us to nothing, not to the legal institutions of England in *Bleak House* and not to the English roads that Bucket and Esther travel in their search for Esther's mother. These objective, concrete referents, these historical facts, belong to the reduced languages of history or social analysis, for in the linguistic moment, it is not the referential power of language that dominates, but its re-creative force, as the individual enters subjectivity and as desire is historicized. The literary language matures the inner relations of the psyche between conscious and unconscious processes and between subject and relational world.

Yet the language of fiction is also referential, and the timely as well as timeless meaning of *Bleak House* is that the institutions of society oppress persons. The transpersonal structures of the social order, where individuals find their relations and positions publicly codified, are indifferent to individuals, not in the sense that these institutions possess an alienated consciousness, but in that their authority is misunderstood. And this difficulty is compounded by the polysemic quality of figural language. The image of the fog, the dominant image of the opening pages of *Bleak House*, as it is taken up, repeated, and enlarged in connection with the Dedlock family and Chesney Wold, will clear up sufficiently to reveal how Dickens represents his England and judges it, and then too how this judgment is synchronized with Esther's story, so that her life, because it too is evaluated, supports Dickens' views of the law.

The fog surrounds, conceals, rolls over, and invades English life. An impalpable and yet obfuscating element in the moral and political atmosphere, it sorts well with the "grasping and floundering conditions" of the High Court of Chancery, where it confounds those who "look in vain for truth" in any cause. It is a murky "afternoon," Jarndyce vs. Jarndyce "drones on," the case that "has been death to many," always ready "to spoil and corrupt" those touched by it. Chancery and its quintessential case go on, enriching lawyers, ruining suitors, in "trickery, evasion, procrastination, spoliation, botheration," defying common sense and justice, perverting language ("groping knee-deep in technicalities") and offending truth. Jarndyce vs. Jarndyce itself is a chimera: its energy, the money that paid its way through the court, is soon to be exhausted, and Chancery, so foggily unaware of the human cost it exacts, weaves about itself that cocoon of soft, dense, and absorbing material that suffocates as it pretends to revive hope. Chancery deflects every effort to penetrate the fog by transforming new information into "mere buds on the forest tree of the parent suit." Chancery exists to thwart understanding, to defy progress. And the world of the Dedlocks in Lincolnshire and London is the same, wrapped up in "too much jeweler's cotton and fine wool."

The social criticism of *Bleak House* persuades and moves the reader with a conviction Dickens is unique in commanding. Its language arouses, too, another set of meanings, not because that eternal mist of legal wrangling itself is so suggestive, but because the entire scene develops with so much passion and enlarges itself with so much internal necessity. Dickens must sustain this note, and that he does so with much variety testifies to his fictional powers; to the reader the fog invades every cranny of the novel, and moreover with what it preeminently and sensuously conveys of a kind of hidden inexistence, for what is, as fog, also is not; it fills and yet leaves empty; it has the look and feel of what is there, like Chancery, and yet it never withstands opposition. Fog is all; fog is nothing. Fog, and Chancery, and the Dedlocks' world, are present as the camouflage of an absence, for each in its individual way conceals by means of a pretence of fullness its own essential vacancy. Its authority evaporates (though for Dickens in *Bleak House* it is not destroyed) by reference to another manipulation of that paternal absence that the legal, social, and political institutions of England have distorted. As a father, Sir Leicester Dedlock fails, and the social authority he commands is exercised in self-preservation. Like Chancery, though without its impersonal malice, Sir Leicester resists inquiry and inspection. If the symbolic father and his law establish the rules of relation, Dedlock and Chancery may be said to insist upon them, but the founder also exists to shape those who will displace him. Chancery and Dedlock turn toward these potential replacements with undisguised hostility. It is the vengeful attitude of the father as rival that meets those who challenge him. The beginning of *Bleak House* recalls this structure of paternal indifference and hatred and of the childish need to eliminate the great obstacle, that protean figure who, if he loves, may also destroy; who hates, even as he invites love. Who then issues the license that makes this narrative so authoritative?

Dickens writes, at the end of the first chapter, "If all the injustice it has committed, and all the misery it has caused, could only be locked up with it, and the whole burnt away in a great funeral pyre, —why so much the better for other parties than the parties in Jarndyce and Jarndyce!" And at the beginning of the last paragraph, the extraordinary present of this narrator's style, with its combination of solemnity and exasperated humor, sounds again: "The Chancellor is about to bow to the bar, when the prisoner is presented. Nothing can possibly come of the prisoner's conglomeration, but his being sent back to prison." Both remote and deeply engaged, this voice is confirmed by reference to another: "I have a great deal of difficulty in beginning to write my portion of these pages, for I know I am not clever"—as clever as that preceding one, of course, *was*. There is a difference emphasized in the contrasting of voices, one that grows into a chasm: present tense, past tense; historical sense, personal destiny; critical intelligence, a feeling heart; objective observation, sympathetic response; judgment, sentiment. What, by this extravagance of distinctive styles, by this risky and, to almost all its critics, aesthetically disruptive shifting of tones, can be achieved? May we imagine, first, another structure and eliminate the obstinate Esther? Even a less drastic alteration, a casting of her story into the third person, destroys what, apparently, Dickens strove at some expense to preserve, that abrupt and unmistakable shift of style and tone. The difference must remain, must in fact be experienced fully. When differences expand into polarizations, the consequence is not a kind of stable opposition but an emphasis, a hierarchy, as one pole of difference begins to assume a negativity. It becomes what the other is not. As the narrative manner of *Bleak House* develops, the removed, authoritative, powerful voice of social observation and deftly plotted coincidence becomes just that negative. Esther's voice lacks power; she insists upon that point. She is negligible, and her only hope is to win some love. In all its assured conviction, the voice of the present tense, while it so firmly speaks, is not Esther's. But the negation never acts to demean the young woman's style. In the intricacies of the novel's progress, a certain trust begins to grow in that girlish narrator, and the impersonal observer finally sub-

mits to her an authority she never claims. It is she finally who judges
Skimpole, who cares for Ada, who suffers, and who loves and is re-
warded. She knows John Jarndyce as that other of her voice never
could. The objective narrator, who all along had observed and judged,
who also condemned and exposed so cleverly Chadband and Smallweed and Turveydrop, and who admired George and Phil and the
Bagnets and transmitted effectively its pity for Jo, that voice supports
and, it must be said, derives from Esther; it is Esther's other voice.[2]

This conception of the narrative peculiarity of *Bleak House* requires that we see Esther's situation in more detail. Lacan has elaborated a psychic structure, Freudian in inspiration and in detail, which
brings the psyche out of a series of relations to the Other that are described as the "Imaginary" and into relations governed by what is
called the "Symbolic," where the "Law of the Name-of-the-Father" is
obeyed. In the imaginary, relations are restricted to the alienating
identifications (and oppositions) that constitute the ego and are the
chief processes of the psychic life. From the originating totality of the
union with the mother to the history of separations and adoptions of
ideals and roles and models, the other exists for the self. Esther's
infinite capacity for adopting other young women illustrates this kind
of relation; she nurtures them as she would be nurtured; she behaves
as that absent mother would have behaved toward her. Imputed to
her by the sadistic Miss Rachael, the guilt of separation and mourning
is transformed by Esther into a life of sacrifice: I am not worthy; you,
whom I love and care for, are the worthy one. Only this mechanism
adequately if not fully takes us into that critical scene of loss when
Ada becomes Esther and kisses the dried roses of Allan Woodcourt.
These relations are not shed like an old skin when the entry into the
symbolic is made.

The transformation in the imaginary makes the symbolic visible.[3]
In Esther's life, the crisis occurs when she develops the smallpox that
kills Jo. She will not be seen, particularly by the beautiful Ada. She has
changed, she believes; what hope she had of a beauty that merely reflected Ada's is now blasted. Others finally challenge her: she is more
beautiful than ever, they say; she has not changed; she is lovely. The
little boy at Boythorn's honestly gives us a clearer picture. Her face has
been altered. Dickens insists on the change when Esther in accepting

Jarndyce's offer admits to her glass that her face is different and then lowers her veil to Allan Woodourt, displaying her disfigurement and so assuming her great loss. Contrary to the apparent drift of these events, Esther's acceptance of the guardian does not apply the injunction against incest. The guardian is still in danger of that crime, but the ward has escaped it by escaping her own image. Her altered appearance cuts her off from close identification with Ada and Charlie and the rest, and when she declares herself ready to become mistress of Bleak House, she enters into a new role. Rather, it may be said that Esther as the designated mistress of Bleak House, when she accepts Woodcourt's affection as pity after exhibiting her face to him, performs the essential act that marks her entry into the law of relationality. She makes the connection between the loss of her beauty and Jarndyce's proposal herself—"But he did not hint to me, that when I had been better-looking, he had had this same proceeding in his thought, and had refrained from it." She reflects upon the guardian's generosity and consideration and upon her duty to him. She confronts herself in the mirror: "And so, Esther my dear, you are happy for life."

No agony is so great as to be determined to be happy in misery because one ought to be, because it is right and good to be happy in making another happy. Self-sacrifice does not comprehend this determination, for what Esther accepts is her position as an adult —not her early roles as Dame Durden when she could dream of Allan, but the familial one, the loving wife. The change is subtle but confirmed everywhere. Ada is still her "beauty," but, after the secret marriage to Carstone, "she was changed." Esther cares for Caddy, at about the same time, over a period of two months and displays again her affection for those young women she befriends, but it is a critical Esther, who, if only in asides, allows Caddy's family themselves to display their meannesses and selfishness: Mrs. Jellyby and Mr. Turveydrop are particularly attended to. In judgment, in acceptance of change, in already disposing herself to be mistress of Bleak House, as in her altered face, Esther is a new Esther, but not in her essential passivity. While she cared for Caddy, a little hint is dropped by the guardian that he has decided not to press his suit and that his darling Esther will after all have her Allan. He asks her, of Allan, whether the young man had experienced some "particular disappointment" and whether she has "heard of anything of the sort."

Of the evident cruelty, however it may be excused, of Jarndyce's secret I have spoken. But this opinion needs review, if for no other reason than that Dickens seems wholly unaware of it. Its corollary too must be examined, for if Jarndyce is not needlessly indifferent to Esther's feeling, can she be as listlessly passive as she seems when she meekly accepts her good fortune just as the guardian feels confident in his right to bestow it upon her? Thematically, morally, the incident will not bear scrutiny. Structurally, it resolves the novel's deepest tensions. Esther accepts almost wordlessly her happiness in the same spirit as she had determined earlier that it was her place to be happy even after learning that Woodcourt loved her. The new Bleak House is the home of the paternal principle, that principle of relationality, which she had acceded to in the old. The movement is in perfect alignment with her more mature grasp of her condition, of her changed beauty, of her relations to Ada and Caddy. She is able to do now what she most deeply wishes as the fulfillment of what is most importantly expected of her—to make Allan Woodcourt the father. This sudden and surprising transference—from the old to the new Bleak House—is a symbolic action in the Lacanian sense, not, that is, as a symbol of something else, but as a transformation of human relationality and an ordering of the processes of identification. The change is experienced as belonging elsewhere than in the private desire that motivates action, and it is also known as a regulation, a manifestation of law, in the expression of that desire. More, the symbolic as it escapes and indeed offers escape from mere seriality redeems time; to the observer of the public narrative style of *Bleak House,* the world is temporalized as a permanent present, an endless series of nows. Because Esther's narrative is the story of the entry of the person into the symbolic, it must make use of that novelistic convention which tells of change and describes the psychological and moral conditions that affect it. Esther's is a "true" story which ultimately converts the specious eternality of the observer's narrative into true fiction.

Early in the novel the analphabetic Krook had drawn his hieroglyphic JARNDYCE before Esther with a certain presumptuous and premonitory glee. Readers respond here with a certain anticipation of mysteries to be unraveled: Will Esther inherit money? Will the secret of the Jarndyce suit be found in the miser's hoard? Nothing like these results will happen, but in his sinister way, Krook tells the tale of *Bleak House.* "Jarndyce" is the weak father, as it is the soul-destroying suit, as it is somehow the very language that as symbolic order must be stated. When the marks become a language, "Jarndyce" will become the father, to be signed again in a different register. The name of the father of course appears everywhere, not only as JARNDYCE, but as Jarndyce vs. Jarndyce, as Chancery, as the Lord Chief Justice, as Dedlock and Snagsby and Chadband and Chesney Wold and all the other remnants, living and dead, moribund or active, of paternal authority that inhabit *Bleak House.* The general action of the novel supposes that Esther's wise passivity, which establishes the positionality of the father in the new Bleak House, also casts back over the voice of the other who tells the public story of the reign of the symbolic order. Esther's narrative lays down the law of signification that permits this larger element of *Bleak House* to be given meaning.

Plainly, it requires this aid. Not only does the social commentary of the other narrative need to be saved from its own irony; it also looks to the orphaned girl for its anchoring in narrative authenticity. Esther's narrative provides that relation to the unconscious processes that the language of fiction, in its phantasmal dimension, always explores and restates. It always exists as the written language, though in what I take to be the metaphorical sense that Jacques Derrida has given that unspoken part of language, that is, as the mark of an absence, though of a mark repressed. The fiction leads back not to the beginning, but to the condition in which a beginning is missed, when desire already sought its lost object, but in its substitute. Lacan's view of the metonymic operation of desire suggests that when the fictional language brings us into the fantasy we encounter in relation to the narrative consciousness another whose language is visible in the words and deeds of the principal agent of the novel. Esther's Oedipal crisis and its strangely unwilled solution attach the objective narrative to a psychic history and affirm therefore an order which that other narrative must realize only in the moral tone of its aroused sympathies and aversions.

In Lacan's recovery of Freud, the subject is what appears in being subjected to a language, to a system of signifiers. It is what is signified among themselves by the signifiers considered as signifiers. This subjection to signifiers does not occur instantaneously in the history of the individual. Already, in the process, for example, of differentiation from the world of objects, which depends on marks of difference on the surface of its own body as well as on the experience of the mirror-stage where identity is joyfully grasped on the model of the unity of the perceived body, the individual had entered processes of signification. And the chain of objects linked to the original (lost) object of satisfaction had already, too, by the time of the more mature accession to linguistic structures, formed a signifying system that will resemble those conscious structures. But in language, again with a retrospective relation to the mirror-stage, where the other is identified with, the subject develops only in relation to that Other that the linguistic system and its capacity to produce meaning must bring into consciousness. A signifier belongs to an outside, to all those differences that place it in language; but the subject, already in the mirror-stage and now with a developed psyche, is also positioned. Earlier in the mirror, the individual is *there*, imaged as a unity; in language, the individual again is placed, and now in that position where meaning is intended: "I say that. . . ." The difference between the positionings corresponds to the difference between Lacan's imaginary and symbolic: in the imaginary the relation to the other belongs to the sphere of being it and not being it, of being captured by it, a stage of subjectification, of the "coagulation of identity in a structure of otherness." The other is the term which separates the self from object, and in language this term becomes that Other from which language issues. In this place, the subject rises as what can be stood in for; it is represented there; it is nothing but this representation, and this representation must do for all subjects. Language creates the place where subjects find each other, where "social communication" occurs.[4]

To communicate is to be different from someone, and the primary difference achieved through the castration anxiety is the sexual one. Sexual identity, won under threat, comes about in relation to the ways in which castration is experienced. The object of the castration threat is figured as the phallus, which not only is the signifier of the primary identity, but of all significance, in that the signifier in this case establishes a link to the (anatomical) referent. The freedom of the signifying system paradoxically operates to create significance in the association of the realm of the signifier with that of the signified. The phallus signifies this relation and, more, the situation of the subject (under the threat of castration) in the signifying system. The place of the signifier as that of the Other is also the location of the relation to the referent, so that in this Other—the realm of the symbolic—the subject finds those cultural orders whose authority and priority she or he cannot question. That is, in questioning them, the subject must question questioning, for the critical, judgmental, monitoring, self-conscious operations of the ego display it as subject within the sociocultural orders.

Perhaps another view of the narrative structure of *Bleak House* may now be mentioned. In an earlier distinction, or rather set of distinctions, the two narrative styles complement one another in their difference, where the very sharpness of that difference insists that the two points of view be held in a kind of relation that must be called structural, that is, a relation that produces and continues to produce a set of meanings. The attitudinal narrative of the observer which judges and discriminates among various aspects of the social order of England at last subsides into a peaceful contemplation of Chesney Wold, with the enmity between Boythorn and Dedlock converted into a kindly meant pretense and with Dedlock's hold on the political life of the country loosened by his wife's death. Now George the stalwart cares for him. At the same time Esther interrogates and exposes the irresponsible Skimpole; when judgment slackens into pity at Chesney Wold, moral outrage moves Esther at Skimpole's house. The same structural view of the novel which allows us to hold the godlike authority of the observer and Esther's needs and impotence in a single glance also extends our franchise over other dimensions of the novel.

Esther's is a life of submission, passive, dominated, and oppressed. Yet her great negation—"I am not worthy of love; I must make myself so"—cannot be allowed to stand so simply credited. Her formal existence in the linguistic structure of the novel allows us to expand her role. Esther is "seduced" by the "father"; that these words require special interpretation does not mean they are inaccurate or employed in some specialized way. The metaphor of sexual behavior and its familial setting describes the structural matrix, the relational world, of desire and its development. By similar extension, we are also permitted to see the second Bleak House as a repetition of the first, to respect the position of the father in both dwellings, to appreciate the fact that Allan Woodcourt replaces John Jarndyce. The same structural necessity does not compel us to put Esther on a couch when we see her as desiring the father. In the relation of older guardian and young ward, there is more than the paternal love of the daughter; Esther loves and submits to the father. Beyond this perhaps not surprising conclusion, which, however, cannot be read too sentimentally, we must venture to interpret Esther's childish guilt as a reflection, again within the Oedipal transformation of emotion, of a wish to eliminate the mother. Nothing in her personal psychology (even if that phantom be allowed to materialize) of course allows this malicious intention. But structurally, and always proceeding with tact and an awareness of the complexity of formal relations in the novel, Esther is guilty of wishing the mother's death (with Bucket, does she hound her mother to her doom?), just as on a more directly apprehensible level, she desires the father.

The outcome of these structural judgments for the Esther-narrative is that more general formal considerations arise, particularly as regards the point of view of that narrative. If Allan occupies John Jarndyce's place, if Esther aspires to the mother's, if, to extend the case only by example, Caddy and Jo become Esther's children and Ada becomes Esther herself in the scene of sacrifice, Esther also, as the center of desire in the novel, must take her place in the disguised scene of incest. In all cases, a position opens to be occupied; immediate feeling may contradict the relation, common sense may demur, causality and temporality may suffer, but the ratios in the relations of positions hold and will be determinative. As for the evident narrative disunity of Bleak House, then, the position of the "subject" of the narration, the declarer, the imaged speaker, the source of intellectual and emotional judgment, also constitutes a formal element of the novel, in this case a dual element of complementarity and opposition. In the phantasmal representation by which the subjective place of the narrative is opened, the reader installs herself or himself without question in that vacancy. What such behavior implies is that the subject, who never is anything other than the one in the subjective position, begins to produce meanings. The situation of a subject in the symbolic order follows upon the recognition of a difference that leads to articulation. On the model of the diacritical system that Saussure located, the individual who matures into sexual differentiation does not perform a biological function but accepts a role in the symbolic realm, in the world of relations. The term *phallus*, as it appears in Lacan, designates this principle of differentiation by which meaning is produced, this introduction into culture, this already existing route for the development of desire, this emergence from imaginary relations with objects. Because the phallus belongs to the symbolic father, to that father in whose name the acculturation of the person is carried out, it is the principle of paternity that may be said to govern narrative, as well as other modes of the generation of meaning.[5] Novels, as institutions, as meanings, as openings into subjectivity (understood in the special sense that a structuralist psychoanalysis gives that term), traverse these fundamental passages with remarkable success, but also with an irremediable lack of completion. Individual readers never tire of the positions of the subject. Meanings are always deferred, always cross the paths of other meanings, and the fantasy in which desire acts out its substitutive satisfaction never ends. What was originally lost is beyond recovery, but what continues to signify is that *subjective* activity, that occupation of a position and that relation to the desire of the Other toward whom articulated demand is directed. Esther continues to want love even as in her love she re-creates the paternal order. *Bleak House* contemplates the evidently permanent state of institutional crisis in the context of a reinstitution of the symbolic order. As it must, that order brings into human fullness individual desire and individual meaning through the creation of the subject in relation to the Other. Like the sons of the dead father, whose murder Freud thought was celebrated in the mythic imagination in order to circle around guilt toward community, readers of fiction honor their own constitution as subjects by entering a shared fantasy. They exchange among themselves that potential for signification that is the sacred fount of the phallus of the symbolic father.

2 "The Captive King": The Absent Father in Melville's Text

RÉGIS DURAND

I   There is a sense in which the question of the absent father should not be posed as such, at the outset, and should not be considered as the fundamental problem, but as only one of its representations or masquerades, a theatricalization of a problem. Should not the fundamental question—if there be such a thing—be posed rather in terms of the eternal Oedipal configuration: desire of the mother (her own, that of the child for her) and hatred of the father? And perhaps even beyond ("before" in the mythic chronology of the unconscious) that configuration, where the problem comes to a standstill at an unpassable and most primitive stage: that of the rivalry, the merciless war between two narcissisms (that of the father, the *Urvater,* and that of the child in happy symbiosis with his mother—the child inside the womb, dreaming of, or reminiscing about, the uterine paradise). From there, one could go on to show how this original conflict generates a whole theater of doubles, reduplications which populate our stories. But fathers are absent conspicuously from Melville's fiction. Mothers, too, for that matter, but the longing is there, the remembrance and the desire to be reunited with the innumerable images and fantasies of cavities, vaults, wombs, penetration, and plunge. One could even find a text to go with the desire, one as explicit and peremptory as they come:

Surely all this is not without meaning. And still deeper the meaning of that story of Narcissus, who because he could not grasp the tormenting mild image he saw in the fountain, plunged into it and was drowned. But that same image, we ourselves see in all rivers and oceans. It is the image of the ungraspable phantom of life; and this is the key to it all. (*MD*, i: 14)[1]

But then, there is *Redburn* and the return of the dead father; and *Pierre* and its obsessive, perverse manipulation of father images, enough to force a reconsideration of the question. The narcissism of the child *in utero* indeed may be the key to it all, but the *fiction* speaks another language. Not only is fiction haunted by the return of the vanished father, but it wagers its very status and existence as fiction on the question of the symbolic father. Its flow, its narrative momentum and shape, are closely dependent on the strategy adopted in connection with that figure. In Melville, images and metaphors, especially those concerning rivers and oceans, weave a parallel discourse in which the questions of time, origins, and death are subsumed under the idea of paternity. And then there is *Pierre*, in which the circle is completed, and the return to narcissism is effected through a complex and painful ritual of introjection and rejection of the dead father and of the doomed fantasy of wholly incestuous origin (something like the desire to be the offspring of oneself with one's own mother). What follows is an attempt to trace some aspects of this intricacy.[2]

II   The Absent Father and the Original Metaphor

In his essay on time in Melville, Georges Poulet quotes a passage from *Moby Dick* which illustrates the fractured, fragmented character of Melville's fictional time. But if we read the passage in question to the end of the paragraph, something else emerges, which touches on the fundamental nature of Melville's fiction and perhaps of all fiction:

There is no steady unretracing progress in this life; we do not advance through fixed gradations, and at the last one pause: through infancy's unconscious spell, boyhood's thoughtless faith, adolescence's doubt (the common doom), then scepticism, then disbelief, resting at last in manhood's pondering repose of If. But once gone through, we trace the round again, and are infants, boys and men, and Ifs eternally. Where lies the final harbour, whence we unmoor no more? In what rapt ether sails the world, of which the weariest will never weary? Where is the foundling's father hidden? Our souls are like those orphans whose unwedded mothers die in bearing them: the secret of our paternity lies in their grave, and we must there to learn it. (*MD*, cxiv:406)

Fathers may be conspicuously absent from Melville's fiction, yet clearly a passage such as this, in its elaborate metaphorical way, shows that the absence of the father is a key psychological and structural element. In order to analyze it, I propose to make use—as a starting point, say as a means to gain leverage—of a neo-Freudian hypothesis concerning the origins of language and of the unconscious.[3]

Recent Freudian theory links the emergence of language, of language as discourse, to the figure of the symbolic father. The Freudian "primal repression" becomes with Jacques Lacan the "paternal metaphor"; access to the order of the symbolic is gained through the agency of what Lacan calls the name-of-the-father. What I want to suggest at this point is that Melville's fiction offers a striking example, an analogue, in fact, and a metaphor of this process. Not of course that process *itself* at work, inasmuch as it is unconscious and, consequently, belongs to an entirely different order of experience, but something *not unlike* it.

From a Freudian point of view, discourse is closely related to the figure of the dead father, a figure which constitutes one of the deepest primitive scenes, one at the very foundations of the unconscious and of the constitution of the symbolic organization. Roughly summarized, the process is the passage from a primitive state in which the subject occupies—or desires to occupy—the position of the real father and is, therefore, in unbearable competition with him, to a *symbolic* identification with the father, the symbolic father, or figure of the law. What Lacan calls the name-of-the-father is the signifier of this symbolic operation, one of those "key-signifiers" placed, as Laplanche and Leclaire put it, "in metaphorizing position." This position implies that the signifiers' role is to order the whole system of human language, to articulate desire to the symbolic order. It is the role of those key-signifiers to make effective the separation, the bar, between signifier and signified. The bar, central to the whole symbolic process, is what makes the emergence of meaning possible: the signified, instead of floating freely, is now pinned down, "captured" in certain specific places (the famous "points de capiton," the "holding down points"). This is really the essential process behind the so-called paternal metaphor which is a repressive gesture, the constitutive repression: a passage from a world of pure difference and meaningless oscillation to an *anchoring*, a stabilization through some key symbols. The paternal metaphor, when it is successful, casts a kind of "signifying mesh" or network and acts as a ballast. When it is *not* completely successful, as in the case of psychotic subjects, what has not been properly repressed and made symbolic becomes foreclosed (*Verwerfen*) and threatens to return in the real as hallucination. The whole symbolic process is affected by the failure of the paternal metaphor (one of the consequences being that it becomes impossible to distinguish between the symbol and the thing symbolized, word and thing presentation, for instance). The message of the psychotic may tend to resemble what linguists call autonomous messages, that is to say messages about words rather than messages using words.

This is obviously an inadequate presentation of a complex question, but if we now return to the passage from *Moby Dick* with which we began, we can see how it relates quite explicitly to the paternal metaphor as we have defined it. This passage summarizes as it were a fundamental uncertainty or hesitation between two types of relations to the symbolic order, which from the point of view of fiction imply two narrative modes. The first would be the successful achievement of the "family romance," a linear and non-contradictory discursive and symbolic mode. It is represented in the first sentence of the paragraph quoted, but negatively, under a kind of disavowal ("We do not advance through fixed gradation . . .").

The other mode, opposed to linear coherence, emphasizes discontinuity, oscillation, and non-differentiation. In the paragraph quoted, it is exemplified in the seemingly psychotic desire to follow the mother into the grave in order to learn there, as Melville puts it, the secret of our paternity. This accounts, as we shall see, for a whole aspect of Melville's writing which always threatens to tear holes in the fabric of narrative continuity. At such times, what had been foreclosed—owing to the partial failure of the paternal metaphor—returns under the form of hallucinations or regressive fantasies. Such a tension between the two modes is not unusual in fiction. But in the case of Melville, I think it has not been properly seen that it constitutes an essential structural element, which accounts for what has been variously and often unconvincingly described as the theme or the obsession of failure.

Most of Melville's novels are voyage or discovery novels. As such they manifest the traditional aesthetic of a genre. But the "quest" seen

from the point of view of the Melvillean protagonist is strangely aimless, without a real objective. It is not merely, I would argue, the
romantic quest for truth or identity that many have read into it. It is
precisely because of its aimlessness that it has invited so much speculation. As it is, the quest is mostly a drifting, an errantry—at best a way
of passing time; at worst a kind of quiet suicide. Think of Redburn,
White-Jacket, Ishmael: what do they do on board, except wait for time
to pass, for the voyage to be over? Is not theirs an aimless circuitous
voyage on which they embarked out of pure resourcelessness or dere-
liction? Their so-called quest, then, is *not,* appearances to the contrary, the inner core of the narrative, its vital generative principle. The
narrative in the form of a voyage, of a discovery, is *superimposed* on
the inner core; it is external to it and structures the novel *like* a narrative and gives it a semblance of a narrative framework. But the core is a
non-narrative, an expectancy, a stasis.

Stasis must be understood here in opposition to narrative flow: it
does not by any means imply that the material is lifeless. The material
which I call primitive—in that it comes before the narrative stream-
lining and remains largely outside of it, outside of the equivalent of the
symbolic process—is in fact very powerful. At times, it forces its way
violently into the narrative: what had been foreclosed, non-symbolized (the Father) returns as hallucination, such as, for example,
Redburn's hallucination of his father in Liverpool. So that the whole
novel (here *Redburn*) appears to tend not toward a new knowledge (of
experience, of identity) but toward the return of the dead father. Then,
in *White-Jacket,* the return of the non-symbolized takes place not in
the form of hallucinations but in the form of an inversion of the narrative (or symbolic) process itself, which turns on itself and explores its
own depths and vehicle. Instead of being a narrative of events, the
novel becomes a description of scenes and places. The core of *White-
Jacket* is a progressive exploration of the hidden parts of the frigate, its
innards, in a series of regressive fantasies. The dominant structure of
the novel is not a narrative (a process of symbolization), but an inven-
tory, a litany of objects, spaces and bodies, as they are invested by a
return of the primitive.

In those two novels, although the narrative process is constantly in
danger of being subverted by the non-symbolized, it manages to retain
its grip, its dominance. In *Moby Dick* and *The Confidence-Man,* on

the other hand, the balance of forces is modified. We no longer have a narrative framework occasionally disrupted by the return of primitive material. It is not that the primitive material becomes dominant because it is quantitatively more important, but that the narrative energy itself seems to be affected by the return of the non-symbolized, *as if the symbolic process itself* (in its fictional form) were weakened; as if the forecluded material now manifested itself not through hallucinations or regressive fantasies, but through a distortion, a perversion of the narrative vehicle. The novelistic discourse no longer provides the seamless continuum which enables the novel to assimilate and to carry various heterogeneous materials. The stasis is no longer a matter of an isolated moment in the general flow of the text. It is the flow itself, the discursive momentum which is now threatened. Naturally, the distinction I am making between *Redburn* and *White-Jacket* on the one hand, and *Moby Dick* and *The Confidence-Man* on the other, is somewhat oversimplified. It is not so much an opposition as a shift of emphasis, a displacement, that takes place from one pair of novels to the other. In the first two, a repression is rigorously maintained, because of the strongly felt presence of what we might call "a narrative superego," which imposes on the writing a clear chronological and causal framework. In the other two, and especially in *The Confidence-Man*, it is as if the original metaphor (that largely mythic, fictitious operation of repression which Lacan calls the "paternal metaphor" —we are dealing here indeed with a metaphor, a theoretical fiction), then, had lost its moorings, had perhaps become contaminated by the instability of the material it was supposed to operate on. So that the powerful presence of the superego is still felt, but it seems at times out of control, at times excessive (too pervasive and too intrusive), at times insufficient (too weak or ludicrous). It is this hesitation between excess and lack which characterizes the two latter novels: both excess and lack refer to an empty enigmatic space where something, as the Lacanian phrase goes, is never quite in its place. But we might want at this stage to look at the texts more closely.

III

In *Redburn*, the scenario of the protagonist's hallucination is in itself extremely interesting. Redburn is reading an old guidebook of the city

of Liverpool, which has been left to him by his dead father. With the
book in hand, he tries to reconstruct the itinerary his father followed
on his visit years before to this city. It is at this point that the traditional pattern of initiatory symbolism is reversed. Instead of having a
father show the way and vanish, the opposite takes place: the guidebook leads to no new knowledge or discovery, but simply to a return
of the dead father: "So vivid was now the impression of his having
been here, and so narrow the passage from which he had emerged, that
I felt like running on, and overtaking him round the Town Hall adjoining, at the head of Castle Street" (R, iii:197). It is reasonable to say
that if Redburn's voyage has any meaning at all it is this: to reach
Liverpool so that this stange encounter may take place—a discreet but
powerful subversion of fictional convention, an intrusion of *Unheimlichkeit* in its purest form.

But of course the moment of transgression is short-lived. Narrative
discourse then takes over firmly (the discourse one could accurately
call *dominant,* because it dominates in several ways: psychically, inasmuch as it represses, it is repression itself; ideologically, inasmuch as it
provides the norm, the expected, acceptable form, the opposite of
Unheimlichkeit). The two operations by which this is effected are
worth examining briefly, because they represent two common modes
of dealing with the return of the symbolic (father) in Melville's fiction.
The first is the translation of the image of the father into a conventional or institutional figure, say a captain, a hero, or a god. All of
those figures go with a hierarchic, linear, and "discursive" vision of
time and narrative, which is evidence that what is at stake is a reassertion of the authority of conventional models. There is, for instance,
this passage: "For Time must prove his friend in the end; and though
sometimes he would almost seem as a neglected step-son of heaven,
permitted to run on and riot out his days with no hand to restrain him,
while others are watched over and tenderly cared for; yet we feel and
we know that God is the true Father of all, and that none of His children are without the pale of His care" (R, xxix:179). The difficulty,
the violence implicit in this reinstatement, shows in the syntax: in the
deployment of restrictive clauses ("and though . . ."), which always
come first and with which readers of Melville are familiar, and which
occupy the stage before the clauses are negated or swept aside by the

principal ("Yet . . ."). By this frequent stylistic trait Melville creates something analogous to disavowal, positing first what must (almost) in the same breath be denied. I say *almost* because in the delay, however short, is a necessary consecutiveness of major importance. It is the stylistic realization of what is affirmed in the first sentence, "For *Time* must prove his friend *in the end*," which is to say the supremacy of chronological time, which regulates and imposes its order. We have a kind of disavowal, then, a dual gesture, and the reader perceives here the bitterness and ambivalence of a freedom which is not really wanted, the desire for a paternal order and a sense of direction. (The word "step-son" hints at this desire for recognition and legitimacy. This should be seen in relation to Ishmael's dream, also a dream of parental authority, but under the negative sign of the tyrannical step-mother.)

In the second operation, also quite interesting, the fantasy, or the vanishing point, is not an authority figure and a desire for order, but transgression of the individual dimension and a projection onto a collective plane:

We are not a nation, so much as a world; for unless we may claim all the world for our sire, like Melchisedec, we are without father and mother. For who was our father and our mother? Or can we point to any Romulus and Remus for our founders? *Our ancestry is lost in the universal paternity;* and Caesar and Alfred, Saint-Paul and Luther, and Homer and Shakespeare are as much ours as Washington who is as much the world's as our own. We are the heirs of all time, and with all nations we divide our inheritance. On this western hemisphere all tribes and people are forming into one federated whole; and there is a future which shall see the estranged children of Adam restored as to the old hearthstone in Eden. (*R*, xxxi:217, italics added)

The question of the father is here extended horizontally, so to speak, to the whole American nation, a nation orphaned not so much because of the absence of the father, but because of a plethora of fathers. An orphan is everybody's son: universal paternity. If such is the case, the problem dissolves, and the individual quest becomes futile. But at the same time, this ideal "political" state of affairs is sufficiently utopian to ensure that its place is only *in the future*. And it is this temporal dimension which, once again, reintroduces order and repression. "And there is a future . . .": to posit the existence of a foreseeable future is to be willing to yield to the higher power of a sequential order, one equivalent to reintroducing institutions and their figures (here Adam, the archetypal father). What remains, however, before (and in spite of) the return to order , is the transitory utopia of a federation of tribes and people, the dream of an end to isolation and of a reunion of all *isolatoes*. A metaphor exists for this state of timelessness and fatherlessness (the two concepts being, we are beginning to realize, closely related): the ship.

The ship is an island, an ark, an "Anacharsis Clootz" federation of all types. What do the members of such a motley crew have in common? The fact that they are all lost sons, drifting purposelessly as they wait for a return. Of all the ships, the most characteristic is the warship:

The Navy is the asylum for the perverse, the home of the unfortunate. Here the sons of adversity meet the children of calamity and here the children of calamity meet the offspring of sin. Bankrupt brokers, boot-blacks, blacklegs, and blacksmiths here assemble together; and cast-away thinkers, watchmakers, quill-drivers, cobblers, doctors, farmers, and lawyers compare past experiences and talk of all times. Wrecked on a desert shore, a man-of-war crew could quickly found an Alexandria by themselves, and fill it with all the things which go to make up a capital. (*WJ*, xviii:94)

What is interesting and new here is the topology: the ship is not, like the Republic, a federation in space. It is a closed world, a vertical world, an organism with its bowels and secret recesses. So that what was returning fleetingly and paradoxically as hallucination in *Redburn* can now invest itself in a particular space, which can then be explored.

The exploration of the frigate in *White-Jacket* is indeed a return of primitive elements, a penetration into cloaca, a bituminous labyrinth of bowels and cables. In chapter 30, for instance, the narrator takes us on a tour of the innards of the ships and their innumerable shadowy activities. The number of regressive features is striking: the fear of becoming lost "in some remote, dark corner of the bowels of the frigate" (158) and of being abducted and molested by a strange character—"I became alarmed at the old yeoman's goggling glances, lest he should drag me down into tarry perdition in his hideous storerooms" (157).

This fantasy of a rape scene revolves around a father figure. It is even more clearly the case in other episodes which concern castration and death. Here is a remarkable example:

They looked like *the gloomy entrances* to *family vaults of buried dead;* and when I chanced to see some unknown functionary *insert his key,* and enter *these inexplicable apartments* with a battle-lantern, as if on solemn official business, I almost quaked *to dive in with him and satisfy myself* whether these vaults indeed contained the mouldering relics of *bygone old commodores,* and post-captains. *But* the habitations of the living commodore and captain—*their spacious and curtained cabins* were themselves almost as sealed volumes and I passed them in hopeless wonderment, like a peasant before a prince's palace. Night and day armed sentries guarded *their sacred portals,* cutlass in hand, and had I dared to cross their path *I would infallibly have been cut down* as if in battle.

The words I italicized constitute a kind of primal scene in which the subject fantasizes a penetration, clandestine and unspeakable, and "justifies" it by the prohibition on the sacred portals and the threat of castration associated with them. ("But" has no logical value here; it is a kind of shifter which permits the passage from one scene to another —more precisely from the scene of the dead father[s] linked with cloacal vaults and threatened penetration to that of the living father[s] and the threat of castration.) The anal character of the ship is everywhere in evidence, but what is interesting is the connection with "family vaults," the loss and the return of the dead father. The return is an aspect of the stasis, the slow surge of a regressive principle which overcomes the whole narrative. The novel tends to become mere description of the innards of the ship, the taxonomy of its huge body: a litany of places, objects, and names.

Naturally, as we indicated earlier, this is only one aspect of this novel. If *White-Jacket* is indeed constantly threatened by the return of primitive elements, what we have proposed to call the "narrative superego" prevails, and the text goes on in tight chapters and clear, lively prose. It is not until *Moby Dick* and *The Confidence-Man* (*Pierre* being put aside for the time being) that the crisis initiated by the (relative) failure of the paternal metaphor spreads to narrative discourse itself. It is to some textual implications of this phenomenon that I now turn. I will take as a guiding thread the question of time and origins, and the related father metaphors, and try to determine some of the strategies—of living, of writing—that ensue.

IV

The question now is to see how the absent father (and associated re-pressed primitive material) determines new narrative strategies in the later novels. But again I am tempted, at the outset, to question this formulation—the verb "determine" in particular. It is not perhaps so much a question of one element determining a change in strategy as it is of a series of related changes taking place. That the problem of the absent father is absolutely central to this process is beyond doubt. That it comes first, or even that it is always clearly identified as such, is another matter, and we have to take into account the series of dis-placements that occurs (it is only in *Pierre* that the problem is explicit-ly thematized again, but even there it is far from being simple).

We might perhaps begin where it all seems to begin again. In *Moby Dick,* chapter 3, a painting is described. The passage is famous for the description of the mysterious floating mass in the middle, the first avatar of the Leviathan, and for the lesson in interpretation Ishmael playfully offers. Among his many suppositions is that the painting is the work of a young artist who, "in the time of the New-England hags, had endeavoured to delineate chaos bewitched" (20). Further down the page, the picture is described, among other things, as "the breaking-up of the ice-bound stream of Time" (20). "Chaos be-witched" and "the stream of Time," stasis and flux, the pool and the cataract: this tension between two modes of apprehending time and life, between two metaphorical registers, is an essential character-istic of the experience of *Moby Dick*. It underlies the "fractured" sense of time Georges Poulet talks about, as well as the dual vision which dominates the novel: the circle and the line, to see and to look, the gaze and the object, the object and the word, etc. But there is more than a purely dualistic element. What matters in fact is the change, the con-stantly varying speed or angle, the sudden accelerations, the ver-tiginous drops, and the immense stagnant pools. It is as if "normal" narrative flow were constantly impeded by obstacles, undertows, changes in terrain—hence, the importance of complex models (neither linear nor circular): spirals, whirls, whorls. Turbulences and tropes are etymologically related—related in their origins as well as *to* the question of origins. *Moby Dick* is concerned with generation and accretion, with how things come to life and are produced by a play of forces, in ice breaking and flood subsiding, connections being made and energy doubling back on itself—all of which is to say: without a father, without a clearly identifiable source. This is how the question of origins comes to be indistinguishable from the symbolic organization, the writing itself.

It is not so much the metaphysics of origins which concerns Melville so obsessively as it is the mechanics of it. What is it that makes a river run, a whale roll, a drop fall? What is the original minimal impetus, the declivity, the *clinamen* that begins it all, as in Lucretius' physics?[4]

Take the letter *H*, breathe it out, and you (almost) have a whale, since "the letter H . . . almost alone maketh up the signification of the word" (1). Or take a roundness or a rolling (or any alternative couple of gestures: a rolling and a pitching; a breathing in and a breathing out; a *Fort* and a *Da* . . .). What is a whale? How does it come to life (how does anything)? Through the excretion of a letter; or through a dual gesture; or an ambivalence, a duality: a whale is where land and sea, container and contained are one:

> —There Leviathan
> Hugest of all living creatures, in the deep
> Stretched like a promontory sleeps or swims,
> And seems a moving land; and at his gills
> Draws in, and at his breath spouts out a sea
> (*Paradise Lost*, quoted on page 4 of *MD*)

Origins and creation are quasi-indistinction, the minimal difference, the *clinamen*, precisely. From there, nothing can flow regularly, no line can remain straight. Take a straight line and lo and behold! It branches out, sprouts branches and twigs. Everything bifurcates and forks out in increasingly complex patterns. Such are Melville's hieroglyphics: traces of countless little acts of creation, of cleavings and fractures. What all that amounts to is the impossibility of a single origin and the challenge to the very idea of paternity. The gesture is

radical and its implications momentous: not only are a substitute
philosophy of life and a new psychology proposed, but a new mode of
discourse is invented, one whose purpose is to prevent the insidious return of repressive discursive order. Let us just take one example and
follow it through. Let us take the line, which plays such an important
part in the novel and is such a rich metaphorical cluster. Say we get
hold of it in chapter 60 ("The Line"), which describes its functions,
its complex connections in the boat, its "hempen intricacies," its "horrible contortions," exalted at the end of the chapter to metaphysical
heights ("All men live enveloped in whale-lines. All are born with
halters round their necks," lx:241). This chapter is followed immediately by a hunting episode (lxi: "Stubb kills a Whale"), which in turn
generates two technical chapters (lxii: "The Dart" and lxiii: "The
Crotch"). The latter opens on the following remark: "Out of the
trunk, the branches grow; out of them, the twigs. So, in productive
subjects, grow the chapters" (lxiii:246). (This generic principle echoes
the remark in chapter 60 that "there is an aesthetics in all things,"
lx:238.) Now, on the crotch in question repose two harpoons: "a
doubling of the chances," indeed (lxiii:247)! The doubling now becomes more and more complex. And since my whole point is precisely
to trace this arborescence, this generation through doublings and re-
coils, I had better quote the whole end of the chapter:

It is a doubling of the chances. But it very often happens that owing to the
instantaneous, violent, convulsive running of the whale upon receiving the
first iron, it becomes impossible for the harpooneer, however lightning-like in
his movements, to pitch the second iron into him. Nevertheless, as the second
iron is already connected with the line, and the line is running, hence that
weapon must, at all events, be anticipatingly tossed out of the boat, somehow
and somewhere; else the most terrible jeopardy would involve all hands.
Tumbled into the water, it accordingly is in such cases; the spare coils of box
line (mentioned in a preceding chapter) making this feat, in most instances,
prudently practicable. But this critical act is not always unattended with the
saddest and most fatal casualties.

   Furthermore: you must know that when the second iron is thrown over-
board, it thenceforth becomes a dangling, sharp-edged terror, skittishly cur-
vetting about both boat and whale, entangling the lines, or cutting them, and
making a prodigious sensation in all directions. Nor, in general, is it possible to
secure it again until the whale is fairly captured and a corpse.

Consider, now, how it must be in the case of four boats all engaging one unusually strong, active, and knowing whale; when owing to these qualities in him, as well as to the thousand concurring accidents of such an audacious enterprise, eight or ten loose second irons may be simultaneously dangling about him. For, of course, each boat is supplied with several harpoons to bend on to the line should the first one be ineffectually darted without recovery. All these particulars are faithfully narrated here, as they will not fail to elucidate several more important, however intricate passages, in scenes hereafter to be painted. (*MD*, lxiii:247)

The model created here is remarkably complex and productive, with its aleatory and multidirectional connection. Yet it adds nothing to the narrative flow of the novel. It is like a bypass, a whirlpool (but active: not a backwater). The flow itself is not threatened—it would be only if such pockets proliferated—but it is locally and temporarily impeded, and the impediment creates its own little whirling and spiraling energy and will not be tamed easily.

This model is syntactic: it rests on a series of markers, each of which creates a new diversion, an accident: furthermore, thenceforth, nor, consider now, when, for, etc. Those markers determine the calms and turbulences of the passage. There are *connections:* and . . . and . . . and . . . ; *undertows:* though . . . though . . . ; *whirlings:* ; . . . ; . . . (   ).

If *Moby Dick* can be said to be an ironic text it is because of that constant dodging of linear flow and single source, that proliferation of doublings, counterfeits, countercurrents, and reversals. To flow against the stream is to negate the entropy of the chronological course —a form of neguentropy. Irony is neguentropy: to hold back in the same breath what has just been uttered, to say it and ruin it at the same time. Or, short of holding it back, to spin it and whirl it a little before allowing it to disappear with the stream. Against the mortal entropy of fathers and narrations, let us pause a moment; let us play the fool, disguise ourselves, and watch the river flow.

The Confidence-Man is a story of the Mississippi. Yet the river is strangely absent from the novel, as absent as the sea is pervasive in *Moby Dick*. Yet, within the quiet day's sailing which constitutes its narrative frame, a violence and a turbulence akin to that of Old Man River are intensely felt, not thematically, but metaphorically: what is in question here, as we indicated, is the metaphorical process itself.

Melville must have had an intuition of this focus when he wrote the fragment entitled "The River," which was discovered with pieces of the manuscript of the novel and written on the same kind of paper.[5] In this fragment, Melville describes the story of the displacement of a father by his son, the story of an usurpation—how the Missouri dethrones his father and refuses to yield to his authority:

The Missouri sends rather a hostile element than a filial flow. Longer, stronger than the father of waters, like Jupiter he dethrones his sire and reigns in his stead. Under the benign name Mississippi, it is in short the Missouri that now rolls to the Gulf, the Missouri that with the snows from his solitudes freezes the warmth of the genial zones, the Missouri that by open assault or artful sap sweeps away fruit and field, graveyard and barn, the Mississippi that not a tributary but an undermine enters the sea, long disdaining to yield his white wave to the blue. (*CM*, 355)

Whether this fragment is directly related to *The Confidence-Man* or not, a relation is here established between the theme of usurpation, of false identity, and the revolt of the son against the law of the father. In reality, what the somber masquerade of the novel reveals, beyond the proliferation of thematic or moral interpretations, is in fact a costumed representation of one capital scene in the theatre of the unconscious. Here the original repression is not so much rejected as grotesquely twisted, played with, and displaced. What characterizes the novel is that the subject seems arrested in a narcissistic stage of the kind that takes over the psychic economy after a severe injury or loss to the self. This takeover has been described by Gilles Deleuze: "The narcissistic ego is inseparable not only from an initial damage, but also from the disguises and displacements woven from one edge to the other, and which produce the change. Masks against other masks, disguises under disguises: the ego cannot be told from its own clowns, and limps along now on a green leg, now on a red one."[6] This, and in fact the whole chapter that follows, could just as well have been written about *The Confidence-Man*. That is the case precisely because the novel stages what the analyst is describing: a sense of loss which will not be transcended into something else, but perversely explores its own mechanism, its own productivity. The emphasis here is on pure play and displacement, on a superego rampaging through the props on stage. Just as the strategy in *Moby Dick* is ironic, here it is humorous, if we take Deleuze's definition of humor as "the art of surfaces," "the art of displacement." So that *The Confidence-Man* is the book of questions without answers, of an increasingly hysterical "punning with ideas." Here the pageant and the mobility point to an everpresent gap, a wound that will not heal, but will only dress itself in bright colors, the lack of that which is always missing in its place: the name-of-the-father, flaunting itself in jest and desperation. Melville now sees the ironist as "a surly philanthropist" and gives his preference to a new breed, a kind of monster, of mutant, "the genial misanthrope":

Now, the genial misanthrope, when, in the process of eras, he shall turn up, will be the converse of this; under an affable air, he will hide a misanthropic heart. In short, the genial misanthrope will be a new kind of monster, but still no small improvement upon the original one, since, instead of making faces and throwing stones at people, like that poor old crazy man, Timon, he will take steps, fiddle in hand, and set the tickled world a'dancing. (*CM*, xxx:154)

This is Autólycus against Timon. To play the fool, a violin in one's hands, and to jive and jibe madly—such is the sensible way to play the fool. There is no need to emphasize the aesthetic and strategic implications of this position. They have been underlined by several commentators, who base their developments on chapters 33 and 44.[7] The character who fits this paradoxical and fatherless stage is "a real original" described in the image of the Drummond light:

The character sheds not its characteristic on its surroundings, whereas, the original character, essentially such, is like a revolving Drummond light, raying away from itself all round it—everything is lit by it, everything starts up to it (mark how it is with Hamlet), so that in certain minds, there follows upon the adequate conception of such a character, an effect, in its way, akin to that which in Genesis attends upon the beginning of things. (*CM*, xliv:205)

What is defined here is the fracture which marks the return of the narcissistic ego, its stasis, its empty time, and its suspension from the very knowlege of the lack. It is a form of "eternal recurrence" in which there is no circularity, but rather a paradoxical combination of linearity and circularity, of form and formlessness, of the kind precisely which the passage from *Moby Dick* I opened with suggested. Again we can follow Deleuze: "eternal recurrence" does not make everything return, but on the contrary affects a world which has rid itself of the defect of the condition and inequality of the agent, to affirm only what is excessive and unequal, interminable and incessant, the product of the most extreme formality. Thus is ended the history of time: it must undo its physical or natural circle, too well-centered, and form a straight line; which, because of its own length, forms another circle, eternally de-centered.[8]

This endless and "empty" transformation of forms is the strategy at work in *The Confidence-Man*, a work of mourning for an unmentionable loss. Between a wounded narcissistic ego and an implacable superego, and between the stasis of grief and the free energy of play, the text has its impossible place, in the margins of the symbolic process.

V The Captive King

But I shall follow the endless, winding way, —the flowing river in the cave of man; careless whither I be led, reckless where I land. (*Pierre*, v,7:126)

And then there is *Pierre,* in which the question of the father for the first and only time is apprehended directly, with extraordinarily acute analytic intuitions. What is presented there is the collapse of a paradise, the world of Saddle Meadows where Pierre Glendinning and his mother live in Oedipean bliss, with the memory of the dead father conveniently tucked away in a marble sanctuary. The agent of this collapse is Isabel, the agent of the return of the repressed. The forces, the desires she unleashes and embodies, erupt powerfully and shatter the original Oedipean stasis. They initiate a series of fantasies which all tend toward a reassertion of Pierre's repressed libido. More important perhaps, they initiate a process of regression, a desperate drive to go back to the beginning and become reborn, with a new self, a new identity which would owe nothing to the parental heritage. *Pierre* is largely the story of this neurotic drive against the father and its inescapable consequences. Isabel triggers the crisis, but it is clear from the beginning that the crisis concerns the symbolic level. Note, for instance, how the different metaphorical levels we have already encountered are held together in this admirable sentence: "Now, unending as the wonderful rivers, which once bathed the feet of the primeval generations, and still remain to flow fast by the graves of all succeeding men, and by the beds of all now living; unending, ever-flowing, ran through the soul of Pierre, fresh and fresher, further and still further, thoughts of Isabel" (P, vii:165).

At the outset, as nearly always, there is a dead father. Pierre's is sanctified in a shrine erected to him, a verdant bower in which the figure of the father stands like a phallic totem: "But though thus mantled, and tangled with garlands, this shrine was of marble—a niched pillar, deemed solid and eternal, and from whose top radiated all those innumerable sculptured scrolls and branches, which sup-ported the entire one-pillared temple of his moral life" (P, iv:79). This bower, in which Pierre's effective and moral life has its foundation, calls to mind the Arsacidean bower in *Moby Dick*. But here, there is no weaver-god, no regenerative exchange between life and death. Pierre's father's mausoleum is lodged in the heart of the living like a worm in a fruit: introjected and ensconced in the heart of his son is the figure of the dead father. It is a marble crypt, a stasis and a petrification of time and waters:

Blessed and glorified in his tomb beyond Prince Mausolus is that mortal sire, who, after an honourable, pure course of life, dies, and is buried, as in a choice fountain, in the filial breast of a tender-hearted and intellectually appreciative child. For at that period, the Solomonic insights have not poured their turbid tributaries into the pure-flowing well of the childish life. Rare preservative vir-tue, too, have those heavenly waters. Thrown into that fountain, all sweet recollections become marbleized; so that things which in themselves were evanescent, thus became unchangeable and eternal. So, some rare waters in Derbyshire will petrify birds' nests. (ibid.)

The discourse of metaphors is here in radical opposition to the idyllic surface of the narrative. We know that in Melville whiteness and petri-fication connote a negation of life, a horror. We also know that what is unchangeable is terrifying, a kind of death-in-life as in the case of "sinister Lima" which Melville mentions often. What this passage describes is the same kind of static stage, before the "turbid waters" of desire have started to flow. There is, as in the case of the yellow-backed rebel son, the Missouri, the fear to yield to a larger stream, to "hurry to abrupt intermergings with the eternal tides of time and fate" (P, vii:166). But the metaphor here is reversed: first, because it is the pure waters of the son which are to be disturbed by the turbid flow of adulthood; second, because the fantasy, the unappeasable urge, is not to flow, but to be at the very spring, at the head. But the spring is the tomb, the mausoleum. The beginning is in the death-drive. When Pierre's artificial paradise crashes down, his first impulse is to rush to the Terror Stone, the Memnon Stone, an enormous rock poised miraculously on a ridge. Pierre slides himself under it, "straight into the horrible interspace, and lay there as dead" (*P*, vii:157). There he lies in what is at the same time a tomb and a matrix, where it all began, where it is all going to begin; where the song of "some sweet boy long since departed in the antediluvian time" is going to be heard; where nothing has yet begun to flow, before the flow and the breath are lost "among our drifting sands, which whelm alike the monument and the dirge" (*P*, vii:159).

There Pierre lies in the jaws of symbolic death and castration, placing himself deliberately at the divide, at the dangerous point, in order to put himself to the test and see "if the miseries of the undisclosable things in me shall ever unhorse me from my manhood's seat." Thus, the sepulchre once more is related intimately to the question of origins —the questioning of origins, to be more precise. Pierre identifies with Memnon, the son of no father, the original son, so to speak, "that dewy, royal boy, son of Aurora, and born King of Egypt" (*P*, vii:159). From the tragedy of Memnon to that of Hamlet, the link (the filiation precisely) is direct in more ways than one: "For in this plaintive fable we find embodied the Hamletism of the antique world; the Hamletism of three thousand years ago: 'the flower of virtue cropped by a too rare mischance.' And the English tragedy is but Egyptian Memnon, Montaignized and modernized; for being but a mortal man Shakespeare had his fathers too" (ibid.). The last sentence—note the plural—marks a turning point in the logic of Pierre's relation to his father. The fantasy ceases to be that of respectful neglect, or disavowal; the subject turns to an eradication and exorcism of all that remains and moves toward a reappropriation of his identity. No more secret crypt, no more relics encrusted in the heart of the living: "Never more will I play the vile pigmy, and by small memorials after death, attempt to reverse the decree of death, by essaying the poor perpetuating of the image of the original. Let all die, and mix again" (*P*, xii:232). No more memorials, no more catacombs—Pierre burns his father's portrait in a decisive gesture of self-recovery: "Henceforth, castout Pierre hath no paternity, and no past; and since the Future is one blank to all; therefore, twice-disinherited Pierre stands untrammeledly his ever-present self!—free to do his own self-will and present fancy to whatever end" (P, xii:234).

The casting off of all trammels liberates a prodigious energy, but one unchanneled, purposeless, and objectless. Hence, the threat of a new stasis: no longer that of petrification, but that of a state in which everything fluctuates and changes direction, something like the pole where the needle "indifferently respects all points of the horizon." The dead secret gone, there only remains the self and its depths. What depths? Those precisely which the need for them, the need for a sense of secret riches, and the need for a sense of direction are going to reestablish. The depths of the self are not so much the result of a discovery or of an exploration: they are an invention, the outcome of the drive to go down into, to spiral down. Hence the creation of a new vault, a new crypt. . . . Identical metaphors return: dark waters, mummies, a sarcophagus, etc. The difference is that this secret space is now no longer built around the relics of the father, but around a void. Witness this passage, one of the most striking in *Pierre*, the closest one ever comes to a direct encounter with the symbolic, with that which cannot be encountered face to face and whose knowledge is by essence always deferred:

Not yet had he dropped his angle into the well of his childhood, to find what fish might be there; for who dreams to find fish in a well? the running stream of the outer world, there doubtless swim the golden perch and the pickerel! Ten million things were as yet uncovered to Pierre. The old mummy lies buried in cloth on cloth; it takes time to unwrap this Egyptian king. Yet now, forsooth, because Pierre began to see through the first superficiality of the world, he fondly weens he has come to the unlayered substance. But, far as any geologist has yet gone down into the world, it is found to consist of nothing but surface on stratified surface. To its axis, the world being nothing but superinduced superficies. By vast pains we mine into the pyramid; by horrible gropings we come to the central room; with joy we espy the sarcophagus; but we lift the lid—and no body is there!—appallingly vacant as vast is the soul of a man! (P, xii:335)

The shock of this transgression can be such that the walls of the self's inner chamber collapse, provoking a catastrophic identity crisis. Pierre experiences it once: "The cheeks of his soul collapsed in him: he dashed himself in blind fury and swift madness against the wall, and fell dabbling in the vomit of his loathed identity" (*P*, ix:201). In order to avoid the disaster of such a brutal realization, the self tends to fill the void of its inner chamber. So it happens that the dead mother finds herself, in her turn, entombed, enshrined in "the profoundest vault of his soul," just as the father was before. The text, incidentally, under-lines "this remarkable double-doom of his parents." The symbolic, like the dream, is familiar with such displacements. And it is indeed with a dream that we must now pursue our analysis. It is of course the well-known Enceladus vision (*P*, xxv, 4:402–09), often referred to but seldom read from the point of view of its own logic, that of the dream and of the unconscious.

It should be noted, first of all, that it is a dream of an archeological nature, a dream of an excavation, that of a gigantic rock, named Enceladus after the Titan, which the boys in Pierre's youth had at-tempted to dig out of the mountain. The first part of the vision, then, is historical and archeological: it recalls the efforts of the boys to help a frightful power ("a form of awfulness") liberate itself from the im-prisoning earth. Their attempts fail and only reveal the Titan's "mu-tilated shoulders, and the stumps of his once audacious arms" (406). Enceladus, then, appears slowly as a horrible vision from beyond the grave, a kind of living dead writhing in agony to escape his condition and return. Here is the end of the dream proper:

But no longer petrified in all their ignominious attitudes, the herded Titans now sprung to their feet; flung themselves up the slope; and anew battered at the precipice's unresounding wall. Foremost among them all, he saw a moss-turbaned, armless giant, who despairing of any other mode of wreaking his immitigable hate, turned his vast trunk into a battering-ram, and hurled his own arched-out ribs again and yet again against the invulnerable steep.

'Enceladus! it is Enceladus'—Pierre cried out in his sleep. That moment the phantom faced him; and Pierre saw Enceladus no more; but put on the Titan's armless trunk, his own duplicate face and features magnificently gleamed upon him with prophetic discomfiture and woe. With trembling frame he started from his chair, and woke from that ideal horror to all his actual grief. (407)

The whole sequence shows clearly that this is a dream of the return of repressed desire. Behind Enceladus, who rises "like a battering-ram," the figure of the dead father is powerfully resexualized and identified with the dreamer's own repressed sexuality. The central knot of the dream is that Enceladus is a father figure *and* the symbol of the incestuous son. The Melvillean narrator, in the analysis of the dream which he himself offers, recognizes this and shows considerable analytic acumen. First, he presents Pierre's own interpretation of the dream and shows its limitations, then substitutes his own. This is obviously a passage of crucial import, and it is essential to follow its intricacies.

What Pierre had seen in the dream was the horror of the return of the repressed, both under the shape of the paternal ghost and under the guise of incestuous desire. For reasons which must now be analyzed, the narrator empties the dream of its unbearable incestuous content and translates it into a more familiar desire: a filial longing, a desire to be recognized. But by doing so, he merely underlines (although he would conceal it) what is intolerable in the dream: the terror of castration. It is necessary, at this stage, to pay again the closest attention to the syntax in which the process of disavowal is inscribed:

Old Titan's self was the son of incestuous Coleus and Terra, the son of incestuous Heaven and Earth. And Titan married his mother Terra, another and accumulatively incestuous match. And thereof Enceladus was one issue. So Enceladus was both the son and grandson of an incest; and *even thus,* there had been born from the organic blended heavenliness and earthliness of Pierre, another mixed, uncertain, heaven-aspiring, but still not wholly earth-emancipated mood; *which again,* by its terrestrial taint held down to its terrestrial mother, generated there the present doubly incestuous Enceladus within him; *so that* the present mood of Pierre—that reckless sky-assaulting mood of his, was nevertheless on one side the grandson of the sky. For it is according to eternal fitness, that the precipitated Titan should still seek to regain his paternal birth-right even by fierce escalade. *Wherefore* whoso storms the sky gives best proof he came from thither! *But* whatso crawls contented in the moat before that crystal fort, shows it was born within that slime, and there forever will abide. (408, italics added)

This is as tight a false demonstration as could be imagined, imposed upon the real experience which tries to make itself heard through the dream. If we were to believe this report, Pierre's whole pursuit would seem to have been "to regain his paternal birthright," to deserve to be recognized by an ideal father, another pathetic sublimation of the need for recognition. But we have seen that, on the contrary, the ideal father

was there at the outset, idolized and petrified in his crypt. Pierre's experience is the destruction of that idol, that false superego, and the
encounter with repressed elements which now return in the real (Isabel). The Enceladus dream is the expression of those intolerable tensions, not at all an idealizing gesture, a gesture of submission. What is
intolerable in them is that they shatter forever the very possibility of
a unity of the subject, as they hurl him into a world of endless
doubling.[9] And what's more, the dream lets him know his predicament. The doubles, the duplication itself, never return to an origin,
but only to empty places, other copies. . . . Melville's text is a long meditation on the impossibility of a return to an origin and a legitimacy
(Ahab was already racked by the same despairing urge, the difference
being that he still thought it possible that malevolent obstacles could
be removed). There is no truth or fundament to return to. For a long
time, we believe the secret lies in the tomb, but the tomb turns out to
be empty. We then turn to substitutes, but those proliferate and vanish
in thin air. Worse still, our substitute fathers turn out to be sons themselves, lost sons. The secret of the absent father is that he, too, is a lost
son. That is what Melville's text reveals and conceals at the same time,
that which the subject thinks he would like to know and cannot
acknowledge.

Many are the stratagems by which this can be concealed: by positing, as does Ahab, a transcendent power beyond, which then becomes
the hated keeper of the secret, the enigma of origins; or, as Pierre does,
by decreeing oneself the son to no one, the product of chance, or of
incest. Behind these stratagems lies the desire to be one's own father
(and perhaps to be the father of others: the desire of paternity itself, in
all its ambivalence). It is the revelation which comes to Pierre when he
visits an art gallery in New York with Lucy and Isabel. Among the
mediocre paintings on display, one stands out because of its excellence. It is entitled "Stranger's Head by an Unknown Hand"(!). In
front of this painting Isabel stops, fascinated by the resemblance to
herself and to the father she has never known. For Pierre, the resemblance is to the portrait of his father he destroyed. We then have this
remarkable disposition: opposite the painting is a copy of Guido's
"Cenci," a portrait of a woman who symbolizes incest and parricide.
Neither Pierre nor Isabel pays the slightest attention to it (only Lucy

stares, riveted). Both are held by the other painting, Isabel because of her narcissistic blindness, Pierre because it opens for him new and appalling perspectives. For Pierre now comes to doubt that Isabel is his sister and sees that his hasty identification of her as his sister may have been the product merely of his "intense procreative enthusiasm" (*P*, xxvi:416), a fancy born of the desire to be a father (the father of his father's daughter). But procreation, paternity, is no simple matter. It now appears that it, too, like the rest, is a question of ambiguous signs. How does one know, exactly?

> How did he *know* that Isabel was his sister? Nothing that he saw in her face could he remember as having seen in his father's. The chair-portrait, *that* was the entire sum and substance of all possible, rakable, downright presumptive evidence, which peculiarly appealed to his own separate self. Yet here was another portrait of a complete stranger—a European; a portrait imported from across the seas, and to be sold at public auction, which was just as strong an evidence as the other. Then, the original of this second portrait was as much the father of Isabel as the original of the chair-portrait. But perhaps there was no original at all to this second portrait; it might have been a pure fancy-piece. . . . (416)

As we progress toward the close of this startling psychoanalytic fiction, the notion of the father itself is caught in the process of reduplication. What is a father? Is there anywhere a "real" father (a father who is not a son—or a daughter)? Pierre has discovered that it is as dangerous to disturb the walls of the paternal vault as it is to challenge the base of our symbolic being or to attack our own organs. The disruption spreads to all areas.[10]

Coda

Before the final hecatomb, Pierre and Isabel are vouchsafed a moment of peace and unity. It is nothing, just a short spell, and by no means a positive resolution of the problems we have analyzed and of the contradictions in which we have our symbolic being. It is just that the writing, in a trancelike moment, by bringing together a series of metaphors which have been running through several novels, offers the mirage of a brief reunion. The distinction is suspended between the sea and the river, the sea and the land, the depths of the vault and the

height of the dome. The river which so often embodied a conflict
between father and son has now become a feminine element; for a
short while, the text dreams of an end to all conflict and all quests, in
the repose of a motherlike presence:

They stood leaning on the rail of the guard, as the sharp craft darted out from
among the lofty pine-forests of ships' masts, and the tangled underbrush and
cane-brakes of the dwarfed sticks of sloops and scows. Soon, the spires of
stone on the land, blent with the masts of wood on the water; the crotch of the
twin-rivers pressed the great wedged city almost out of sight. They swept by
two little islets distant from the shore; they wholly curved away from the
domes of free-stone and marble, and gained the great sublime dome of the
bay's wide-open waters. (418)

A Clown's Inquest into Paternity:

       Fathers, Dead or Alive,

       in *Ulysses* and *Finnegans Wake*

       JEAN-MICHEL RABATÉ

It is because the Unconscious needs the insistence of writing that critics err when they treat a written work in the same way as they treat the Unconscious. At every moment, any written work cannot but lend itself to interpretation in a psychoanalytic sense. But to subscribe to this, ever so slightly, implies that one supposes the work to be a forgery, since, inasmuch as it is written, it does not imitate the effects of the Unconscious. The work poses the equivalent of the Unconscious, an equivalent no less real than it, as the one forges the other in its curvature. . . . The literary work fails or succeeds, but this failure is not due to the imitating of the effects of the structure. The work only exists in that curvature which is that of the structure itself. We are left then with no mere analogy. The curvature mentioned here is no more a metaphor for the structure than the structure is a metaphor for the reality of the Unconscious. It is real, and, in this sense, the work imitates nothing. It is, as fiction, a truthful structure.[1] (Jacques Lacan)

What is a father? Who is the father? What is common between my father, your father, me as a father, the man next door, the mailman, the commercial traveler or He whom we picture walking in the clouds? A father as Viconian giant, thundering, farting, belching, castrating sons and daughters alike, with his pockets full of sweets to lure little girls astray, or cakewalking as the cake that you can both eat and have in his last triumphal march, just to provide critics with one of their great white whales? Who can be sure to be the father, who can be so self-confident as to utter without faltering, "I am a fa . . ." and not crash down into the frozen lakes of doubt and incest that have nonetheless been safely crossed? Thus, *Finnegans Wake:* a list of names, all dubious, corrupted by tradition and oral distortion, voluntary

manglings and unconscious censorship, all of which try to pin down
the father to a definition or to a precise spot on earth. Among those,
one appellation seems to offer a clue, which might serve as a point of
departure: "apersonal problem, a locative enigma" (FW, 135.26).[2]
This can lead to three sets of preliminary remarks. A father is not
simply an "individual," but mainly a function; paternity is that place
from which someone lays down a law, be it the law of sexual difference, the law of the prohibition of incest, or the laws of language. A
father is not a person but the focal point where castration can be
brought to bear on the structure of desire; as such he is the knot binding the anarchic compound of drives and the realm of cultural codifi-
cation. Next, a father is not a "problem," but a nexus of unresolved
enigmas, all founded on the mysterious efficacy of a Name, which in
itself remains a riddling cipher. And lastly, Joyce's formulation helps
us to replace the question of designation by an exploration in positioning; if, as we shall see, a father is defined by his absence, paternity and
patriarch are set adrift in a world of substitutes, in which everybody is
endlessly elsewhere.

I am not setting out to give a psychoanalytic reading of "the father
in *Ulysses* and *Finnegans Wake*"; indeed Lacan's epigraph should
rather come as a warning not to apply Freudian hermeneutics to a text
which already uses and makes fun of so many Freudian, Jungian, and
Rankian tags. Lacan's statement could also suggest that a psychoanalytic interpretation, although now wary of unlocking the "author's
psyche" behind his text, has its limits, to be found not in a textual
uniqueness or irreducibility, but in the deliberate manipulation of un-
certainties through which Joyce sought to infinitize the possibilities of
language. If the unconscious works like a text, as a text, what Joyce
may imitate of its effects in his "epical forged cheque" (FW, 181.16)
of "many piously forged palimpsests" (182.2) only bursts through at
times as symptoms. And the symptoms do not so much betray Joyce
himself as a state of language in its overdetermined and complex
articulation with politics, sexuality, and history. In these language-
symptoms, released and not simply created by Joyce, the role of paternity is perhaps not so ominous as one could be tempted to believe,
yet surely more problematical, more elusive, and more perverse. As we
move from *Ulysses,* which seems hinged to a careful delimitation of

the various functions of fatherhood, to *Finnegans Wake,* where the father, struck dead or hidden, is slandered at every page, the nature of the link between the two sets of problems will have to be more explicit. Many mistaken assumptions arise from too strict an application of the overall pattern of *Ulysses* to the symbolic liquidation of the father *Finnegans Wake* achieves.

Ulysses begins in the atmosphere of the pervading presence of the mother and ends with a hymn to femininity; the reader can even conjure up the unwritten text that would join Molly Bloom's final "yes" to Stephen's melancholy musings on his dead mother, if the circularity of *Finnegans Wake* could apply to *Ulysses.* It is fitting to remember that the concept of "atonement" is dropped like a brick upon Stephen's theory of paternity in *Hamlet* precisely by Haines, the usurping Englishman coming to rescue Mulligan the Irish usurper: "I read a theological interpretation of it somewhere, he said bemused. The Father and Son idea. The Son striving to atone with the Father."[3] Despite the vagueness of the reference, an imprecision which Stephen would never allow since he almost always quotes by name, this remark only then prompts Stephen's thoughts on the "consubstantiality of the Son with the Father." Now, the very origin of this "interpretation" ought to invite suspicion and prevent us from too glibly glossing over the text in the same way. Moreover, at the close of the book, the question of atonement is met with an offhand dismissal in the abortive conclusion to Bloom's proposal that Stephen (as Telemachus who has found Ulysses at last) should spend the end of the night in his house. Bloom ponders on the difficulty he will have to keep in touch with the young poet as he meditates on the "irreparability of the past" and remembers an incident which had taken place in a circus: "once . . . an intuitive particoloured clown in quest of paternity . . . had publicly declared to an exhilarated audience that he (Bloom) was his (the clown's) papa" (*U,* 657). The answer is the curtest of the sarcastic comebacks contained in the catechistic chapter of Ithaca: "Was the clown Bloom's son? / No." This little scene quite deftly sketches the whole structure of the book, placing Stephen as clown, jester, or fool, not too far from the laughing audience; it shows, by a kind of *reductio ad absurdum* of the basics of the theme of paternity, that the "fusion of Bloom and Stephen" which Joyce had contemplated, as the Linati scheme reveals,[4] was at best temporary and bound to fail. Therefore, the claim to paternity on which the greater part of *Ulysses* seems founded is now challenged by the widening gap which sets "father" and "son," like Bloom and his notched coin, drifting further apart. "Had Bloom's coin returned? / Never" (ibid.).

If the "possible, circuitous or direct, return" Bloom had hoped for never really occurs in *Ulysses*, this failure points to the scene of *Finnegans Wake*. I shall try to trace out the path opened by the concept of "atonement" in *Ulysses* to show how the shift from a living "impossible" father[5] to a dead father, one reduced to his pure function, governs the basic unit of the family and generates a radically new orientation in the language of fiction. If the father is a "legal fiction" in *Ulysses*, in *Finnegans Wake* he opens the door to the laws of fiction as "truthful structure."

I   The Figures of Incestitude

"Investigations into paternity are forbidden." (Code Napoleon, 1804, article 340)

One of the basic elements of *Ulysses* is the duplication of the father figure, and the relationship between the real father (Simon Dedalus) and the symbolic father (Bloom as Ulysses) is a first key to the function of paternity in the book. The dissociation is established progressively between the two, and at the start there seems to be a close link between Stephen and his father; at least there is evidence for this link in the words of others as recalled by Stephen. Two physical motifs, the voice and the eyes, recur to stress this resemblance, so that a certain degree of "consubstantiality" seems to unite father and son in the flesh. The editor of the newspaper exclaims that Stephen is a "Chip off the old block!" (*U*, 134) when Stephen suggests a pause in a pub; likewise, Kevin Egan had told him in Paris: "You're your father's son. I know the voice" (*U*, 40). In the same way, when Bloom thinks about Rudy, his only son who did not live, he mentions the two features: "If little Rudy had lived. See him grow up. Hear his voice in the house. . . . My son. Me in his eyes" (*U*, 81). Late until the *Walpurgisnacht* of the Circe chapter, Stephen, who tries to kill the "priest and king" in his mind, has not killed his father yet, for he still imitates his prodigal father by being consistently prodigal: "Play with your eyes shut. Imitate pa. Filling my belly with husks of swine. Too much of this. I will arise and go to my. . . . No voice. I am a most finished artist" (U, 491–92). Stephen imitates the mannerisms of his father when he sings, but in his drunken state, the blindness and the voicelessness alone reveal that Stephen is closest to his real father: he is about to return, although he represses the mention of his father. No voice, no eyes, a closed, opaque body—already caught up in the cycle of repetition in which failed artist and failed gentleman merge their shortcomings. In fact for Joyce the voice and the eyes seem to have embodied the true clues to affiliation, since when he proudly announces Giorgio's birth to his family back in Dublin, he writes, "The child appears to have inherited his grandfather's and father's voices. He has dark blue eyes,"[6] and this is enough of a description.

These distinctive features loom out again when Stephen imagines the love-making of his parents. But, though his vampiric and necrophiliac fantasies revolve around his mother's corpse, they are blended with theological speculations on paternity, for Stephen identifies himself with a divine form, revealed in the likeness of physical characteristics (eyes, voice), a form which lends to his contingent existence the ineluctable necessity of a law. "Wombed in sin darkness I was too, made, not begotten. By them, the man with my voice and my eyes, and a ghostwoman with ashes on her breath" (U, 35). Stephen implies that he has not merely been generated in the flesh by his parents, but has been *made*, or willed eternally by a divine Creator. The transmission of a pure form thus seems instrumental in canceling all reference to the sexual role of the mother, and the *lex eterna* of the father's law prepares the way for the assertion of a "divine substance wherein Father and Son are consubstantial."

But Stephen is betrayed by the ambiguity of his images, as he feels locked in a post-mortem embrace with a mother who haunts him, and he only refutes the Arian heresy to fall into the trap of an unnamed heresy which would interpret the "substance" as the womb of imagination. If Stephen's first temptation is to rule out the Oedipal triangle so that he may enhance a dual relationship to his Maker, it then appears that he has never killed his mother and cannot take his father's

place. For him, to kill the mother would mean to deny this substance
without an origin which fascinates him, and whose truth he ultimately
discovers in the materiality of the act of writing: "Belly without blem-
ish, bulging big, a buckler of taut vellum, no, whiteheaped corn, orient
and immortal, standing from everlasting to everlasting. Womb of
sin!" (U, 35). The white vellum or parchment is Eve's sin as well as
the future blank page kept waiting for Stephen's traces and signs,
"signs on a white field."

By a very telling shift in Stephen's reflections, which shows the
ambivalent nature of the *lex eterna,* the imagined voice of Simon
Dedalus proceeds with an attack, although oblique, on the incestuous
potentialities of the family pattern. Just after these thoughts, Stephen
wonders whether he will visit his aunt: "Here. Am I going to Aunt
Sara's or not? My consubstantial father's voice." Stephen is deterred
from such a visit by the sneers he has often heard: "Did you see anything of your artist brother Stephen lately? No? Sure he's not down in
Strasburg terrace with his aunt Sally. . . . And and and and tell us
Stephen, how is uncle Si? . . . . And skeweyed Walter sirring his father,
no less. Sir. Yes, sir. No, sir" (U, 35). Through Simon's voice, we hear
uncle Richie's stammer and Walter's obsequious sirring. This voice
conjures up a series of vivid pictures in a spirited ventriloquism which
fuses with the rhythm of Stephen's musings. The "old artificer" even
parodies the Daedalan myth in a sordid fall: "Couldn't he fly a bit
higher than that, eh?" Such a flexible idiom lends itself perfectly to
mimicry and abuse while it achieves its aim: the scene is so effectively
reconstructed that Stephen, walking along the strand, passes the house
and forgets to call on them. The father's voice has been powerful
enough as to shunt Stephen's thoughts to another track, and yet reveals even more of the incestuous nature of his link to his "in-laws,"
and by way of another detour, to Bloom's possible fosterage.

All this becomes clearer and more pointed when the same sequence
recurs in a different context, during the funeral procession, as Bloom,
Simon Dedalus, and friends are driving to the churchyard. Bloom tells
Mr Dedalus that he has just spotted Stephen, "your son and heir,"
walking on the beach, thus giving the cue for what seems to be one of
Simon's clichés: "Down with his aunt Sally, I suppose, Mr Dedalus
said, the Goulding faction, the drunken little costdrawer and Crissie,
papa's little lump of dung, the wise child that knows her own father"

(*U*, 80). Simon Dedalus no longer responds to Walter's servility but Crissie's love, and his insinuations modify the previous remark made by Stephen about Crissie ("Papa's little bedpal. Lump of love," [*U*, 36]); now the scatological abuse makes clear the incestuous relationship between Richie Goulding and his daughter. For Simon, this is what characterizes the mother's side of the family: it is a faction involved in a continuous intrigue, always plotting against the supremacy of the real head of the house. As such, it threatens the orthodoxy of the father's law; it questions the original atomic or adamic structure. The mother's family is a constant reminder of degradation ("O weeping God, the things I married into," [*U*, 35]). When Stephen is tempted for a while by this possible shelter, he may well be looking for a temporary substitute home, by anticipation finding in his "fraction" of an old decaying unity the maternal and heretical shelter only Bloom can offer. The displacement of the incestuous nexus toward Bloom's paternal attitude is then made more obvious before reaching a climax in Molly's dreams of seducing a "sonhusband" (as *Finnegans Wake* neatly puts it in 627.01).

The specific meaning of incest entails a pun on blindness and insight contained in the verb *to know*. The phrase "wise child that knows her own father" echoes proverbially and also recalls *The Merchant of Venice*. Launcelot tells his blind father who does not recognize him, "Nay indeed, if you had your eyes you might fail the knowing of me: it is a wise father that knows his own child" (ii:ii). But then he adds confidently, "Murder cannot be hid long: a man's son may; but, in the end, truth will out"; Bloom, who must be confusedly remembering those lines, distorts their impact as "The body to be exhumed. Murder will out" (*U*, 92). Bloom also has his skeleton in a cupboard, and through the associations with the Childs murder he is led to his own fifteen-year-old daughter Milly: "She mightn't like me to come that way without letting her know. Must be careful about women. Catch them once with their pants down. Never forgive you after. Fifteen" (ibid.).[7] The equating of love-making with murder—soul-murder, as Schreber would say—is a typical feature of the Oedipal fantasies linked with the hallucinated primal scene. We shall see how this association determines the father and son relationship in *Finnegans Wake*, replacing the father and daughter relationship of *Ulysses*.

Bloom and Richie Goulding thus have been connected, for the reader at least, heaped together as they are by this "lump of love." This connection is emphasized by the parallelism of their situation in *Sirens*, when both are silently listening, enthralled by Simon's superb tenor voice; "married in silence" they talk a little.

A beautiful air, said Bloom lost Leopold. I know it well.
Never in all his life had Richie Goulding.
He knows it well too. Or he feels. Still harping on his daughter. Wise child that knows her father, Dedalus said. Me? (*U*, 259)

On the one side, there is a "Master's voice," the voice of a man "full of his son" (81) and endowed with a rich voice all others admire; on the other side are two fathers who are hampered by their half-conscious incestuous wishes and who can only literally "harp" on that theme. Bloom is quite right to describe the "relations" of the two "brothers-in-law" with the musical simile: a rift in the lute (263). Thus, will it finally "make the music mute / And ever widening slowly silence all."[8]

The gap between the right lineage and the maternal line of descent already introduces the contrast between the symbolic order as defined by the law of the father and the prohibition of incest, and an imaginary realm where the fantasies of incest merely cover the wish to return to the womb. This contract explains why a qualification needs to be made about Bloom's role as a symbolic father. To be a father, symbolically, does not imply merely a real paternity; on the contrary, it takes death, absence, and radical otherness into account. Bloom can be said to become Stephen's father only after they have parted; it is when they are closest that this relation is impossible. Contact is the reverse side of the coin of mystical fatherhood. Because of Bloom's offer and Stephen's subsequent refusal of hospitality, Stephen has to choose for himself in order to father himself: he accordingly begins the new cycle of dawn while Bloom is getting buried in his deep night (according to the Linati scheme).[9] A symbolic father is not simply the father of a son, as such can be left to the real father's function; a symbolic father is as it were the father of a father—a grandfather, in a way—who fades away to become increasingly identified with a pure name. But Stephen's new home can be only a text which he still has to sign as he incorporates Bloom's name to it.

The way to such a symbolic father can only be discovered if the refusal of any acknowledgment it implies is based on the ignorance of the real father. Stephen and Simon, in spite of their objective complicity, have to ignore their respective presence in the blind link which prevents them from knowing each other. Simon Dedalus fails to recognize his son several times, as for instance when Lenehan praises him with, "Greetings from the famous son of a famous father" (*U*, 248). Simon's "Who may he be?" expresses his lack of concern, and after he has admitted his oversight ("I didn't recognize him for the moment") he rapidly shifts the conversation to another subject. Stephen similarly does not aspire to have "a wise father who knows his own child": such would be the imaginary father as Bloom dreams of himself ("Now he is himself paternal and these about him might be his sons. Who can say? The wise father knows his child" [410]). Stephen has had the opportunity to reflect earlier in life upon certain ambiguous expressions of his father's; for instance, the scene in the pub during the visit to his father's hometown in the *Portrait*[10] showed the rivalry to be more apparent. Stephen would probably have failed by his father's standards and those of his friends: "Then he is not his father's son, said the little old man. —I don't know, I'm sure, said Mr Dedalus, smiling complacently" (*P*, 94). What a wry remark on the dictum, *Pater semper incertus!*

But this uncertainty cannot be pushed to its end in a denial of filial or paternal ties. And Stephen makes an interesting parallel between John Eglington (Magee) and himself when in *Ulysses* he accuses Magee of "denying his kindred" (*U*, 195). Magee deals the most decisive blow to Stephen's theological and para-psychoanalytical theory of creation in Shakespeare when he says, "What do we care for his wife and father? I should say that only family poets have family lives" (ibid.). Stephen's paradox lies precisely in the fact that he needs to present Shakespeare in the midst of family rivalries, usurpations, and treacheries in order to free paternity as creation from the power of the mother. Magee is in fact a sort of alter ego for Stephen, but is as yet unaware that he has had to deny his heritage in order to live on romantic and outdated principles. Stephen thinks: "He *knows* your old fellow. The widower. / Hurrying to her squalid deathlair from gay Paris on the quayside I touched his hand. The *voice,* new warmth, speaking. Dr Bob Kenny is attending her. The *eyes* that wish me well. But do not *know* me" (195, italics added). The widower refers to

Stephen's father, and the phrase "He knows your old fellow" was said by Mulligan about Bloom, whom Mulligan jokingly suspects of pederasty ("He knows you. He knows your old fellow. O, I fear me he is Greeker than the Greeks" [189]). Bloom is already the "jewgreek" combining incest with homosexuality.

It is only then that Stephen finds the courage to develop his theory with the famous statement, "A father is a necessary evil" (195). While Magee places Shakespeare as a creator alone in a mythic space, surrounded by the figures of Falstaff and others, Stephen sees him as the representative of paternity as artistic creation: this "mystical estate" can only be transmitted to a son; it cannot be made conscious. Thus, "Fatherhood, in the sense of conscious begetting, is unknown to man" (ibid.). The "mystery" of fatherhood is this unconscious begetting through which an artist feels the unconscious to exist. The consciousness is reserved to the mother: every man "knows" his mother and "does not know" his father, because his father himself is unaware of the nature of their link. Only a mother's love can mean truth, since the evidence of the senses proves the filiation and also since the son shares with the father the unmentionable privilege of having crossed in person, once at least, the threshold of her womb. "What links them in nature? An instant of *blind* rut" (196, italics added). *Amor matris,* a true "genitive" subjective and objective, but *Caecitas patribus,* an "ablative" plural: desire and castration, places and replacements. This blindness anticipates the full treatment of the incest theme and of the post-Oedipal symbolic castration. Stephen has already defined incest, following St. Thomas, as "an avarice of emotion" (194), which he relates to the Jews, "the most given to intermarriage." Stephen still attempts to reach a definition of the "mystical father," and he gets lost in his self-contradictory developments; he finally locates the elusive relationship in a complete refusal of incest. For Stephen, there can be no reconciliation without first a "sundering," and the father and son are "sundered by a bodily shame so steadfast that the criminal annals of the world, stained with all other incests and bestialities, hardly record its breach" (196). Incest marks the negative limit of paternity, incest literally taken as the love between father and son. In the vast array of perversions one taboo still holds, stronger than the forbidden yet tempting intercourse of the son with the mother. The "bodily" shame is confirmed by the common "transgression" of the mother's sex. Therefore, if the rapport between the mother and son is one of prohibition and transgression, the relation between father and son is what constitutes the essence of the law; it lies at the very core of the Oedipal pattern which introduces the subject to the symbolic realm of language. Without the mother, the son could not *not know* his father. But the mother by herself is unable to tell her son the way to his origins, or his name even.

The famous remark of Telémakhos to Athena in the first book of *The Odyssey* underlines all this discussion: "My mother tells me that I am his son [of Odysseus], but I know not, for no one knows his own father." Through language, a play of absence, difference, and incertitude are brought to bear upon one's own kinship. The mother's voice is not forceful enough to prove the truth of her motherhood: her love has to be true since it can do without proof. Now, as soon as the subject attempts to define himself, he needs the symbolic order of language as conditioned by the absent father, so that he may wander through meaning in quest of a father. For Lacan, the acquisition of language is contemporary with the Oedipal stages.[11] When first I speak, I accept a symbolic castration in that I have to renounce my intense desire for fusion with the mother: as I learn the rules of language, I accept the externality of a symbolic code which existed prior to my unique connection with the other and even predetermined it. The Church is for Stephen such a symbolic world of discourse and culture, which ought likewise to renounce the lure of a madonna "flung to the mob of Europe" (195) in order to found its world "upon the void," "upon incertitude, upon unlikelihood." If the mother's self-sufficiency is denied, the father is not, for all that, a presence embodying the legitimate succession. Language is a system of differences, a power of death and absence in which he too is caught up. This paternal complicity explains the guilt lying within language's very foundation, the guilt of having to displace the mother and to kill the father as presence. Hence, the shame which makes up the voice of the artist, "Shame's voice" as the voice of Shem the artist in *Finnegans Wake*.

Castration and incest thus are played off one another to define the symbolic order of the written text. Paternity is reduced to being a name, which can be separated from the bearer and transmitted to an heir, as Shakespeare did when he transferred his power to Hamlet. Hamlet, "disarmed of fatherhood, having devised that mystical estate upon his son" (*U*, 195). The divine procession of the Logos needs no virgin to encourage believers, but a name is necessary. It is then striking to notice that the first time Joyce wrote the phrase "legal fiction" to define fatherhood, he used it in connection with his own son's name: "The child has got no name yet, though he will be two months old on Thursday next. . . . I don't know who he's like. . . . I think a child should be allowed to take his father's or mother's name at will on coming of age. Paternity is a legal fiction."[12] The same expression sounds quite different in *Ulysses*, since Stephen has to ascertain at once the fiction of paternity and the ineluctable power of a name; this difference explains the shift to a modal phrase ("Paternity may be a legal fiction"): any "definition" of paternity has to be hypothetical. And the suspension of the imposition of the name cannot last very long, since a name implies this "mystical" function—a mystique without love or belief—binding heredity to the law. The name becomes a signifier, as Lacan expresses clearly: ". . . the attribution of procreation to the father can only be the effect of a pure signifier, of a recognition, not of a real father, but of what religion has taught us to refer to as the Name-of-the-Father."[13]

Stephen does not really claim his name. It is imposed on him from the outside; even his listeners refer his subtle digressions back to his name: "Your own name is strange enough. I suppose it explains your fantastical humour" (199). Although a name explains nothing in such a direct way, indeed its function is to raise the physical resemblances (eyes, voice) to the power of a symbolic signifier. Only a signifier can be related to a voice, in a pattern which opposes name and bearer, inherited signifier and speaking subject. Stephen has then to choose a delicate balance between usurpation and right lineage. He says: "I am tired of my voice, the voice of Esau" (ibid.). Thus, although he is really the first-born and hardly seems to care about his brother Maurice, he is both Esau and Jacob in his double role of actor and acted upon: as actor, he displaces both brothers and father; as acted upon, he obeys the mother's wishes ("Act. Be acted upon."). The course of his self-generation is a journey through writings, from the Bible to Shakespeare, in which he sets out to assume his father's name in full

("Dedalus"), after having passed the labyrinths of his own logics: "Lapwing. Icarus. *Pater, ait.* Seabedabbled, fallen, weltering. Lapwing you are" (199).

So the voice is less of a clue revealing one's descendance than a symptom of a division within the subject; it is less "his master's voice" as Paddy Dignam exclaims (451) than a cracked reproduction which splits asunder in the effort to maintain warring opposites in the same position of discourse. Just before Dignam's exclamation, Father Coffey's voice was heard: "Namine. Jacobs Vobiscuits. Amen," in a sacrilegious variation on Jacob's biscuits.[14] The name-of-the-father as received must be written down to be efficacious as signifier, but in this very movement, the play of differences opens up and fastens the subject in a knot tying Jacob to Esau. Stephen had wondered: "What's in a name? That is what we ask ourselves in childhood when we *write* the name that we are *told* is ours" (198). This statement is a new departure from what Telémakhos said when he mentioned that no one knows his father by himself. No one knows for himself, but everyone, even a poor schoolboy has a signature, a name that becomes a coat of arms, a personal emblem or simply the illegible cipher of the most common signature: "a crooked signature with blind loops and a blot. Cyril Sargent: his name and seal" (25). A name entails a writing, a hand re-appropriating what another's voice says of it. This hand and voice are here locked together in the blind gaze of a signifier which has to reconcile the name-of-the-father with the mother's desire. Now, the voice of Esau is twice absent: a first time because it has been usurped by Jacob's voice, a second time because it has been replaced by his handwriting. When this problematic knot is linked to the creation of a text, the antagonistic elements are integrated into the machinery of sense which adequately uses the brothers' conflict to bring about the father's fall. Such a scenario adumbrates the nuclear organization of *Finnegans Wake*.

In *Finnegans Wake*, the story of Jacob and Esau, exploited to satiety, offers the model of a potent performative function of language, a paradigm even more interesting than the divine *fiat lux*, since it works with a deceived paternal namer. Isaac, whose name is already a pun ("laugh!"—"When is a pun not a pun?" asks the textbook in 307.1–2, with the answer "Isaac" in the margin, suggesting that the answer is "when it is a name"), cannot alter his benediction after he has realized Jacob's ruse. Now Esau stems from his father's side; he is the natural heir of patrilineal descent, while Jacob the second-born is his mother's favorite. The mother needs the paternal benediction to place Jacob at the head of the family: she needs the ritual power of a name. Jacob obeys his mother's *voice;* Rebekah tells him, "Only obey my voice" (Genesis 27:13). When later the blind father feels his son's body hidden beneath a goatskin, he seems to renew a sensual contact with his wife. His lyrical benediction takes the form of a fresh alliance with a feminine earth: "*See,* the smell of my son is as the smell of a field which the Lord hath blessed." In his blind vision, through the almost homosexual contact of a trembling hand with a son's fake skin, the old father turns back to the mother and her heir to bless the erotic gift of food and a body fetishistically identified by hair. All this is bartered against this name. In his voice, something is inexorably written, a signature which becomes a fate: *fari fatum.*[15] Speech is a production which entails irreversible action as soon as it is undersigned by a name: "Speech, speech. But act. Act speech. They mock to try you. Act. Be acted on" (*U,* 199).

The same division between name and bearer reappears in Bloom's complex relationship with his father's name. This theme is introduced when Bloom remembers the words his father was fond of quoting: "Nathan's voice! His son's voice! I hear the voice of Nathan who left his father to die of grief and misery in my arms, who left the house of his father and left the God of his father. Every word is so deep, Leopold" (68–69). These lines from the play *Leah* are said by Abraham, a blind Jew who recognizes the voice of the villain, Nathan, a recanted Jew who changes his name and abjures his faith. He persecutes Leah (who bears the name of one of Jacob's wives in the Bible), a jewess, as he attempts to erase his origins. The scene, vividly evoked by Bloom's father, recurs in Bloom's mind to mark his guilt when he thinks of his father's suicide. The coming anniversary of his death sends Bloom's thoughts spinning around his inheritance of a changed name, a name which is never exactly fitting nor properly placed. "Bloom" is a translation from the Hungarian name "Virag," which means flower. Hence Bloom's pen-name of Henry Flower. In this exile from an origin, the name has suffered a certain degradation. This instability is enhanced by the absence of any male heir in Bloom's family. Throughout the book Bloom mourns both his father and his son, poised between a transcribed origin and a nameless issue. As such, he can only imagine a substitute heir, like Stephen, and must also use pseudonyms. This prudence makes him unable to sign his own real name; that is confirmed by the gossip in a pub: "O Bloom has his good points. But there's one thing he'll never do. / His hand scrawled a dry pen signature beside his grog" (167).

Whereas Stephen balances between a father's and a son's name, Bloom's own signifier is unstable, a prey to transformations: "Bloom" will never acquire the status of symbolic signifier. One relevant instance of that general distrust for his name—which, like the name of Odysseus, *Outis*, allows for all sorts of puns—lies in the obvious legal action which changed Virag to Bloom. Martin Cunningham explains the procedure to his drinking companions: "His name was Virag. The father's name that poisoned himself. He changed it by deedpoll, the father did" (321). The pub idiom ("father's name that") opens a significant ambiguity here, since the sentence could even imply that the name was poisoned by itself(!), or simply that the father's suicide could be due to a certain flaw in his name. The same type of idiotism occurs to question Bloom's ability to stand as a real father. A certain J. J. continues with: "... every male that's born they think it may be their Messiah. And every jew is in a tall state of excitement, I believe, till he knows if he's a father or a mother" (ibid.). Here, of course, father and mother refer to "father of a son" and "father of a daughter" but if we are to take this literally, Bloom is then only a mother, an insinuation which will be acted out in one of the most paroxysmal hallucinations of Circe, when he gives birth to eight children.

The transformation of the name and the suicide can then arise from similar causes; a suicide like that of Rudolph Bloom is a desperate act, committed in isolation, while the *deedpoll* which ratified his new name is a deed executed "by one party only" (it is quoted on page 644: "I Rudolph Virag... hereby give notice... at all times to be known by the name of Rudolph Bloom"). To poll means to cut off or to cut even, as with a sheet of paper for instance; this practice of polling the edge of the paper is opposed to the practice of indenting it, which suppposes two parties at least and is meant to reconstitute the original sheet, "each section being later fitted if necessary to the sections having an exactly tallying edge as proof that the sections are parts of an original authentic document" (*Webster's Dictionary*). *Finnegans Wake* mentions for instance a certain Mr Cockshott, "present holder by deedpoll and indenture of the swearing belt" (524.17) in a passage introducing the father's bisexuality. Since the change of names has been, in a way, unilateral, its symbolic function as name-of-the-father is more than problematical. The real *symbolon,* an object cut into two halves that can be reconstituted as a token of identity, implies that dented edge which is lacking in the case of a deedpoll. "Cockshott" is here a signifier of the phallus; one of the most enigmatic recurrent names of *Finnegans Wake,* he unites the broken line of the symbol (indenture) and the clean edge of castration (deedpoll). It is no surprise then to see Bloom's grandfather, Leopold Virag, in one of the visions of Circe, holding a parchmentroll, which among other things is the text of his son's deedpoll (he provides us with a hint when he exclaims "Pretty Poll!" [*U,* 489]). The old Virag, more than Rudolph Bloom, appears as Bloom's real father in this scene, since he at least is an authority on sexual matters: "(He taps his parchmentroll energetically.) This book tells you how to act with all descriptive particulars" (488). He is also a master over his son's fate and toys with the anxieties of his grandson: "Consult index for agitated fear of aconite. . . . Virag is going to talk about amputation" (ibid.). Sex and death are reconciled in Virag's hysterical ramblings, and the sequence of the first names: Leopold-Rudolph-Leopold-Rudy offers a pattern which goes beyond the change of surname. Virag in fact initiates the series of metamorphoses which affects the Blooms; Virag calls up the apparition of Henry Flower in persona and is described aptly as "sloughing his skins, his multitudinous plumage moulting" (483). As "Basilicogrammate," he is "Lord of letters"; like Thoth, the god of letters Stephen invokes, he welcomes all the travesties, transsexualisms, and metempsychoses of the book.

It is not because Stephen and Bloom are not really father and son that they fail to "atone," for Stephen sees even less of his father during Bloomsday; it is because Stephen is the son-type in the process of fathering himself, approaching the creative stage, at least one hopes, and Bloom is the imperfect father in the process of husbanding all his

forces to find himself. Bloom's absence from home, his Homeric pil-
grimage, has started in 1893, at the time when he had his last complete sexual intercourse (i.e., coitus non interruptus) with Molly; his
physical and intellectual absence has increased ten years later, in
1903, since his daughter Milly's puberty (696). The wider frame of
Absence covers the minor "temporary absences" in which Bloom feels
his freedom inhibited by the female alliance of Molly and Milly. The
nine months and one day that have come between the "consummation" of her puberty and the date of 16 June 1904 indicate that Molly's
adultery with Boylan is nothing but the natural outcome of the symbolic incest which both links and separates Bloom and his daughter.
So the different triangles overlap and displace each other successively.
We shift from Molly—Bloom—Rudy, the early Oedipal triangle
ended by the death of Rudy, to Molly—Bloom—Milly, the familial
triangle, and to Molly—Bloom—Boylan, the triangle of adultery. The
next triangle would of course be Molly—Bloom—Stephen, a triangle
that would be both incestuous and adulterous, since "the way to
daughter led through mother, the way to mother through daughter"
(656). Molly, who entertains thoughts of seducing Stephen, could still
be a foster mother for him; by the possible offer of her daughter, she
would become Stephen's mother-in-law, thus finding a new point of
return to her husband, freed at last from his Oedipal infatuation with
his daughter. Hence the impossible superimposition of the two basic
triangles, Molly—Boylan—Bloom and Molly—Bloom—Stephen,
ideally would give rise to the one stable lozenge, Molly—Milly—
Bloom—Stephen. But this superimposition does not happen.

   Such a combination would bring about the ideal fusion of the con-
tradictory "French triangles" Stephen had discovered in Shakespeare's life and creation. "You are a delusion, said roundly John
Eglington to Stephen. You have brought us all this way to show us a
French triangle" (202). Their fusion would build one of the *French
lozenges* which are passed around in Bella's brothel: "No objection to
French lozenges?" (499). This pattern will in turn be included in the
expanding sex of the mother who *Finnegans Wake* presents with "the
no niggard spot of her safety vulve, first of all usquiluteral threeingles"
(297.26–27): she is drawn as A.L.P / παλ (293), and her figure
sums up the different possible positions in the family: ". . . it will be

lozenge to me all my lauffe" (299.28, with a note referring to the sigla of the family).

In the *Portrait,* the young Stephen who still has to "encounter" experience denies family ties as well as all triangular relationships. He seems to be a victim of the delusions of grandeur that, according to Freud,[16] accompany those family romances most children evolve around their origins. Stephen stands aloof and in proud isolation, cut off from his relatives despite his father's awkward attempts at intimacy with him (". . . I treat you as your grandfather treated me when I was a young chap. We were more like brothers than father and son" [*P,* 91]. Typically, Stephen sees himself as the foster child of Irish lore: "he felt he was hardly of the one blood with them but stood to them rather in the mystical kinship of fosterage, fosterchild and fosterbrother" (98). His vocation of artist, which is yet a pure promise, implies a severing of the most immediate ties, and this process goes on well into *Ulysses.* But in the *Portrait,* this romantic attitude is left without any complementary positive father figure, and his temporary hope to "save" his family from chaos, thus becoming too slackly his parents' father, is undermined by parodic economic metaphors, much in the same way as the image of a "cash-register" comes to debunk the masturbatory enthusiasm of his first creative act, the composition of his villanelle.

Stephen then tries to use his family as a secure bolt-hole from which he could define himself, in spite of its evident frailty. The values embodied by the family could have served as a "bulwark" or a "mole" against the mounting "tides" of desire which threatened to overcome him, but the only effective check to his impulses can come from religion. Stephen generously places the money he got from his school prizes at the disposal of his family, hoping to give a new vitality to their life, "by rules of conduct and active interests and new filial relations" (*P,* 98). But, as soon as the money is spent, "the commonwealth fell, the loan bank closed its coffers and its books on a sensible loss"; Stephen is no longer able to resist the call of Nighttown. The latent ironical tone of some sentences which stress his wish to promote quasi-usurious practices, all in a noble cause of course, shows Stephen "press[ing] loans on willing borrowers so that he might have the pleasure of making out receipts and reckoning the interests on the sums lent" (ibid.). This situation is paralleled in *Ulysses* as the hesitation between squandering and lending at interest takes on heightened significance when Stephen explains in the library that for St. Thomas incest is a kind of usury of emotions (*U,* 194). The "breakwater of order and elegance" which Stephen wants to erect was a desperate attempt at limiting the circulation of desire to the little microcosm of the family, and when it crumbles for want of money, he measures his failure in terms of a renewed sundering of ties: "He had not gone one step nearer the lives he had sought to approach nor bridged the *restless shame* and rancour that had divided him from mother and brother and sister" (*P,* 98). The single difference is that here the "shame" does not apply to his relationship with the father. In *Ulysses,* a physical shame dividing father and son gives them both the impetus to travel to the ends of the world in order to avoid meeting the other with the same voice and eyes.

A father is "what went forth to the ends of the world to traverse not itself" (*U,* 479): the prohibition of the shameful proximity of parenthood brings about a circuit, a bend and swerve through language, thanks to which the subject indeed traverses himself precisely because of this movement of self-avoidance. The subject travels through the panorama of styles, literatures, and speeches, and generates the complementary image of self as other. This very movement finally rests upon the assertion of a capitalized Other,[17] a place where the unconscious molds from the outside the serial discourses through which one passes, dying and being born again. In Stephen's musical theory, the father and the son are compared to the "fundamental" and the "dominant" on a scale, as Stephen plays a series of "empty fifths" on the piano: they are "separated by the greatest possible interval which is the greatest possible ellipse consistent with the ultimate return" (ibid.).

The greatest possible interval is both castration as embodied in the father's law and the tabooed, almost perverse, love of castration for itself. In Lacanian terms, Stephen is the phallus[18] for Bloom even more than for Molly, the phallus as a signifier of absence; this representation triggers the movement of ellipse back to the mother. In *Ulysses,* ellipsis is constantly a precondition to the ellipse or transmigration through language: the ellipsis or omission of the prohibited love for the father.[19] This condition also explains why Stephen refuses religion not as a structure of thought, but as a theology of divine and human love. The ellipsis of sexual intercourse conditions the heavenly and terrestrial ellipse centered around Gea-Tellus, Molly as *ewig weib-liche*. And Molly, who is perhaps the only "present" character in a text woven by the apparitions and fade-outs of various absent males, can rightly pun on Bloom's omissions and her own emission. At one point, she remembers the doctor who was to cure her venereal disease that was contracted during her too frequent masturbations due to Bloom's inspired erotic letters: ". . . that doctor one guinea please and asking me had I frequent omissions" (730). She still thinks he had guessed the cause of her ailment, which she of course "omits" ("and I said I hadnt are you sure O yes I said I am quite sure"). When she later con-siders diverse ways of seducing Bloom, she imagines his discharge on her drawers: "then Ill wipe him off me just like a business his omission then Ill go out" (740). Bloom, the "commercial traveller" who follows his son in his wanderings, has perhaps chosen the longest loop round sexual commerce; but if this "wiping out" is by no means an "atone-ment," no more than a promise of a fulfilled and generative sexuality, it can tentatively point to an issue. After all, to cancel an omission may asymptotically approach the shortest route to a direct statement. The father's loss is his gain, in a perpetual displacement; the lack of inter-course finally spins the courses and recourses of the Viconian history on which *Finnegans Wake* elaborates.

II   A Patricidal or a Matricidal Writing?

A. Inter-penetration and Inter-perpetration

A scribicide then and there is led off under old's code with some fine covered by six marks or ninepins in metalmen for the sake of his labour's dross while it will be only now and again . . . that a gynecure was let on to the scuffold for taking that same fine sum covertly by meddlement with the drawers of his neighbour's safe. (*FW*, 14.21–27)

Ulysses opens with two closely linked paradoxes: Stephen, whose mother has just died and who still has a father, is supposedly in search of a father ("Japhet in search of a father," [*U*, 16]) not of a mother; but the mother haunts Stephen's consciousness much more than the living father; the dead mother is alive—the living father is dead. Fathers in Joyce's work keep repeating that they are not yet dead, in a denegation which gradually loses all credibility as it echoes from the *Portrait* to *Finnegans Wake*. The shifting perspective Joyce offers on those successive dead fathers can be read as a very simple play on pronouns. In the *Portrait*, Mr Dedalus' asseverations encompass Stephen's fate in the damned circle of his degradation: "*We*'re not dead yet, sonny. No, by the Lord Jesus (God forgive me) not *half* dead" (*P*, 66, italics added). Stephen will have to take up the cue, distinguishing a living half from a dying half within the composite entity which juxtaposes father and son. The use of a first person plural is quite deliberate; it departs from the original words as transcribed with probably more accuracy and hate by Stanislaus Joyce: "Just *you* wait. *I*'m not dead yet. No, by God, not half dead. Who-op! What do *you* think?"[20]

In *Ulysses*, one section of the Wandering Rocks presents Simon Dedalus who tries to dodge past his daughter Dilly, who has come to demand some money to feed the family before he drinks it away; in his vividly mocking and mimicking voice, Simon parallels his own future death to that of his wife: "An insolent pack of little bitches since your poor mother died. But wait awhile. . . . I am going to get rid of you. Wouldn't care if I was stretched out stiff. *He*'s dead. The man upstairs is dead" (*U*, 225). Although he has played a part in "killing" her, as has Stephen, to him her memory is now sacred, even as her death marks the end of the libidinal and economic balance of drives in the family. Simon then perceives quite rightly in Dilly's cold rage at his irresponsible squandering a desire to see him dead—Dilly voices earlier the terrible "Our father who art not in heaven" (214)—and Simon projects his own wake in a mourning fantasy: he is a corpse, stretched upstairs like Father Flynn's body in "The Sisters." Through his projected death, he can get rid of those who want to get rid of him, since he already is a third person, an absent reminder of the past in the impending future of a symbolic threat. The father will fit, therefore, in his role of dummy in the game; he will elude and escape, while remaining the stabilizer of a symbolic order defined by his name.

In *Finnegans Wake*, the father never really speaks in person; for instance, he never exactly utters the original words said by Tim Finnegan in the famous ballad: "D'ye think I'm dead?" The initiative always belongs to the others, to the collective cries of the mourners: "Macool, Macool, orra whyi deed ye diie?" (*FW*, 6.13); and the father always speaks as the object of their wishes (he would say: "D'ye think *me* dead?") not as a subject: "Anam muck an dhoul! Did ye drink me doornail?" (24.15). The father is in a way like the king about whom Freud quotes a French joke: to the King who asked to be made the butt or subject of a joke, a wit replied: "the King is no subject."[21]

And as soon as the mourners see Finn about to resuscitate, they persuade him to lie back, and they eventually force him to stay in his bier: "lie quiet and repose your honour's lordship! Hold him here, Ezechiel Irons . . ." (27.22–23). The conclusion is straightforward: "Repose you! Finn no more!" (28.35). They go on to explain that he can rest in peace, since a substitute has already been found, for now comes Earwicker the publican, Finn's "namesake": "For, be that samesake sibsubstitute of a hooky salmon, there's already a big rody ram lad at random on the premises of his aunt of the hungred bordles . . ." (28.35–29.1). Finn is the dead giant whose dreams spin universal history; he is buried in a landscape limited to Phoenix Park and the outskirts of Dublin, and Anna Livia flows on to the sea with her continuous feminine prattle.

So it seems at first that the same pattern as in *Ulysses* can be applied to *Finnegans Wake:* a split between a real and a symbolic father contrasts the dead father identified with the law against a living father whose shortcomings, failures, and perversions are the talk of the town. In fact, the relation between Finn and his substitutes (for they are perhaps more than one) is never quite clear, as nothing is clear in this dream book of a language merging into a night of all languages; but we already can state that the archetypal father is not "consubstantial" with his sons or substitutes. *Finnegans Wake* leaves a logic of substances to enter one of relations, which means that the principle of "incestitude" is now operating at the very level of language. The language is in such a perpetual confusion and hesitation about its own objects that everything is moving in a reversible world centered around a mysterious guilt. Even if the father appears to be the origin of the guilt, he is not a Christlike persona; he is no host or "corpus meum." His first function is to bequeath a symbolic debt inside language to the community.

Finn seems to be equated with a place, Phoenix Park, whose name can be superimposed onto the title of the book—the spark of the embers consuming the Phoenix negates (nix in German) the end (finis, fin): Fin-negans, Wake! If such a majestic father lies at the root of all history, he can be expected to inform it in some way, to offer some kind of vital source, some heroic blood through a continuous transubstantiation. But what a close analysis of the text reveals is that no communion is ever possible, because the origin disintegrates under the inquisitive eye of seekers and followers alike. Finn's body seems to be arrayed for its consumption in a parodic last supper; the mourners even say grace before eating it: "Grace before Glutton. For what are we, gifs a gross if we are, about to believe. So pool the begg and pass the kish for crawsake. Omen" (FW, 7.6–8).[22] Fittingly enough, the parts of his body seem about to turn into bread and ale, "But, lo, as you wold quaffoff his fraudstuff and sink teeth through that pyth of a flowerwhite bodey behold of him as behemoth for he is noewhemoe. Finiche!" (7.2–15). The sacred salmon of divine wisdom becomes a "behemoth," a gigantic monster fading away in the landscape. As white whale swallowing everything and everybody—Noah as well!— yet remaining invisible; this absent father is of course the Wake itself, both the ritual that is going on with its disappointed mourners and the bulk of the book which must also frustrate the efforts of the readers: ". . . he is smolten in our mist, woebecanned and packt away. So that meal's dead off for summan, schlook, schlice and goodridhirring" (7.17–19). The "salmosalar" is now a canned herring, destined to be exported rather than eaten on the spot: the textual metamorphosis thus evaporates the text, referring each sentence back to all the others. The father is now his own son, smolt (young salmon) and milt (male ova) fusing in the dense fog of universal mythology. The meal is ended before it started, and the baffled revelers only say "good riddance" to the lure of this "red herring." The text parades its eucharistic nature only to expose it as illusion; the "someone" who might have been exhibited to us is nothing but a "sum-man," an addition, a combination of all past sins. As the communion can never by achieved, the sense is lacking, and the mythic totality can never be (re)constituted.

Whatever the exact degree of "inconsubstantiality" between Finnegan and Earwicker may be, they share the uncomfortable privilege of having committed a misdemeanor: both are implied in the endless trial which sets out to determine the reason of their "fall" and to ascertain the extent of the guilt which stains everybody else: "What then agent-like brought about that tragoady thundersday this municipal sin business?" (15.13–14). From the start, Finnegan's fall from a wall "in erection" epitomizes an original sin's having a collective and political significance. The whole book is just an immense reiteration of the manifold interpretations of such a transgression. Since the guilt is collective, the absence of the dead father prepares the scene for what appears to be a symbolic debt which establishes the realm of the law. As Lacan writes: ". . . if this murder [of the father] is the fruitful moment of debt through which the subject binds himself for life to the Law, the symbolic Father is, in so far as he signifies this Law, the dead Father."[23] Joyce follows the hints he had from Freud closely enough, since he too reduces collectivity to the family.

We have seen how Stephen had attempted to cancel his filial debt, beforehand as it were, by setting up his family's lending bank; in *Ulysses* his strategy of irresponsibility declares him insolvent and makes him unable to relieve the evident bankruptcy of his "house of decay." In *Finnegans Wake*, everything is bolted around the very name of the dead father, Finn. The dead Finn becomes "finis," the end, and also the beginning of the father's symbolic life: "Finn is." Thus, he becomes his family, transformed as he is into the Irish clan or *Fine*.[24] The Fine was not limited to a nuclear family; it included several septs. The sept itself is a further stage before the nexus of the Oedipal family; indeed, the sept as punned by Joyce into the French "sept" or "seven," and the basic family in the *Wake*, is made up by seven characters, the parents, three children, and two servants, Joe and Kate. The title of the book could well be "Urges and Widerurges in a primitive sept" (267, right margin, capitalized). The Fine includes the larger family, with the twelve customers in the pub, and the four old men. For instance, the Irish Brehon Law acknowledged the solidarity of all the members of a Fine; everyone is responsible for each other's crime. It also fixed a price for all offences; the legislation stipulated a fine for murder, theft, etc., so that in this system the family is determined by a system of obligations and mutual responsibility. This collective commitment renders all the members of the Fine "sinnfinners" (36.26): they pay the fine for the sin, and as they acknowledge their kinship, they stand as politically subversive, at least in the eyes of the other law, the imposed English law. But since they pay their fine, they soon become accusers, and this is why the father has to answer for his offences to his parents first; Earwicker says this exactly: ". . . I am woowoo willing . . . to make my hoath to my sinnfinners. . . ." The Sinn Feiners are now sin finders.

Moreover, Earwicker's name is often traced back to "Eric," the Scandinavian name; when the inquirers search for the possible origins of the father, they list ". . . the Earwickers of Sidlesham . . . offsprout of vikings who had founded wapentake and seddled hem in Herrick or Eric" (30.7–10). An *Eric* is precisely the price one has to pay for an offence; one paid a murder-eric, a theft-eric, etc. *Finnegans Wake* echoes this many times; "I will pay my pretty decent trade price . . . the legal eric for infelicitous conduict" (537.12–13), declares Earwicker as repentant sinner[25]. Hence the price the clan has to pay for the father's murder is the murder-eric, which places Earwicker in the following dynastic succession:

> Finn (the dead father)
> FINE (the family and familial debt)
> Eric as Earwicker, substitute and scapegoat.

The family's origins are linked to the primal murder of the old ancestor who with his name countersigns the symbolic debt without which there could be no offspring. Shem likewise praises his father: ". . . his farfamed *fine* Poppamore, Mr Humhum, whom history, climate and entertainment made the first of his *sept* and always up to *debt*" (173.22–24, italics added). We now understand better why every time the buried hero offers to stand up, the crowd taunts him with derisive jeers: "Hahaha, Mister Funn, you're going to be fined again!" (5.12). A father never can be de-fined.

For Joyce, as for Vico, the family is the basic unit of civilization. In the family lie the seeds of the *polis* and the political order, yet the historical passage to the system of families is marked by a return to particularism and even to autarky. For example, Vico's theory[26] posits a certain catastrophe at the source of history, a catastrophe connected with the Biblical Flood. According to him, the early giants, who indulged in unrestrained copulation in the open, were frightened by the thunder, which they took for a divine remonstrance; they then went into caves and there founded the rites and customs such as religion, decency, moral laws, the prohibition of incest, all of which make up the family.

Subsequently, every family possesses "its own religion, its language, its territories, its matrimonial ceremonies, its name, its weapons, its government and its laws" (*SN*, §630). Joyce uses this independence to build an autonomous language, a sort of idiolect of the family. Vico's analysis of the familial organization anticipates in many ways Freud's theory of the primal herd in *Totem and Taboo,* as Vico sees in the father's law a despotic power: law and legacy are intrinsically connected; and using this right to leave a legacy, the father has often transformed the system of heredity into despotism, which can range from ordinary paternalism to absolute tyranny. Jupiter, as "Jus-Pater," represents the absolute authority of the fathers during the age of families. The first families also extend their limits; those "gentes" shelter clients (*famuli*), or runaway slaves, along with the nuclear family. Vico's analysis of the *Roman Twelve Laws* is fascinating because it displays an awareness of the link between names, inherited from the symbolic father, the prohibition of incest, and the dialectics of revolt against the father's law. The family is soon cleft by struggling parties; the rebel slaves are joined by the sons who are not much better treated and fight against the autocratic rule of the father. This rebellion breaks down the old unit and brings about the birth of a political state. Kings are chosen by the *patres* to subdue the rebellious *famuli*, replacing thereby the domestic authority by the civil one; the state, in place of the family,[27] then controls property.

The case of the Roman plebeians is typical: they rebelled not to claim more political power, but simply to be granted the right to marry "like the Fathers" ("connubia patrum" and not "connubia cum patribus," stresses Vico, [*SN,* §598]). Without the rites of the fathers, marriage was not sacred, and the plebeians could not *name* their father, "non poterant nomine ciere patrem": they could not prove their heredity, nor could they be part of a symbolic order. Vico clearly relates the lack of a name to the impending risk of committing incest: "the plebeians . . . who could not prove the legitimate ties which linked them to their fathers . . . incurred the risk of engaging, like animals, in incestuous relationships with their mothers or their daughters" (*SN*, §567). If we can generalize from this case in point, we may then notice that the sons react violently against a paternal tyranny which comes near to imposing a potential incest upon them. But, by so doing, and this is where *Finnegans Wake* goes a little further than either Freud or Vico, the sons who finally defeat the father—if they do—unwittingly violate the most prohibited of the incest taboos: when they murder him, strangle him, shoot him, they are in a way having sexual intercourse with him. To bear this out in details, I will now turn to *Finnegans Wake* and the exemplary story of Buckley and the Russian General.

The essentials of the story are simple enough: Buckley, an Irish soldier fighting against the Russians at Sebastopol during the Crimean War, one day catches sight of a Russian General alone in a field. He is about to shoot him, but when he realizes that the General simply wants to defecate, he falters; then the General wipes himself with some grass, and Buckley, disgusted, braces himself and shoots.[28] The story is enacted with slapstick effects by Butt and Taff, appearing on a television screen in a pub. Joyce, who had heard this story narrated by his father, had enormous difficulties in inserting it in the *Wake,* despite the straightforward relevance of the classical Freudian themes. He could only include it after Beckett had given him a nationalist key to its conclusion: "Buckley shoots the General because he wipes himself with a "sod of turf," offering "another insult to Ireland." The political theme is then grafted onto the Oedipal sequence of provocation and ritual murder. Earwicker is the incestuous father *par excellence;* an "earwig," he is also an "insect," and insects abound that can connote incest: "Insects apalling, low hum clang sin!" (*FW,* 339.22). The General seduces Butt's beloved sister ("odious the fly fly flurtation of his him and hers!" [352.7]), and this brings about the final insurrection: "We insurrectioned. . . . I shuttm!" (352.13–14).

The father's sacramental aura is what prevents the sons from murdering him at once. They try to come nearer to a sacred space and to "divulge" it: "Divulge!" (340.31) shouts Taff to his brother. They are both involved in an "interpretation," since, according to Vico's false etymology, "interpretatio" derives from "interpatrari," which means "to penetrate the fathers": "The first interpretation applied to the divine laws and was made by means of auspices, earning thus the name of interpatratio" (*SN*, §448).

The sons' interpretation does not render them intrepid: "And may he be too an intrepidation of our dreams which we foregot at wiking when the morn hath razed out limpalove and the bleakfrost chilled our ravery!" (338.29–31). Their "trepidation" wishes the father to be only a nightmare, a pure fantasy produced by their own guilty unconscious. The father as "necessary evil" is nevertheless part of the "nightmare of history" from which the sons hope they will awake in the morning. And when the day comes, near the end of the book, the mother uses similar words to calm a dreaming child: "Hear are no phantares in the room at all, avikkeen. No bald bold faathern, dear one. Opop opop capallo, muy malinchily malchik" (565.19–21). The Russian phrase (my little boy) calls up the Russian context of the story of Buckley, while the General has become the panther of Haine's nightmare in *Ulysses* ("the black panther was himself the ghost of his own father" [*U*, 394]). He is also the Roman centurion who "polluted" Mary in the revised catechism expounded by Virag in Circe. Any father is but the ghost of himself; he conditions the myth and the unconscious of the sons by his name. To forget the father means to hope for a mute awakening in the sad detumescence of a chilly morning. But happily for us, there is no waking out of the Wake, no place unaffected by the power of the name; and when the sun "raises out his lump of love," he also castrates the night's wet dreams. The father is the tribal totem, the bear ("Urssian," 352.01; "ussur ursussen," 353.12, blending U.S.S.R. with an Irish—bear, not bull) attacked by a pack of hounds. These dogs shout "Bog curse" (339.6)—"Bog" is "God" in Russian—meaning the curse of God/Dogs, but also the curse of the bogs, of peat and turf. As old bear, this father "reveals" himself and exposes himself to the interpretation in that he "bears/bares" his name: "Of the first was he to bare arms and a name" (5.06); he is thus a "forbear" who bares his body, his arse specially, inviting his own immolation.

Butt, though, repeatedly acknowledges that he had not the courage to shoot, and Taff pushes him along. To underscore this ideological block, Taff relies on the very machinery of the story itself, and a title is enough to suggest that something must have happened somewhere, and the recurrence of titles is as great as that of proper names. They all play the same role: "Since you are on for versingrhetorish say your piece! How Buccleuth shocked the rosing girnirilles" (346.18–20). Once Butt has been convinced that he must act, he becomes confident, garrulous even, while the General starts accusing himself of all the sins in the world, and Taff seems more and more reserved about the revolution. And when Butt tells the audience that he finally shot the General (the problem is never to know whether the action actually takes place or not; what matters is that he has been brought to express himself), Taff appears both critical of his brother and aware that he is merely attempting to replace the father:

Taff (camelsensing that since they have given bron a nuhlan the volkar boastsung is heading to sea vermelhion but too wellbred not to ignore the umzemlianess of his rifal's preedings . . . effaces himself in favour of the idiology alwise behounding his lumpy hump of homosodalism which means that if he has lain amain to lolly his liking—cabronne!—he may pops lilly like a young one to his herth—combrune—). (352.16–22)

The revolution is going to triumph, and the boatmen of the Volga are heading to the sea under a red flag, but this Easter rising is merely boast by the vulgar, the people (Volk), and Taff poses now as the aristocratic liberator (Yeats) who does not know what to do with his gunmen. Taff "effaces himself" in favor of the ideology: he must blot out all the signs marking his difference. The new state which will replace the old will have as totalitarian an ideology as the former, with its insistence on a state religion (Butt is seen in the next paragraph with "his bigotes bristlying," 352.27); Butt has simply taken his father's place, and Taff uses the same title when he congratulates him: "And Oho byllyclaver of ye, bragadore-gunneral!" (352.23). Taff's indulgence for the past links him to his father, whose sins he shares ("homosodalism," for instance); like his father, he erases himself and disappears. As Shem the Penman, he will incur the same reproaches and insults, while his brother refuses the guilt which he yet betrays by constant slips of the tongue.

The "ideoloogy" is the linguistic process which unites the two brothers in one person: "Butt and Taff (desprot slave wager and foeman feodal unsheckled, now one and the same person . . .)"

(354.7–8). The desperate wage slave and the feudal yeoman represent the alliance of the proletariat with the small landowners in an
"ideal reconstitution" (355.01). But if the father's death may well
have taken place in the reality defined by the confluence of their fantasies, the father still lives at the symbolic level of myth: their victory is
"umbraged by the shadow of Old Erssia's magisquammythical mulattomilitiaman" (354.9–10). The General was only another disguise
for Finn, the dead hero who survives by bequeathing his inheritance of
guilt and debt: "As to whom the major guiltfeather pertained it was
Hercushiccups' care to educe. . . . and the law's own libel lifts and
lames the low with the lofty" (355.11–12). This ideology will be even
more perverted in the next cycle, when the freed slaves are reduced to
the role of victims or accomplices of the Nazi terror: "Forwards! One
bully son growing the goff and his twinger read out by the Nazi priers.
You fought as how they'd never woxen up, did you, crucket? It will
wecker your *earse*, that it will!" (375.16–20, italics added).

B. The Language of the Earse/Aerse

Beckett's suggestion gave Joyce a convenient relay, enabling him to
move from the murder of the mythical ancestor to a wider interroga-
tion about a role and place of the mother in language. Not only does
Joyce fully "nationalize" the story,[29] he also universalizes the national
problem and shows its relation to idiom, idiolect, and ideology. Even
the systematic opposition between anal and phallic elements threads
through all the languages which really contribute to burst the mother's
tongue. The most obvious symbols that are paraded in this story reveal
that it reenacts the struggle between phallic and anal drives. Butt with
his gun is also called "Bod" (penis in Gaelic), and he taunts the father's
"jupes": "Come alleyou jupes of Wymmington!" (339.26). This
correspondence points to the father's transvestism and feminizes his
arse ("zhopa" means arse in Russian). Similarly, Stephen had been
struck by the expression "les jupes" used by a Jesuit to refer to the
Capucin dress, and he associates the priests' dresses with "the delicate
and sinful perfume" of the "names of articles of dress worn by wom-
en" (*P*, 155). The brothers' several attempts at insurrection are all
failed uprisings against the Tsar or "Sur of all Russers" (340.3–5)

("ser" means "shit" in Slavonic languages, and "sur" is the Tsar in Russian),[30] and though Butt's fly is unbuttoned ("and your flup is unbu . . ." [341.02]) he needs no less than three pauses and numerous exhortations before the actual shot. Taff's entreaties are unequivocal: "Whor does the pene lie, Mer Pencho? Ist dramhead countmortial or gonorrhal stab?" (349.1–2). His venereal diseases should not prevent Butt's "ramhead" from butting into the father's arse. Yet, in spite of this abundance of anal/phallic themes, the role of the mother cannot be neglected, and indeed it affords a key for comprehending the shift from the different initial positions of the sons and father.

During one pause in the duet of Butt and Taff, a news report gives a clue to the interpretation of the overdetermined relation between all members of the family. The news ends with a horse race in which the father has the lead as "Emancipator, the Creman Hunter" (342.19) —we recognize the reversed initials of H.C.E., Earwicker as Here Comes Everybody—followed by "three buy geldings," while two young mares ("too early spring dabbles") are "showing a clean pairof-hids to Immensipater" (342.25–26). The incestuous position of the Emancipator/Immense pater is blatant: he emancipates his doubled daughter (or his wife plus his daughter) just to abuse them, and he conversely castrates the sons who are mere "geldings." They, in turn, have only one alternative: to castrate or to be castrated. When the father seems about to get the upper hand, the horrified crowd witnesses an exhibition of incestuous relations and their associated perversions: "Sinkathinks to oppen here! To this virgin's tuft, on this golden of evens! I never thought of sinkathink" (342.26–28). This disclosure of the virgin's pubic hairs is another hint about the perverse nature of H.C.E., who perpetrates the same insult as the offense to the "Virgin Soil" (title of a book by Turgenev which Joyce had in his library about Ireland).[31] Butt and Taff cannot bear the family's secret to be revealed, so they fall back on the pretext of an insult to a virgin sister or mother to enable themselves to shoot the father. The alliance of symbolic castration of a penis and patriotism in order to defend a phallic mother constitutes what Joyce calls ideology. The "virgin's tuft" will then have to be transformed into the "sob of tunf" with which the father wipes himself: "beheaving up that sob of tunf for to claimhis" (353.16).

As he wipes himself, the father claims the soil of the country as his; he soils it and makes a "s.o.b." of each son in this perverting action. The insult against national values and national honor—the customers shout "For Ehren, boys, gobrawl!" (338.3), joining "Ehre," honor in German, and Erin go bragh—can be reversed, turned back onto the father: he himself becomes a "son of a bitch." Taff thus exclaims: "The lyewdsky so so sewn of a fitchid!" (340.1). He is not uninhibited enough to say, "The lewd son of a bitch" outright, and his guilt makes him stutter ("so so sewn"); he also disguises his statement as Russian, and, translated in Russian, the sentence equates the General with mankind ("lyudskoi," human). Through this piece of abuse, the father shrinks to the stinking role of a son of a polecat (fitch, we find "polecad" in 341.1), and "son" is rewritten as "sewn" because in Russian "sewn" is pronounced "shiti," which contributes also to "fitchid." The General is "sewn" with children; he is the "monad" or unity about to disseminate its fragments of go(l)d ("scutterer of guld") in a golden rain which multiplies him by twenty (fichid in Gaelic).[32] The multifaceted complexity of a father's persona is literally made up by his sons. Hence, the primary sin is to stand in the relation of father and son: "son" in Russian is said "Sin" (CGH); "sewn of sons" and "soiled by shit" are almost synonymous. The father has to pay the penalty for his own paternity, while the son can only wash away the sin of sense through this murder, which yet links him more closely to the shameful reproduction and incarnation of his father. "Shit" must then be replaced by "shoot," as the extremes meet when phallic becomes anal and anal phallic; in the process of "atonement" is no redeeming value, but the simple reproduction of the father's ideology.

We now enter the matrix of the *Wake*, this nexus of transformations which constantly turn the tables on the father and his sons, since their libidinal places are interchanged; the brothers attack the father's anal perversions in the name of the mother's honour, only to repeat the same shift from orality (Shaun) to anality (Shem). When the General makes his confession shortly before the shot, we read: "He wollops his mouther with a sword of tusk in as because that he confesses how opten he used to be obening her howonton he used to be undering her" (349.30–32). He wallops his mother as he wipes his mouth with the famous sod of turf, which implies a whole inversion of the passage between mouth and anus, all this related to a mother tongue. "Mouth" replaces "arse" because it is linked to a maternal language, but the phallic connotations of "sword of tusk," nevertheless, show that the General's sin is to make love as often underneath his wife as on top of her. His corruption of the mother language lies in his creation, since he "lowers" it when he perverts it in his obscene writing, open to all aberrations. Bisexuality is a necessary element in his nature[33]—we learn for example that he is "smooking his scandleloose at both ends of him" (343.24–25). But while bisexuality is part of the "General's" polymorphous perverse disposition, homosexuality, because it has been repressed from the ideology of "normalcy," contaminates the brothers' struggle for liberation. Butt is at one point identified with Oscar Wilde, one of the archetypal figures of inversion in *Finnegans Wake*,[34] and he takes his cue from the mention of "pedarrests" (349.33). What is meant simply by Wilde's pederasty is onanism in the Biblical sense: ". . . the whyfe of his bothem was the very lad's thing to elter his mehind" (340.14–15). This passage does not only refer to the fact that his wife was no obstacle to Wilde's homosexuality: the text says that the "wife of his brother" was the "very last thing to enter his mind." Classical homosexuality (bottom, behind) is related to Onan's sin, the refusal to afford a posterity to a sister-in-law after the brother's decease. Onan spills his seed to the ground, refusing to raise the house of his brother: he does not want to be a father in his brother's name. And Joyce knew the medieval correlation established between onanism, contraception, and sin. What is more relevant is the confusion some theologians made between "parricide" and "sodomy," John T. Noonan sums up the whole issue in this way: "Thus Lactantius treats homosexuals as parricides: his implication is that they destroy potential human beings. It is entirely in keeping with this approach to treat the users of contraceptives and abortifacients as parricides or homicides."[35] Joyce does not treat homosexuals as parricides, but parricides (and who has not dreamed of killing his father?) as homosexuals. Women, spurned or raped, are the only fixed or stable points of reference in this reversible universe: but they are merely exchanged, taken as a pretext of the perverse male struggle for power.

At this level, the General lays the archetypal function of the drunken patriarch, Noah, who exhibits his arse, not his sons, "sham! hem! or chaffit!" (351.26). The drunkenness is another form of paternal blindness, while the open and deserted ark, after the flood has subsided, is now Noah's own anus; Stephen had already punned on this possibility in Circe: "And Noah was drunk with wine. And his ark was open" (*U*, 538, the sentence follows a recall of his theory of incest, "Queens lay with prize bulls," see page 196). Noah must be covered by a son walking backwards; the similar perversions of the General and of the Tsarist times ("those thusengaged slavey generales . . . in sunpictorsbook," [351.22–24]) are inverted once more by the new puritanical order: "I did not care . . . for any feelings from my life privates on their reptograd leanins . . ." (351.26–28). The renaming of St. Petersburg as Leningrad is part of the devious strategy focused on the obscene arse of the father. "Reptograd leanins": walking backwards with retrograde leanings toward the father. Noah's ark becomes Joyce's Trojan Horse, or Wellington's "big wide harse" (10.21), since we shift easily from *horse* to *arse* to *ark*, and then to *aerse* or *erse*.[36]

The father who exposes himself cannot be reduced to anality alone. When he is represented "exposing his old skinful self tailtottom" (344.16), he is not only exhibiting himself, but masturbating and mixing the different levels, top, tail, and bottom all the while tempting the peeping Tom with his tail; then follows a surprising declaration of love from Butt: "as I love our Deer Dirouchy" (344.32), *ushi* meaning father in Russian. The love for the father is finally defeated by the alliance with the mother, so that, through the father's actual death, his name may live. Thus can he be invoked under the name of "Old Erssia's magisquammythical mulattomilitiaman" (354.10).

All this tends to imply that Erse, the grand old forgotten language the Citizen extolls in his pub, plays in *Finnegans Wake* the role of a "father-tongue": it appears as the metamorphosis of a native language, voiced and soiled by the father, returning to the materiality of loam or humus. Only then can it really fertilize the earth. When the father has completed the irrevocable outrage, he intones a song, "an exitous erseroyal *Deo Jupto*" (353.18). His royal arse which is offered to be kissed—"he can kiss my Royal Irish Arse" (*U*, 137)—is a new "King's English" in which the proximity of the paternal arse displaces the mother tongue.

The mythic giants Vico places at the origin of history stem directly from Cham, Shem, and Japhet (*SN*, §369), but their exact genesis is not so "patrilinear"; it is referred to the neglect of their own mothers who abandoned them, "let them roll naked in their own filth" in the post-diluvian primal forest. Left to themselves, "living in the midst of their excrement, the nitric salts of which constituted an excellent fertilizer for the earth," they then attempted to clear a way through the forests, "without any fear of gods, fathers or masters" (ibid.). Here, the mixture of earth and manure, with the added dimension of onanistic pollution, contributes to the mythic origins of civilization: it creates a new language, one blended with body products, that amalgamates "humus" and "human nature" in a type of very special "humor." Shem inherits this language from his father (although he derives his inspiration from his mother and his subjects from his sister), and this explains why he threatens to wipe the English language off the face of the earth: "he would wipe alley english spoken, multaphoniaksically spuking, off the face of the erse" (178.6–7). Shem will use all the other languages to break down the English rule; English will become a spook through the action of his spuking and diarrhoea. *Arse* and *Erse* allied to a multinational *earth* both effect the murder of the mother language. The murder of the father is in fact only a dialectical climax in this indefinite struggle.

Such an unsteady blend of language and substances asserts nothing but its own regenerative power to live and die when it explodes the overgreat proximity of a native tongue. Accordingly, *Finnegans Wake* never ceases commenting on its own material appearance of living printed letters scurrying across a white page: "Owlett's eeggs . . . are here, creakish from age and all now quite epsilene, and oldwolldy wobblewers, haudworth a wipe o grass" (*FW*, 19.11). The sacred *terra firma* which would come as an ideal synthesis never wipes out the sexual and textual "hesitancy":[37] the epicene neutralization of sexual differences applies to the moments when ideology is about to triumph —the fusion of Butt and Taff, or the coalescence of Burrous, Caseous, and Anthony after the regicide, or the victory of St. Patrick over the Druid who stands for the whole book, as Joyce said.[38] The text stages there its own defeat when the language of ideology blurs the differences; but the text thrives on defeat paradoxically, for the adverse criticism only triumphs after it has produced a piece of synthetic tissue in order to wipe the text afresh: "wipenmeselps gnosegates a hand-caughtscheaf of synthetic shammyrag" (612.24–25). *Aerse* as a language is no synthesis, but rather a *coincidentia oppositorum*, playing as often as not the ambiguities of the written word of anal production against the multiple puns afforded by spoken dialects and distorted pronunciations; from *ae*rse to *ea*rse, it turns to the root of P-earse O'Reilly's ear and pierced eardrum.

The theme of the *aerse* as a father-language is to be paralleled with what Stanislaus reveals in his *Dublin Diary*[39] when he notices the frequency with which the word "arse" crops up in his brother's mouth:

Pappie has been drunk for the last days. He has been shouting about getting Jim's arse kicked. Always the one word. . . . I am sick of it, sick of it. I have a disposition like a woman, and I am sick of this brutal insistence on indignity. I writhe under it. I try to regard [it] as drunken, drivelling lip-excrement, but it is too strong for me. Ugh! It is a word that is scarcely ever out of Jim's mouth. He has been remarked for it and *playfully* accused of being a bugger because of the way he pronounces it. (*DD*, 49–50)

James and his father seem already linked in an ambivalent inheritance of anal abuse, while Stanislaus, instead of being accused of homosexuality, stresses his own femininity. But the most telling detail is this: "Jim's criticisms of these notes of mine are characteristic. One of them is this: 'An' do ye be sittin' up here, scratchin' your arse, an' writin' thim things.' He pronounces 'arse' something like 'aerse' " (*DD*, 148). Expressing his virtuous contempt for the objective complicity of his idol, James, with his tyrant, their father, Stanislaus pins down the characteristic symptom with accuracy and reveals too that he does not want to have anything to do with "aerse." Stanislaus voices his loathing for his father because his father is Irish ("*Irish,* that word that epitomizes all that is loathsome to me" [*DD*, 23]), and he almost reproaches James for being too indulgent, as if he felt that Jim had in fact kept the inheritance of gift and guilt left by his father: ". . . and towards Pappie, who, too, represents feudalism to [Jim], his mind works perversely. But his sense of filial honour, as of all honour, is quite humoursome" (*DD*, 55). For Stanislaus, his brother is placed in the same perverse attitude when confronting the Church, the country, and the father: a delicate mixture of respect and contempt, of rejection and imitation, is at work in his mind, revealing a pattern which imposes its own duplication. The cunning debunking of the father who nevertheless is idolized defines a complex stance, parodic and patristic simultaneously; this is the position of "patriody," whose symptoms show in the pronunciation of "aerse."

These symptoms do not tend to betray new biographical aspects; they matter as the seeds of a future textual scene which will appear only in full with the episode of Butt and Taff. The notes of Stanislaus are relevant as literature, for we know that Joyce kept reading them and used many details in his later fiction, from *Dubliners* to *Finnegans Wake*. It is no accident, for instance, that Stanislaus claims the paternity of interior monologue since he experiments with it in his diary (*DD*, 167), a technique he himself imitates from Tolstoi's rendering of the thoughts of a dying officer in his *Sebastopol Sketches*. Joyce finally may have acknowledged his "debt" when he placed the scene of Buckley's shot near Sebastopol. Stanislaus is of course only part of the elusive figure of Butt, yet what remains of him in the character is his keen eye for easy justifications and escape in his brother's strategy, an escape which James Joyce finally achieves through the multiplication of an English rooted in an Irish soil, with the added force of all other possible idioms: "Jim is thought to be very frank about himself, but his style is such that it might be contended that he confesses in a foreign language—an easier confession than in the vulgar tongue" (*DD*, 110). And this was only written in 1904!

In his "foreign" language, Joyce makes the crudest of all confessions, as he recognizes his "perverse" filiation to a despot who cannot be done away with simply and safely. Unlike Stanislaus' blunt rejection, Joyce's exile brings him back, after the journey through the languages, to a place where words are buried alive to be exhumed again and again. Aerse as language destroys what would be on a first level an enslaved mother tongue which obeys the dictates of Rome and London. One of the first ironies of *Ulysses* is the attempt made by Haines, the Englishman, to reappropriate a language that the old Irish peasant cannot even understand: she mistakes his Gaelic for French. "Aerse," nevertheless, is not a thing of the past as Gaelic appeared to Joyce: it opens the individual discourses to a historical dimension; Taff expresses this possibility when he exhorts Butt: "Ath yetheredayth noth endeth, hay? *Vaersegood!*" (346.23; italics added).

Yesterday, which will be this today (yet here today), is not finished yet. The assent to this dynamic drive in which past and present exchange their qualities and properties means a release of all the historical dramas that show how the father's murder is equated with an incestuous sharing of perverse anality. Even castration, as a symbolic weapon wielded by the father, or as imaginary retaliation of the sons, participates in this *soiling* of a soil, "To the dirtiment of the curtailment of his all of a man?" (353.4). Uncivility bounds on both sides, yet it is this desperate fight which gives birth to cities and civilizations.

When Taff is absorbed by the "son-ideology" which will replace the "father-ideology,"[40] he notes the "umzeamlianess" of his rival's "preceedings" (352.18), that is to say the "unseemliness" or else the appeal to the spirit of a maternal earth: *um* means "spirit," "intelligence" in Russian, and *zemlia*, the "earth." But in the next sentence, even the distinctions between father and mother get blurred, for Taff calls God his "maikar" ("wiz the healps of gosh and his bluzzid maikar," 352.35–36); "help" is written so as to let A.L.P., or Anna's initials, come to the fore, and "maikar" unites maker and mother in Bulgarian (maikar). The foreign writings lay waste what would be paternal propriety or maternal place. Playing the game of "patriody," Joyce never criticizes perversion; he simply shows its comic or parodic fallout, inasmuch as it affects the father figure. And with this anal or analogical writing, endlessly multiplying the definitions which constitute the propriety of a language, he frees the words from their frozen meanings; he thereby short-circuits the illusion that there can be a mastery over meaning, a mastery which would correspond to a fixed position of the subject in his discourse and in society. Such a language woven with writings resembles a Penelopean tapestry to be pieced together by the reader, for it sets the names adrift, spins the codes round, while it continues to mime a historical process. History becomes equated with a cyclical process of renaming, the laws of history being easily reduced by Joyce to the laws of language. "The only difference," he said to Jacques Mercanton, "is that as with the dream, I perform in a few minutes what it sometimes took whole centuries to produce."[41]

Joyce considers his breakthrough in literature as an insurrection and often sees himself in a state of war; his numerous comparisons prove it: "What the language will look like when I have finished I don't know. But having declared war I shall go on *jusqu'au bout.*"[42] This war is indeed a war against English, against a mother tongue which is used to the limit, mimed, mimicked, exploded, ruined. This scorched-earth policy—the earth being the still maternal soil of words —has to be complemented by the anal fertilization of all the litters, fragments of works, pieces of mythologies, literary odds and ends which are left to proliferate in the text. When, at the conclusion of "Exiles," Richard, the artist, feels a "deep wound of doubt" arising from the agonizing incertitude over his wife's fidelity, when Stephen declares that paternity is the mystery of the void, and when Shem refuses to join the Irish Easter Rising because he "pray[s] to the cloud Incertitude" (178.31), they all reproduce the same pattern, a pattern constituting a feminine receptacle of language through the acceptance of a symbolic castration "which can never be healed." The fusion of womb and wound creates the only possible link between tomb and womb: in its unstable fusion, the father's perversity and the mother's constancy are merging, bridging the gap between the feminine flux of liquids, rain, water, urine, menstrual flood, and the anal idiom of aerse with all its litters and letters.

This self-canceling "ideolect" sets out to reveal an unknowable original sin in a quest without end or aim even, since what Joyce demonstrates is that original sin is the sin of sense as believed to be an origin: this "since" recurs in the *Wake* to date the barred origin, "since the flood. . . ." Stanislaus was then entitled to say later that "original sin . . . was to be the subject of *Finnegans Wake.*"[43] Whether origins are alternatively identified with the father's law or with the dual relation to the mother, the fall has already separated the text from the hallucinated meaning. There is no devouring of the host, no communion, in a word, that is not a prey to the convoluted circuit of the father's bowels. If, as Atherton writes, original sin is for Joyce God's creation of the world,[44] this creation is marked off from the start by a certain failure, a miscarriage, a collapse. The happy fall (*felix culpa*) is acknowledged, but the doubt about its origins can never be raised fully. It may be phallic as well as anal; we never really know as we get lost among the seemingly haphazard digressions of the speakers at the *Wake.* "It may half been a missfired *brick,* as some *say,* or mought have been due to a collupsus of his *back promises,* as others looked at it" (5.26–28, italics added). Once more, though, the vocal emission is connected with the penis (prick), while the eye is connected with the arse.

Joyce's aim is to prick the bubble of narcissistic self-sufficiency, but not merely by a manic abandonment of the subject to the untamed flows of desire. He prefers to present the father in his symbolic role of dead ancestor casting his blessing on a realm of names, and to use this mythical figure as a basis for diverse replacements; with all the surrogate figures, Joyce exhibits what wounds, what hurts. With the Russian General, killed or castrated by the sons uniting against him, Joyce demonstrates "the itch in his egondoom" (343.26): not only the painful preservative which prevents full conception and generation, but also the *id* inside the kingdom of the *ego.* As Freud phrases it, "Wo Es war, soll Ich werden."[45] The different fathers can be placed on a descending scale that would seem to parody Vico's stratification between gods, heroes, and men: Zeus, Polypheme, and Ulysses are thus seen on a descending scale. Zeus, like Finn, is the absent father whose symbolic name only can be invoked, and often in vain; the fact that he castrated his own father must be repressed from consciousness. Polypheme, the Cyclops, is the real father who transgresses all the laws and breaks the code of hospitality. This "impossible" father has to be overturned time and again by the sons whose fusion builds up the unstable figure of the imaginary father: this place where Stephen's and Bloom's unconsciouses were supposed to intersect appears now as the moment of the ritual murder, which, in the last analysis, aims not so much at a displacement of the father's guilt as it aims at the complete recasting of the mother tongue. As the process is exhibited, the entire play of decomposition consists in letting the elements which constitute the father interchange with one another.

C. *The Laws of "Anonymoses" (47.19)*

To say that we never know whether the father's sin was anal or genital means that one cannot ascertain the priority between his attempt to seduce his daughter or to exhibit his "white arse" to the buggering sons-soldiers, although the biblical pattern would tend to imply that

Earwicker, like Lot, is seduced by his daughter(s), whereas he rather provokes his sons like the drunken Noah. This distinction concerns the "real" father as Earwicker the publican; if we now consider the divine "Loud" of creation who thunders among the clouds, his creative sin must have been anal; there is no doubt here for Joyce, and it echoes in the repeated hundred-letters thunder-words. This Lord is like the God of Moses who showed his "back parts" to him instead of his face.[46] In many respects, the Russian General is like Moses, the man Moses of Freud's last "historical novel." When the sons shoot him, they both shoot the tyrannic and monotheist leader and destroy their awe-inspiring idols. Butt says, "I shuttm" (352.14) to call up Shittim, the place where Moses is supposed to have been murdered, according to Freud and to Sellin.[47] Like Noah, Moses is related to an ark, or two arks rather, the first being the ark of bulrushes where he was miraculously found, and the second the ark of alliance with God, this ark of "Shittim wood." From the obscure legend which tends to preserve the purity of his Jewish origins to the empty ark containing the text of the law, we there find in a nutshell the dialectics of mystical fatherhood. Moses, too, is a father who founds paternity upon the void, upon a cloud of incertitude which hides his own God, upon the living doubt which abhors material or maternal representations.

To forbid the adoration of visible forms is a way of barring the way back to the mother, back to a feminine goddess of sexual fertility. Thus, the law of the father is asserted against the sensible evidence of the mother's hieroglyphics. There is no doubt that, like the Russian General, Moses is killed because of an "insult to the mother," and that, like him, he is at the source of the written character. Freud mentions that the invention of the alphabet may have been derived from the scribes of Moses, who, "being subject to the prohibition against pictures," "would even have had a motive for abandoning the hieroglyphic picture-writing while adapting its written characters to expressing a new language" (*Moses and Monotheism*, note, page 43). Moses, like Earwicker, stuttered—Moses, according to Freud's version of the biblical legend, because he was in fact an Egyptian who spoke Hebrew with difficulty. Earwicker is a Norseman, a Viking invader who tries to speak Irish. As such, both are foreign invaders: "The unnamed nonirishblooder that becomes a Greenislender overnight!" (378.10–11). Nevertheless, their patrilineal rule will in the end "give omen name" (279.4–5), give a name to everything—the ominous and the numinous having been approached at last.

We started with the initial paradox of *Ulysses* in which the dead mother is living and the living father is dead. *Finnegans Wake* asserts the primary function of a dead symbolic father who allows for all the substitutions around his name, his "normative letters" (32.18), H.C.E. The living mother Liffey flows on the contrary toward her "bitter ending" when she finally meets Death in the form of her ocean-ic father at the close of the book. Since the mother in *Finnegans Wake* is the "only true thing in life," she too is undeniable; she feeds, con-dones, preserves. The father is constantly denied, dethroned, negated, but also reestablished for a new cycle, to prepare a new fall. He is ab-sent in such a way that he generates the falls, flights, and flourishes of fiction. The legal fiction has really become the law of fiction, linking the performative power of language to the serial signatures of collaps-ible fathers.

Joyce's patrilineal fervor always has been determining, even when he decided to explore the limitations of the father's function.[48] As far as his own life is concerned, he even tried to rewrite his biography to put his father in a more favorable light. When Gorman wrote in the draft of Joyce's biography the very rhetorical question, "Of whom was he the spiritual son, and where would he find the Mystical Father?," Joyce abruptly inserted the following rejoinder: "His spir-itual father is Europe, to which his natural father constantly urged him to go."[49] By the time he was writing *Finnegans Wake*, Joyce's exile had to be considered as a flight from a motherland of bondage and into a new country still to be created. Yet, Joyce needed the assent of his real father (his "grandolgrossfather" [*U*, 538]) in the new fiction of a biography, acknowledging his debt of paternity even if doing so meant a slight distortion of the facts.[50] Thus could he attempt to become his own spiritual father's father: he can still appear today as the absent father of much that is being written in Europe and elsewhere, in spite of some of our "bulldozers" pouring not earth, but tons and tons of printed matter on his Babelic burial mound. We could perhaps simply repeat Lucia's exclamation when she was told of her father's death: "What is he doing under the ground, that idiot? When will he decide to come out? He's watching us all the time."[51]

ANDRÉ BLEIKASTEN

La mort du Père enlèvera à la littérature beaucoup de ses plaisirs.
S'il n'y a plus de Père, à quoi bon raconter des histoires? (Roland Barthes)

Faulkner's father figures range from such well-meaning weaklings as
Reverend Mr. Mahon (*Soldiers' Pay*) or Mr. Compson (*The Sound
and the Fury*) to comic villains like the blandly predacious Anse Bundren (*As I Lay Dying*), from dour disciplinarians like McEachern
(*Light in August*) and arrogant despots like Thomas Sutpen (*Absalom,
Absalom!*) to venerable patriarchs like Virginius MacCallum (*Sar-
toris/Flags in the Dust*); and whether living or dead, present or absent,
domineering or feckless, malevolent or benign, they loom large in
most of his novels. There would be little point, however, in categoriz-
ing them or in looking for some father archetype, for what seems to be
at issue in Faulkner's intricate family chronicles is not the father as
a person (a character), nor even the father as genitor, as the actual
begetter of sons and daughters, but rather the haunting question of
fatherhood, in its psychoethical as well as in its wider cultural implications. Far from being confined to the performance of a parental role,
fatherhood appears throughout Faulkner's work as a complex function, both private and public, a symbolic agency operating on various
scales and levels and within various patterns, and to discuss it only in
terms of blood kinship and family structure would be to miss much of
its deeper significance.

1 Pater semper incertus est

An astronomer knows whether the moon is inhabited or not with about as
much certainty as he knows who was his father, but not with so much certainty
as he knows who was his mother. (Georg Christoph Lichtenberg)

Paternity is problematical from the outset. If motherhood is a plain fact, a natural given of experience, fatherhood, as Faulkner's novels suggest time and again, is not. Of the former, childbearing and childbirth provide incontrovertible evidence; the latter is always a matter of conjecture, if not sheer speculation. Moreover, who the father is appears to be of little moment in terms of biological reproduction. For the generation and perpetuation of life all that is needed is the father's seed; the father himself is dispensable. As Fairchild points out in *Mosquitoes*, " A woman conceives: does she care afterwards whose seed it was? Not she. . . ."[1] Lena Grove, the earthy mother figure in *Light in August*, is a case in point: she has set out on a long quest-journey to find Lucas Burch, the rascal who seduced her and made her pregnant, but what she is actually seeking is just a father for her child, and it is quite immaterial to her whether his name is Burch or Bunch. It is noteworthy in this respect that most of Faulkner's pregnant girls and women—Caddy Compson, Dewey Dell, Milly Hines, Lena Grove, Laverne Shumann, Eula Varner—are unwed, and that the husbands of those who eventually get married are seldom the natural fathers of their children. As a consequence, many of his characters never come to know the true identity of their genitor. Januarius Jones, for instance, the frantic womanizer of *Soldiers' Pay*, "might have claimed any number of possible fathers."[2] Miss Quentin, Caddy's illegitimate daughter, is "fatherless nine months before her birth,"[3] and so is, quite literally, Joe Christmas, whose begetting causes the murder of his—Mexican or Negro?—father by Doc Hines. In *As I Lay Dying*, Darl taunts his half-brother Jewel, Addie's adulterine son, with the question, "Your mother was a horse, but who was your father, Jewel?"[4] and his cruel question is echoed in *Pylon* by Jiggs' asking little Jack, Laverne's son by Shumann or Holmes, "Who's your old man today, kid?"[5]

Faulkner's world abounds in orphans and bastards, and whenever we discover in his adolescent or adult characters an acute sense of lostness, whenever his novels dramatize a failure to establish an identity of one's own and to come to terms with reality, there are fair chances that the roots of the tragedy are to be sought in the bafflements, frustrations, anxieties, and resentments of a deprived and disturbed childhood. And among the fatherless and/or motherless we must include the Compson children as well as Joe Christmas: having both their parents does not prevent Quentin and Caddy from feeling forlorn and doomed.

Fatherlessness is not so much the absence of a relationship as a relationship to absence. Besides, it should be noted that in Faulkner's novels the father's absence always casts a real shadow, and that whenever the actual genitor is dead or missing, his role is taken over by some collateral relative—an elder brother or cousin, an uncle, a grandfather —or, as in Christmas's case, by a foster father. In Yoknapatawpha no one, not even an orphan, can escape paternal tutelage totally, and one may well wonder if, in the end, it makes any significant difference whether the fatherly functions are assumed by the actual begetter or a surrogate, for in a sense all fathers, the "real" ones as well as their substitutes, are more or less *outsiders*, representing, within the family, a power that transcends familial bonds, and, therefore, is vested with an authority by no means "natural" in the way a mother's is. As Ike, another of Faulkner's fatherless sons, realizes during his lengthy argument with McCaslin Edmonds in "The Bear," "even fathers and sons are no kin."[6] What comes first is the self-enclosed intimacy of the primal, nuclear relationship of mother and child; as to the father, he will always be at some distance from his progeny. Mutual affection may sometimes reduce the distance; it never conquers it completely, and at some point in the child's development this sense of remoteness will inevitably turn into hostility. As Gail Hightower recalls the fears and anxieties of his desolate childhood, he comes to liken himself and his mother to "two small, weak beasts in a den, a cavern, into which now and then the father entered—that man who was a stranger to them both, a foreigner, almost a threat. He was more than a stranger: he was an enemy. He smelled differently from them. He spoke with a different voice, almost in different words, as though he dwelled by ordinary among different surroundings and in a different world."[7]

2   Father and son

For the child, then, the father is first of all a stranger and an intruder, the one—or rather the *other*—whose arrival portends the fatal breakup of the dual unity of mother and child. Yet of all strangers he is beyond doubt the closest and the most familiar. What is more, even though in the child's experience the father comes after the mother and represents an unwelcome addition to and disruption of the primordial couple, it does not take him long to find out that the father has been there before he was and has possessed the mother before he did. As John T. Irwin notes, "In his rivalry with the father for the love of the mother, the son realizes that no matter how much the mother loves him, she loved the father *first*. Indeed, the son carries with him in the very fact of his own existence inescapable proof that she loved the father first and that the son comes second."[8] Priority in time is one of the very sources of the father's power, and since time is irreversible (except in fantasy), it is to the son a continual reminder of how little power and freedom he can negotiate for himself.

Priority is what gives the father mastery over the son; one might add that it is also what makes his mastery fully legitimate. Uncertain as far as its biological foundation is concerned, fatherhood badly needs the support and sanction of a cultural community. Originally, father power is derived or delegated power, and only social consensus makes it into a rightful one. All authority is *established* authority, the more easily accepted and the more unanimously acknowledged as it proceeds from the unbroken continuity of a cultural tradition. Paternal authority, therefore, is the more firmly settled as time has erased its contingent and hypothetical origin and hallowed its prerogatives as an undisputable "natural" right.

From these issues are derived some of the manifold complexities and contradictions of the father-son relationship. As a figure invested with legitimate power, the father inspires fear and envy, but also commands respect; as a rival for the love of the mother, he provokes both hatred and a strong sense of guilt. Moreover, if we believe Freud, all of experience urges the son to take the father as his first model, his first *pattern:*[9] the little boy "would like to grow like him and be like him, and take his place everywhere."[10] Indeed, the father is the very object of his first *identification;* and as several (but not all) of Freud's statements on the subject seem to suggest, this identification process may occur even earlier than the Oedipal crisis and precede any definite object-choice.[11]

Yet, whatever the time of its occurrence in the son's libidinal development, identification with the father is marked from the very first by ambivalence, and, therefore, is bound to result in unconscious conflict during the phallic phase, when the wish to be like the father comes to coincide and collide with the desire to replace him with regard to the mother. Hatred is then at its most murderous, but, however fierce, it does not preclude a measure of love, since in the "complete" (positive and negative) Oedipus complex an ambivalent attitude persists toward both parents.[12] Which is to say that, contrary to the simplistic assumptions of vulgar Freudianism, the father-son relationship is reducible in none of its stages to mere antagonism. It is essential to remember, on the other hand, the crucial function which psychoanalysis assigns to the father in the dialectic of desire and law that, under normal circumstances, leads to the achievement of selfhood. In the Oedipal triangle the father appears as the obstacle to the fulfillment of the incestuous wish; he bars the son's access to the mother, yet by the same token he also forbids the mother exclusive possession of the son. He thus releases the latter from the constraints and tensions of the family circle, allows him to move on to other object-choices, and furthers his entry into the system of alliances which rules and regulates the wider world of human exchange. In prohibiting and preventing incest, the father indeed performs a major cultural function, especially if, as Lévi-Strauss argues, the universal incest taboo is to be understood as the very cornerstone of human society.

His, then, is primarily the role of interdictor, of legislator through whose authority the maintenance of the cultural order is ensured within—and without—the family. Not that he is himself the author of the law: what authority he possesses he owes to society and its traditions or, to put it in more structural terms, to the specific *place* which he comes to occupy within the family configuration in relation to mother and child—a place previously held by other fathers, now dead, and which he will have to yield in turn to his son, a place "marked in life by that which belongs to another order than life, that is to say, by tokens of recognition, by names."[13] At this point it becomes obvious again how far the paternal function transcends the individual existence of the biological father. Or we might say that what matters most in the last resort is not the living father so much as the dead father, not the real father so much as the *symbolic* father or what Jacques Lacan calls the "name-of-the-father," "the symbolic function which, since the dawn of historical time, has identified his person with the figure of the Law."[14]

Whether Freud's theory of fatherhood and its structural reformulation by Lacan possess universal validity is of course debatable. Yet as far as the classical, father-focused, Western family is concerned, they offer extremely suggestive models of interpretation. My purpose, however, is not to "apply" these models to Faulkner and to approach his novels as literary illustrations of psychoanalytic concepts, as there is, on the one hand, no transparent and irrefutable discourse of science and truth, and, on the other hand, there is no shadowy, delusion-ridden discourse of literature. Rather, I would suggest, Freud's and Faulkner's texts are to be read as differential versions of common concerns and, perhaps, of a common quest for knowledge, the former attempting to articulate in theoretical terms what the latter is trying to express through the language of fiction.

With both, one might note, there is an abiding fascination with the question of fatherhood. Paternity is central to Freud's interpretation of the Oedipus complex as well as to his account of the formation of the superego; it is central, too, in *Moses and Monotheism* and *Totem and Taboo*, his later, highly speculative essay on the origins of religion and culture. As to Faulkner, his interest in fatherhood is attested throughout his work from *Flags in the Dust/Sartoris* to *A Fable*, and in at least four of his major novels—*The Sound and the Fury, Light in August, Absalom, Absalom!, Go Down, Moses*—the father-son relationship is assuredly one of the crucial issues.

3 Väterdämmerung

Dead, but still with us, still with us, but dead.
(Donald Barthelme, *The Dead Father*)

Faulkner's life-long preoccupation with sons and fathers must have arisen out of the depths of some private need, yet it seems safe to assume that it was also related in many ways to the particular society into which he was born and in which he spent most of his life. Faulkner was a Southerner writing about his native land; his questionings and probings cannot be dissociated from the unique context of Southern culture and Southern history. Southern society was almost from the outset a family-centered society. Indeed, in the Old South the patriarchal family typified to a large extent the proper relations between ruler and ruled and so supplied the primal model for social organization and political government. Father and master in one, the slave-holding planter of the prewar South was the source and locus of power: as *paterfamilias*, he claimed full authority over wife and children; as "massa," he felt entitled to demand filial subservience from his slaves. He thus presided over an extended family, white and black, and, as Eugene D. Genovese has demonstrated persuasively in his re-evaluation of Southern slave society, this sense of extended family came to inform the whole network of race and class relations.[15] The planters, it is true, were only a minority, and one should beware of oversimplification: the social order of the ante-bellum South was more complex and more fluid than well-established stereotypes would have us believe. Yet the plantation system conditioned all of Southern life, and the patriarchal and paternalistic values of the ruling class permeated Southern society at large. Whether paternalism mitigated the evil of slavery will long remain a matter of dispute among historians, but there can be no question that the father metaphor played a major role in the rhetoric of white male power, nor can it be denied that it had become a key concept—or rather a key fantasy—in the ideology of the South.

The *Väterdämmerung* set in after the Civil War, when the socio-economic foundations of autocratic father rule began at last to crumble. The defeat of the Confederacy meant the end of slavery. Paternalism no doubt survived for many years among the remnants of the plantation system, and so did the patriarchal family structure till the early decades of the twentieth century. But the lordly father image associated with the planter ideal had become an image of the past.[16] In the impoverished South of the Reconstruction years, fathers surely had as many responsibilities as ever, and their tradition-hallowed authority allowed them to keep control over the family. In the upper classes, however, their field of power had shrunk irretrievably. Compared to that of their predecessors, theirs was indeed a diminished role and one they must have filled the more self-consciously as they could not help but feel dwarfed by the formidable ghosts of their forefathers.

Out of the nostalgic memories of a lost world and out of the nightmare of a lost war, an imaginary South had arisen, as if to obliterate the real one—a collective mirage in which the old Cavalier legend blended into the Confederate myth born from the exploits of Lee, Jackson, Stuart, Forrest, and all the lesser heroes who had bravely fought and died for the Southern cause. And out of this compelling mirage grew Southern shintoism and its wistful rituals. Probably nowhere else in America, not even in New England, was the ancestor ever held in so much reverence as he then was in the South, nor had he ever been such a powerful and omnipresent phantom.

Fatherland had become a haunted and haunting ghostland, and so the Southern father image was bound to become a divided one, at least in those families—generally of the upper middle-class—that had a sense of continuity and tradition. On the one hand, there was the glorious ancestor, the idolized dead father, safely enshrined in myth, intact and intangible in his godlike remoteness and the more indestructible for being timeless; on the other hand, the human, all too human, progenitor, the hopelessly prosaic real father, born into a time and place in which there was no longer use for the dazzling deeds of heroic gentlemen. How, then, could he be expected to serve as a model to his son? And with whom was the son most likely to identify in his youthful search for an ideal self if not his grandfather or his great-grandfather?

4   Dead ends and re-beginnings

Even Fate is, in the last resort, only a later projection of the father.
(Sigmund Freud, "Dostoevsky and Parricide")

Let us now turn to the opening scene of *Sartoris,* Faulkner's first Yoknapatawpha novel:

As usual, old man Falls had brought John Sartoris into the room with him, had walked the three miles in from the county Poor Farm, fetching, like an odor, like the clean dusty smell of his faded overalls, the spirit of the dead man into that room where the dead man's son sat and where the two of them, pauper and banker, would sit for a half an hour in the company of him who had passed beyond death and then returned.

Freed as he was of time and flesh, he was a far more palpable presence than either of the two old men who sat shouting periodically into one another's deafness while the business of the bank went forward in the next room and people in the adjoining stores on either side listened to the indistinguishable uproar of their voices coming through the walls. He was far more palpable than the two old men cemented by a common deafness to a dead period and so drawn thin by the slow attenuation of days; even now, although old man Falls had departed to tramp the three miles back to that which he now called home, John Sartoris seemed to loom still in the room, above and about his son, with his bearded, hawklike face, so that as old Bayard sat with his crossed feet propped against the corner of the cold hearth, holding the pipe in his hand it seemed to him that he could hear his father's breathing even, as though that other were so much more palpable than mere transiently articulated clay as to even penetrate into the uttermost citadel in which his son lived.[17]

Sartoris begins with the ritual, almost necromantic invocation of Colonel John Sartoris, the founder of a family line as well as the first creator of a family myth.[18] It begins, that is, with the invocation of the beginner, the begetter, the origin, the absolute father—a figure long dead, yet more alive than the living and compellingly present to those who invoke his name. As such, he is much more than a character in the novel: an uncanny, pervasive presence-in-absence, a *deus absconditus* controlling the fates of the Sartorises from invisible heights. While alive, John Sartoris vainly had pursued his "dream," but in death he found the power to "stiffen and shape that which sprang from him into the fatal semblance of his dream."[19] "Death" means, more precisely, what his descendants have made of death in the process of transmuting his destiny into legend.

To survive and prosper, vampires need fresh blood, and so the dead only prey upon the living insofar as the living allow themselves to be preyed upon. John Sartoris' spectral potency has in fact no other basis than the fantasies of his offspring; his prestige is pure magic,[20] yet everything happens as though its fascination were irresistible. A rigid pattern has been set up, a paradigm of being and behavior for all his male progeny to emulate, so that none is ever permitted to evade the family doom.[21]

The crucial confrontation, then, does not take place between son and father, but between son and forefather. One might object, of course, that young Bayard, the novel's twentieth-century protagonist, shows no clear awareness of the familial past[22] and that his sole obsession is with his dead twin brother. True, Bayard's despair and death wish may be said to result primarily from his intense emotional involvement with Johnny's death. But Johnny, the loved, admired, and secretly envied twin, appears in the novel as a reincarnation of Carolina Bayard, Colonel Sartoris' daredevil brother, who was killed in the Civil War: three generations later, his reckless gallantry duplicates that of his great-granduncle, and so does the flamboyant manner of his death. Johnny, as it turns out, is the namesake of his equally heroic great-grandfather and may be seen, therefore, also as a twentieth-century avatar of the glamorous colonel. These three interrelated figures thus become as many exemplifications of the same myth, and as many illustrations of the Sartoris way of death. Johnny is the last to meet the demands of the myth with proper panache, Bayard the first to fail in his attempt to fulfill its obligations.

That they are twins points ironically to their likeness—a likeness never to be resolved into sameness. To young Bayard Johnny is at once brother and father, rival and model, a double in whom he recognizes himself as other and with whom he finds it therefore impossible to merge. For while being his alter ego, his mirror image, the twin brother also represents his inaccessible *ideal* self. Eventually he will manage to kill himself and join his twin in death. But just as his life is a degraded version of Johnny's, his death is but an empty travesty: Johnny's jump from the flaming plane, at least as perceived and remembered by Bayard, its rapt and horrified witness, was a gesture of triumphant self-affirmation; Bayard's violent but trivial end, on the other side, completes a process of sullen self-destruction begun long before. And the suspicion lingers that it might be an act of revenge as well as expiation, as if in killng himself Bayard also killed the internalized brother-father.[23] Through his death the compulsive mythic pattern has been reenacted once again, yet repetition has ceased to be proof of its lasting power. The paradox of Bayard's death is that it is both an escape into myth and a flight from myth, the last victory of an exacting past and its ultimate defeat.

To his descendants Colonel Sartoris bequeaths a name and a game: a name with "death in the sound of it,"[24] a "game outmoded and played with pawns shaped too late and to an old dead pattern."[25]

Sartoris depicts a Southern family in which reverence for the ancestor has gone to the extreme of necrolatry, and the cult of the dead has degenerated in turn into a murderous fascination with disaster and a frantic search for death. For whether identification with the heroic forefather succeeds or fails, it necessarily ends in self-destructive violence. In point of fact, identification with him *is* death: there is no other way to equate him, no other way to placate him. In *Sartoris* the dead father no longer functions as a symbol of cultural order, as an index to tradition and a guarantee of its maintenance; he has ceased to be a tutelar spirit presiding over the community of the living. An arrogant statue towering above a *graveyard:* this is the last glimpse we get of Colonel Sartoris.[26] There could be no more apposite emblem of his role in the novel.

5 Battling with ghosts

Decline and death are also major concerns in *The Sound and the Fury,* admittedly a very different (and far better) novel, but one in which the relationship between past and present, dead and living proves just as central an issue as in *Sartoris.* In *The Sound and the Fury* the narrative does not span four generations as it does in the latter novel, nor is there anything like the deliberate counterpointing of Civil War and World War I events. The historical and genealogical perspective provided by *Sartoris* is clearly missing here, or so it seems at least at first glance, and there is, consequently, less emphasis, too, on the presence and persistence of a family myth. Yet again there is a young twentieth-century protagonist confronted with the legacy of his forebears, and again the confrontation ends in tragedy.

Different from Bayard, however, whose progenitor has been dead for eighteen years when *Sartoris* begins, Quentin Compson has a father. One might then assume that in *The Sound and the Fury* the prime confrontation is that of father and son. In a sense it undeniably is, and there can be no question that Mr. Compson occupies a key position in Quentin's drama. Yet his role is hardly that of the repressive father, nor is Quentin's that of the rebellious son. It would be mistaken, therefore, to reduce their relations to mere antagonism and to interpret them in unqualified Oedipal terms. In *The Sound and the Fury* the father-son relationship is both central and tantalizingly elusive. To understand its significance, it is essential to trace its development through all its puzzling obliquities.[27]

To start with the most obvious, Mr. Compson turns out to be an extremely weak and ineffectual father. What authority he possesses is the authority of failure, and failure is all he will bequeath to his son, even as failure was all his own father had bequeathed to him. As Faulkner himself pointed out in one of his interviews: "The action as portrayed by Quentin was transmitted to him through his father. There was a basic failure before that. The grandfather had been a failed brigadier twice in the Civil War. It was the—the basic failure inherited through his father, or beyond his father."[28] In light of the author's comments, one sees more clearly what, in the last resort, determines the filial impasse in *The Sound and the Fury*. If Mr. Compson is totally unfitted to assume the function of fatherhood, it is because he has himself never ceased to be a helpless son. Too weak to be an active mediator between desire and law, he has nothing to offer to his son but the corrosive rhetoric of his nihilistic aphorisms, and all he does during the lengthy debate recorded in the novel's second section is to teach Quentin the devastating lesson of a man's inescapable defeat. This lesson Quentin learns so well that toward the end of his monologue the father's voice almost blends with his own: the father, then, is in the son, but as an alter ego rather than a superego.

Again, we might note, there is a blurring of differences, a confusion of roles. Just as in *Sartoris*, in which Johnny, the twin brother, had become in death a compelling father image to young Bayard, so Mr. Compson, the father in *The Sound and the Fury*, is to Quentin a kind of disillusioned, cynical elder brother, showing him the way to disaster. Again, there is a process of doubling, a repetition in difference with fatal effects. Father and son are amazingly alike in their psychological impotence. With the Compsons, impotence is so to speak a hereditary disease, striking each generation anew, and the only son to be spared is, significantly, Jason, a Compson only by name.[29] Instead of being a threat, a means of intimidation, castration is an inherited condition, a condition aptly symbolized at the opening of Quentin's monologue by the grandfather's watch—"the mausoleum of all hope and desire"[30]—given to him by Mr. Compson. The watch is of course an emblem of man's bondage to time, the ultimate castrator, yet in the specific context of the novel it might be seen as well as a paradoxical reminder of the Compsons' alienation from time. For theirs is a family not unlike the Sartorises, a family for which time has ceased to flow and in which everyone is fated to senseless repetition, which means that nothing of real import can ever happen between father and son: their encounter is an encounter of shadows, for there is neither father to be obeyed nor father to be challenged, neither son to be directed nor son to be punished.

Hence, there is Quentin's tragic bewilderment; hence, too, his morbid fascination with incest. Since Mr. Compson fails him as lawgiver, who could possibly protect him from incest's lethal lure? There is, however, much more to Quentin's incest wish: as I have argued elsewhere,[31] the point is that incest is conceived from the outset as an affront aimed at and *confessed* to the father, and that through the intended confession Quentin secretly seeks to provoke paternal retaliation, i.e., to force Mr. Compson to play at last the part of avenging father and so to acknowledge the son's manhood in the very act of threatening it.

Castration as an act would cancel out castration as a condition. Yet the challenging confession does not take place; the incest with Caddy is not committed. Quentin's devious and desperate strategies are little more than the fevered fantasies of a neurotic mind. Nothing happens and nothing can happen because something *has happened* in a remote past, a past beyond Quentin's personal memory and yet weighing on him like the corpse of an invisible giant: "It was a—something had happened somewhere between the first Compson and Quentin. The first Compson was a bold ruthless man who came into Mississippi as a free forester to grasp where and when he could and wanted to, and established what should have been a princely line, and that line decayed."[32] So there is after all a strong Oedipal father in *The Sound and the Fury*—save that he has long been dead and that to discover him we must trace the family line back to its founder, Jason Lycurgus Compson.[33] True, the latter is never mentioned in the novel, and when Faulkner made these comments, he may well have been reading some of his later books into the earlier one. Yet for a true understanding of his total *oeuvre*, intertextual connections may prove just as relevant as intratextual evidence. With the founder-figure of Jason Lycurgus, we are assuredly given a major clue to the decline and fall of the House of Compson. One might even argue that without him the Compson story would have no plot, that without him it would be indeed what it seems to be: mere "sound and fury."

Insofar as they are all three failures, Quentin, his father, and his grandfather duplicate one another; they form a timeless, frozen series of identical units, not an unfolding sequence of differential terms. Jason Lycurgus, on the other hand, makes for a sense of beginning and a sense of succession: he "established what should have been a princely line," and if he too failed, his was at least an active, inaugural failure; if he sinned, his was at least an original sin.

The founder's failure has become a curse upon his heirs. Whichever generation they belong to, they are all the impotent sons of the same father. It should be clear by now that the pattern thus disclosed is the very pattern that we found in *Sartoris*. Again the ultimate antagonist is no other than the *great-grandfather*. Quentin is confronted with the overpowering ghost of Jason Lycurgus just as young Bayard was with the formidable shadow of Colonel Sartoris. And like Bayard, Quentin plays a losing game, a game that can only end in defeat and death. For the match can never be an even one, and the confrontation with the forefather turns out to be a mockery, even as that with the father was. Where Mr. Compson was too close, Jason Lycurgus is too remote; where the former was too much of a brother (of a narcissistic double), the latter, in his mute and massive transcendence and his forbidding otherness, is too much of an inaccessible god. Neither can be considered Quentin's opponent in any real sense, because each is too elusive to be countered in active resistance. With reference to his own family, Mr. Compson is indeed right when he tells his son that no battle is ever won or even fought.[34]

Yet Mr. Compson's bleak wisdom does not settle the matter, nor is Quentin's escape into death the only way out. Quentin has two brothers, and if Benjy, the idiot, is his whining double in impotent sonship, Jason ultimately emerges as a grotesque father figure (a half-repressive, half-incestuous father to Miss Quentin, a castrating one to Benjy). That he bears the first name of the founder of the line is another of the novel's many ironies: with Jason, too, history repeats itself, but this time as a grim farce.

On the other hand, the question of father and son should also be raised in relation to the novel's mythic pattern. It is of course not fortuitous that each of the four sections corresponds to a day in Holy Week, and that the last one climaxes in the joyful celebration of Easter by the black community. Quentin's pointless "passion" and absurd death are thus contrasted with the redemptive self-sacrifice and glorious resurrection of Jesus Christ, that is to say, with the very apotheosis of sonship that Quentin had in mind on the day of his suicide. One can see here a further irony, but the final section also offers the suggestion of tensions at last resolved, of conflicts at last transcended—if not in reality, at least in myth.[35]

6 White father, black son

All religions are in essence systems of cruelty.
(Friedrich Nietzsche, *On the Genealogy of Morals*)

In *Sartoris* as well as in *The Sound and the Fury* and *As I Lay Dying*,[36] Faulkner dramatized conflicts within a single famly; in *Light in August* he seems to have been much more concerned with individuals in their relationship to society at large, and it is quite significant that in this novel all the major characters are at once aliens to the community of Jefferson and solitary figures without normal family ties. Yet their alienation from the community does not mean that they are estranged totally from its values. Indeed, all of them—with the possible exception of Lena Grove, who seems to exist in a space of her own—have absorbed and internalized these values so well that their conflict with society is always a war on two fronts, a war both without and within. That *Light in August* is a novel about alienation *from* society and its horrendous costs in violence and suffering is obvious enough; one should not forget, however, that it is as much—if not more deeply—concerned with the various forms of alienation inflicted on individuals *by* society.

It will not do, then, to reduce Faulkner's outsiders to more or less criminal deviates from the communal norm.[37] Their minds have been patterned by their cultural environment; no matter how distorted, their mental categories and moral standards are those of their fellow citizens, the more inescapably so because in the closed, intolerant society in which they have to live no viable alternative is at hand. And in many ways they are representatives of that society. Not that any of the novel's protagonists can be identified with the average member of a given social or ethnic group (Faulkner's realism is a realism of extremes, not of averages). Eccentrics they are, yet each of them may be said to dramatize some essential aspect of the rural South in the early decades of the twentieth century. Thus, Gail Hightower embodies its obsessive involvement with a romanticized past, while Joanna Burden, the shunned "nigger lover," appears as an obverse reflection of its sexual and racial fantasies as well as of its puritanical sense of guilt. As to Christmas, the outcast *par excellence*, what makes him supremely significant is not at all his supposedly mixed blood, but his divided self, for it is through the splitting of his psyche, through the deadly combat between his "white" and "black" self-images that he comes to stand as a starkly truthful symbol of the tensions and contradictions of Southern society.

At the same time, however, Christmas is also a living challenge to his culture and its value system. Of the two identities available to him, he chooses neither, and what bewilders and infuriates the community more than anything else is precisely his stubborn refusal to meet its expectations, to conform to its standards, to act either as a "nigger" or a white man.[38] Identity, in the world of *Light in August,* is above all a social imperative: people are required to fit into established classes and categories and to confirm through their normalized behavior the arbitrary divisions and hierarchies upon whose maintenance the very survival of the existing social arrangement depends. Those who cannot or will not fit must be expelled, therefore, from the body of society: Hightower and Miss Burden, the minor offenders, are relegated to the outskirts of Jefferson; Christmas, in punishment for his crimes, is castrated and killed.

Scapegoats are recurrent figures in Faulkner's fiction,[39] yet in no other of his novels (except *A Fable*) does the putting to death of an outcast so strongly suggest the religious dimensions of sacrificial murder. In *Light in August* Faulkner resorts once again to Christian symbolism, but the way in which he uses it is far more complex and ambiguous than critics have been willing to acknowledge. Little insight is gained by calling Christmas an "inverted Christ" and leaving it at that. In fact, the analogies with Christ serve as much to emphasize the character's essential duality: just as he is both "white" and "black," he is both Christ and Antichrist— symbol of radical innocence in his agony and death as well as an emblem of extreme guilt.

Furthermore, Faulkner's tragic (rather than purely ironic) version of the Christ myth is given additional significance through its association with the novel's sexual and racial issues. Officially, Christmas' crime is the rape and murder of a white woman by a black man, and as soon as he has been identified as a Negro, no further proof is needed to establish his guilt. So he must die, and it is noteworthy that the circumstances of his death are a reverse repetition of his misdeeds: the killer is killed, and the rapist castrated. More than ruthless retaliation is involved, however, and there are other debts to be paid. The guilt Christmas is made to expiate is not only his; it is also the guilt unconsciously projected and discharged upon him by the whole community.

What does Christmas stand for in his role of *pharmakos*? On what "other scene" is the final act of his tragedy performed? At this juncture it may be helpful to recall briefly the psychoanalytic interpretation of Southern racism attempted by Joel Kovel.[40] In traditional, white-dominated Southern society, Kovel argues, the Oedipal conflict finds a kind of collective and institutionalized solution,[41] with the white woman in the position of forbidden mother and the black man cast in the dual role of incestuous son and rival father: "the Southern white male simultaneously resolves both sides of the conflict by keeping the black man submissive, and by castrating him when submission fails. In both these situations—in the one symbolically, in the other directly —he is castrating the father, as he once wished to do, and also identifying with the father by castrating the son, as he once feared for himself."[42] Cross identifications, cross projections, desire, hatred, and fear—these are precisely the feelings and mechanisms at work in the putting to death recounted in *Light in August*.

It will be remembered that Christmas' birth cost the lives of both his parents, that his first crime was the attempted murder of his foster father, and his second the rape and murder of a white woman. One might recall, too, that his story offers intriguing analogies with the Oedipus legend.[43] Everything, in fact, urges us to see him as a new fictional avatar of the guilt-laden son figure. Yet if it is true that all sacrifices are to some extent symbolic reenactments of the primal patricide—the collective crime in which, according to Freud, all human societies originate[44]—then Christmas also functions as a vicarious father. In the phantasmal scenario, his castration and murder represent the fulfillment and punishment of a single wish. As to Percy Grimm, the priestlike sacrificer, his chiasmal relationship to Christmas is at once that of father to son and of son to father. The places they occupy are exactly the same, but not their roles: while Christmas, the defenseless sufferer, is two victims in one, Grimm—in what we might call his *ambiviolence*—acts both as defiant son and avenging father.

Doubling is everywhere, and we even find it programmatically inscribed in Christmas' very name: "Joseph," the name of Christ's father, given to him by Doc Hines, the first surrogate father, the fanatical inquisitor who later turns out to be his grandfather; "Christ-(mas)," the name of Joseph's son, given to him in profane mockery by the dietitian, his starkly parodical nursing mother, and the other "sluts" of the orphanage.[46] So Christmas is son and father through his name as well as through his sacrificial role, and in this respect, too, he is not unlike Christ, the divine Son partaking of the omnipotence of his heavenly Father. Yet the Christ he is associated with is the secularized, humanized Christ of the Transcendentalist tradition rather than the Messiah and Redeemer of orthodox Christianity, the humiliated and tortured son rather than Christ in his power and glory; and we might also note that his first name is not the name of Jesus' "real" father, but that of his pallid human substitute. In the father-son duality the emphasis falls obviously on the second term: Christmas is Christ in his passive suffering, in the agonies of his Passion, and his "resurrection" in the memory of myth is little more than the pathetic reminder of a crucifixion endlessly rebegun.

As to the ultimate addressee of the sacrificial message, he is neither a God of mercy nor even a God of justice. If one insists on relating him to the Judeo-Christian tradition, one might say that he is much closer to the jealous Jehovah of the Old Testament than to the Man-God of the Gospels. The metaphors designating him in *Light in August* as well as in some of Faulkner's other novels tell us quite clearly what he is: the "Opponent,"[47] the "Player,"[48] a power more infernal than celestial, manipulating men as though they were pawns or puppets and dragging them on inexorably toward disaster and death.[49]

This God is a perverse and cruel tyrant, a terrible father. Conversely, the novel's paternal figures all act as if they were the duly mandated representatives of "the wrathful and retributive Throne."[50] Never doubting that they have been personally chosen to carry out the Lord's will, Doc Hines and McEachern play God to Christmas. To the sons fall the duties and debts, to the fathers all the prerogatives of power. If the dominant social values in *Light in August* are those of the white male, it is only in fatherhood that masculinity realizes its claim to absolute mastery. In its social organization as well as in its ethos and religion the early twentieth-century South portrayed by Faulkner is still a patriarchy, although a debased one.[51] Fathers control, command, and punish. Small wonder that the God of Yoknapatawpha appears as their magnified and idolized self-projection.

Of the inescapability and destructiveness of father power there is no more chilling evidence than Christmas' tragedy. Yet in the lives of Joanna Burden and Hightower its crippling effects are just as readily discernible. Joanna's fate is sealed in early childhood, on the day when her father takes her to the cedar grove where her grandfather and half-brother are buried. At once spiritual testament and baptismal rite, the father's pronouncement over the grandfather's grave is, in the fullest sense of the term, a speech *act:* it loads the four-year-old Joanna with the "burden" of her name and heritage, assigns her a place in the chain of patrilineal succession[52] as well as in the endless chain of the doomed and damned, and so fixes the rigid pattern of her life. She will try to break out of it, and her affair with Christmas may be seen as a desperate attempt to reaffirm her repressed femininity in the face of her puritanical fathers; in its third and final "phase," however, the latter have regained complete possession of her mind and body, and she eventually dies for having both obeyed and disobeyed their injunctions. Accursed she is indeed, but the curse upon her is in fact nothing but the searing trace of an evil utterance, a male*diction*. Fatality, in Faulkner, is clearly no metaphysical or theological issue, but a matter rather, of language, of words said and heard, remembered or forgotten, and of the unpredictable ways in which they rebound and reverberate from generation to generation, trapping people in their tyrannous echoes.

Hightower's is a different story. His prime obsession is not with the "black shadow," but with "a single instant of darkness in which a horse galloped and a gun crashed . . . [his] dead grandfather on the instant of his death."[53] To Hightower the ancestral past is not so much a burden to be borne as a private theater in which he can play out every night his heroic fantasies.[54] Just like Joanna's, though, his destiny has been preempted by the family ghosts. Born after what should have been his life and death,[55] dead before having been born,[56] Hightower hovers in a vacuum, outside time—"a shadowy figure among shadows, paradoxical."[57] In providing him with an imaginary surrogate for manhood, his compulsive, ritually repeated identification with the "apotheosis" of the Confederate cavalryman grandfather has prevented him from achieving separate identity. Hightower's identification with the dead father is too passive to be acted out in suicide; it condemns him, however, to the absurd condition of death-in-life.

No matter how different the destinies of Hightower, Joanna Burden, and Joe Christmas, they resemble one another in that they are all determined by patrilineal filiation, and what strikes us again as decisive is the relationship to a figure more remote than the actual father. This holds true for Joanna and Hightower, who are both inheritors of a family tradition, but also for Christmas, the foundling, the seemingly rootless orphan. For he, too, has a grandfather, and it is Doc Hines' heinous, petrifying gaze that fixes and fractures his self and points the way to disaster. Christmas' early childhood is overshadowed by dead parents and a living grandfather, while Hightower's and Joanna's are by living parents and a dead grandfather. In none of these cases does the mother play an active part. Christmas' mother died in childbed,[58] Hightower's wasted away in helpless frustration, and about Joanna's all we are told is that she was Nathaniel Burden's second wife and had been sent for by him like an item out of a mail order catalogue.[59] As to the fathers, their sour-faced stolidity stands in revealing contrast to the raw ebullience of their own progenitors. For all their fierce puritanism, Joanna's and Hightower's grandfathers were by no means contemptors of life; they avidly grasped what it could offer and, much like Colonel Sartoris or Jason Lycurgus Compson, they had been shaped in the heroic mold of pioneers and warriors. Hines surely does not belong with them, yet in his demonic turbulence he strikes us as an obscenely caricatural reminder of their militant faith and, in relation to Christmas, his are indeed the godlike privileges of ancestral power.

If Christianity is the religion of the saving son, there is little Christianity in the society portrayed in *Light in August*. Neither is the patriarchal religion of Yoknapatawpha County that of the Old Testament. No covenant has sealed the mutual recognition of father and son, no angel stops Percy Grimm from killing Christmas. Grimm himself is the "angel"[60]—an avenging angel with a butcher knife. And, contrary to the crucifixion of Jesus, the putting to death of the sacrificial victim serves no redemptive purpose. What we have here is patriarchy at its crudest and most savage: a system of self-perpetuating violence and cruelty, based on endless cumulation of guilt and endless repetition of revenge. Christmas dies in payment of a debt, but the debt is not discharged nor can it be. *Les dieux ont soif....*

7   Fatherland revisited

Et rêve de la filiation masculine, rêve de Dieu le père sortant de lui-même dans son fils, —et pas de mère alors.... (Stéphane Mallarmé)

In *Absalom, Absalom!* Faulkner abandons the contemporary scene to delve into the dusky depths of the Southern past. In most of his previous novels there was no doubt a haunting sense of the past; in *Absalom, Absalom!*, however, the past and its meaning for the present become the very objects of the writer's quest or, more precisely, of the writer's quest for, and inquest on, the past, as dramatized by the feverish speculations and conjectures of his four narrators; the novel itself is not a neatly completed tale, but the random process of a telling; not a "historical novel" in any traditional sense, but the hazardous reconstruction of problematic events, a fiction about the making of fictions (including history).

As a genealogical novel, *Absalom, Absalom!* invites comparison with *Flags in the Dust/Sartoris*. Both novels span several generations of (what might have been) a Southern dynasty, and counterpoint past and present. In *Flags in the Dust* the two polar extremes were Colonel Sartoris and young Bayard, his doomed twentieth-century descendant; a similar polarity links and opposes Thomas Sutpen to Quentin Compson. Yet Quentin is no kin to Sutpen nor is he a direct participant in the family drama. *Absalom, Absalom!* is the first of Faulkner's novels to be set in nineteenth-century Mississippi, and Thomas Sutpen is clearly its hero. There is, then, a definite shift in narrative focus, and this shift entails in turn a complete rearrangement of the narrative discourse itself.

So far the figure of the ancestor had been little more than an intriguing shadow. Now he is made flesh, moved to the foreground and made into the focal point of the *story*. The heir figure, on the other hand, ceases to be the novel's protagonist. Quentin's role, however, though functionally different from Bayard's in *Flags in the Dust,* is no less central: if he loses his status as *dramatis persona*, he becomes the major agency of the *narrative*. And in his desperate endeavor to give the story shape and significance, he might be seen as well as the potential artist, i.e., as a fictional double of the novelist in the very process of creation.[61]

Absalom, Absalom! reexplores and rearticulates issues already dealt with in Faulkner's previous novels, yet it is much more than a brilliant summation of familiar themes. Not only is the novelist's vision projected onto a larger canvas; it is projected in such a way as to sharpen our perception of the problematic procedures of his art. What is thus lost in mimetic illusion is regained in awareness of the conditions and effects of its production. By calling attention to itself as structuring process, the novel engages us to renounce the lay pleaures of pure fiction and to join in the narrators' search for possible meanings. Faulkner's complex strategies in this extremely self-conscious text are designed to provide critical distance, to make room for imaginative freedom, to stimulate reflection and expand awareness; their ultimate purpose is clarification, not obfuscation.

Indeed, much of what, heretofore, had been submerged rises at last to the surface. In *Absalom, Absalom!,* for the first time, the ancestral ghost is encountered face to face, and the Hamletlike confrontation with his "questionable shape" is played out both on the scene of fiction and the scene of writing. For sonship and fatherhood, as we come to realize in reading the novel, are not merely capital issues in the fictional world it represents; they relate back to the writer as fiction-maker and designate the very stakes of his perilous game with language.

Quentin Compson is part of the game, and that Faulkner resurrected him from his suicidal drowning in *The Sound and the Fury* to make him the central narrative and interpretative voice in *Absalom, Absalom!* is of course highly significant. One may choose to consider Faulkner's novels as discrete, autonomous units; it is no less legitimate to read them as so many fragments of a single text, each novel functioning as a supplement to the previous ones and requiring in turn the supplementarity of its followers—not to be made whole, but to allow the process of completion to continue. Seen in such a light, *Absalom, Absalom!* would appear as a monumental postscript to *The Sound and the Fury*. Many critics have noted the striking analogies between the story Quentin tells in *Absalom, Absalom!* and his own story, as revealed in the earlier novel, and it is indeed tempting to read one through the other and to decipher them in superposition, as if they belonged to the same palimpsest. Both stories are about father and sons, sister and brothers, and both revolve obsessively around seduction and revenge, desire and death. In *The Sound and the Fury* Quentin is in love with Caddy, attempts to avenge her seduction by Dalton Amers, fails to do so, and commits suicide when he realizes that his sister is irrevocably lost; in *Absalom, Absalom!* Henry Sutpen feels similarly attracted to his sister Judith,[62] tries to possess her vicariously through his beloved half-brother Charles Bon,[63] and eventually kills the latter after learning that he has Negro blood.

In telling their story, Quentin identifies quite naturally with the quixotic, death- and incest-haunted Henry, but he identifies as well with Bon, the unacknowledged son. As John T. Irwin has pointed out, the two Sutpen brothers objectify the enemy halves of his split self and play the roles in which he has so lamentably failed: Bon, the dark brother, assumes the envied yet guilty part of *seducer,* while Henry ends up as the bright *avenger.*[64] The Sutpen story, thus, can be read as a *mise en scène,* an acting out, in the uncanny space of fantasy, of Quentin's internal struggle in *The Sound and the Fury*. As Faulkner himself suggested in commenting upon the relationship between the two novels, Quentin "tells his own biography, talking about himself, in a thousand different terms, but himself."[65] In many devious ways

Absalom, Absalom! is indeed his autobiography, a text in which he (re)presents himself—as fabulator—and attempts to tell (and read) the secret story of his own life.

Most autobiographies are fictions of and for the self. Conversely, fictions are perhaps the only truthful autobiographies. *Absalom, Absalom!* does not tell the truth about Thomas Sutpen and his children, the heroes of the tale; it tells us infinitely more about its tellers, especially about Quentin, the tale's ultimate sender and receiver. The reasons of his fascination with the Sutpen story are not far to seek, but it is not enough to point to the resemblances between that story and his own. For beyond the shock of recognition there is the discovery of the difference, the discovery—or the retrospective illusion—that his destiny might have taken a different course if he had lived in another time, a time when people were "simpler and therefore, integer for integer, larger, more heroic . . . not dwarfed and involved but distinct, uncomplex [people] who had the gift of living once or dying once instead of being diffused and scattered creatures."[66] In this respect *Absalom, Absalom!* might also be viewed as an abortive "family romance,"[67] a phantasmal scenario in which Quentin rearranges his family situation in such a way as to compensate for his sense of lack and loss. True, the Sutpen story is a bleak tragedy, not a fairy tale. Still, its actors, as perceived in retrospect by Quentin as well as by the other narrators, possess an impregnable *wholeness*. Each of them has played his part to its bitter end; death has fixed their lives in the final closure and patterned completeness of a destiny. Paradoxically, these shadows of the past seem to have more substance, strength, and solidity than the "diffused and scattered creatures" of the present.

With two of these shadows Quentin identifies and through this dual identification fully appropriates the claims and risks of sonship, which is to say that he puts himself in a position enabling him at last to face the father he had not found in Mr. Compson. In the formidable figure of Thomas Sutpen he encounters the double of his own great-grandfather, Jason Lycurgus, who belonged to the same race of "bold ruthless" men and likewise "established what should have been a princely line."[68] As we have seen, Faulkner traced Quentin's failure back to a mysterious event in a remote past: ". . . something had happened somewhere between the first Compson and Quentin."[69] It is precisely that arch-event, that enigmatic "something," that Quentin is at pains to elucidate in *Absalom, Absalom!* through the conjectural reconstruction of the Sutpen story.

Along with *Go Down, Moses, Absalom, Absalom!* is Faulkner's most archaeo-logical[70] novel, the one most deeply concerned with the time of the beginnings. To Quentin, Thomas Sutpen first appears as a paradigm of the origin, as the father in his absolute priority and plenitude of his creative (and destructive) powers. No sooner has the novel opened than he "abrupts" upon the scene, materializing out of nowhere, like a demon or a demiurge, to "drag house and formal gardens out of the soundless Nothing and clap them down like cards upon a table beneath the up-palm immobile and pontific, creating the Sutpen's Hundred, the *Be Sutpen's Hundred* like the oldentime *Be Light*."[71] This Jehovahlike image of Sutpen creating his domain *ex nihilo* is transmitted to Quentin by Rosa Coldfield, the least reliable of the book's narrators, so that there is good reason to call her vision in question. Yet it is with this compelling image in mind that Quentin embarks upon his quest, and despite ulterior reevaluations by the other narrators Sutpen remains throughout a fabulous founder figure —so much so that as late as chapter 7 Quentin reflects that "maybe [it took] Thomas Sutpen to make all of us."[72]

Indeed, in no other of Faulkner's novels is fatherhood surrounded with so much of a mythic aura, and in his tremendous energy, in his indomitable will, and in his ruthless pursuit of the "design," Sutpen is assuredly the most virile and most heroic of the novelist's father figures. But *Absalom, Absalom!* is no celebration of the father myth, and as we learn in chapter 7 Sutpen's grand "design" is in fact but a plan of revenge for the affront he suffered as a boy, when he was ordered by a "monkey nigger" to the back door of a Tidewater mansion. Sutpen had then considered killing the plantation owner, but eventually chose to become like him: "So to combat them you have got to have what they have that made them do what the man did. You got to have land and niggers and a fine house to combat them with."[73] Instead of rebelling against the Southern ruling class, young Sutpen decides to join it by becoming as rich and powerful as the planter who insulted him. His career begins like any other Oedipal "family romance": in betraying his class and in repudiating his family, Sutpen rejects his poor "white trash" father to pay allegiance to one of better birth. Supplanting the feckless real father, the planter becomes his ideal father, the model of mastery on whom he will pattern his life.[74]

Born of the memory of outrage and of the furious need for self-vindication, Sutpen's "design" is to acquire land, to build a stately mansion, to found a dynasty, i.e., to appropriate all the attributes that defined social leadership in the Old South. Yet his "wild braggart dream"[75] should not be mistaken for the vulgar ambitions of the parvenu. Social success and prestige are only means and signs, the metaphorical objects of an impossible and appallingly "innocent" desire: the desire to defeat time, to free the self from the bondage of flesh and death and to achieve absolute permanence. To Sutpen it is not merely a matter of replacing one father by another, but of having no father at all, of being both one's own father and one's own son—*causa sui*, self-generated, self-enclosed, and self-sufficient. Sutpen is no god, but he would be god. Autogenesis. Sutpen fantasizes it as a purely masculine filiation: the son born of the father, the father reborn in the son. *Et pas de mère alors*. No earthy Eve, no "natural" generation to compromise the design. No (m)other to obstruct the reproduction of the same. Sutpen will need a wife, of course, but only "incidentally."[76] And his children will be his, with faces that are "replicas of his face."[77] To Sutpen fatherhood and sonship are in fact only complementary modes of his ideal self, which means that for him the begetting of a male heir is a symbolic act transcending the procreative urge. Contrary to appearances, his is not the dynastic dream of a genealogy unfolding in time, as what he aims at is not biological perpetuation, but ontological self-expansion. So just as he denied his father, he must deny his sons, for if he acknowledged them as sons he would have to abide by the law of patrilineal succession and to envision the transmission of his power to his descendants. In other words, he would have to face the ineluctability of his death, the very necessity that his "design" is intended to negate.

In *The Sound and the Fury* the father-son relationship fails because of the father's incapacity to exercise his prerogatives; in *Absalom, Absalom!* it is blocked because of his reluctance ever to yield his authority to anyone. Much like Sutpen's wives, his sons are only there to be used in the pursuit of his egotistical scheme, and once they have ceased to be "adjunctive and incremental to [his] design"[78] they are promptly discarded—hence Sutpen's repeated refusal to *recognize* his first-born son. Although Charles Bon poses no threat whatever to Sutpen's design in social terms, his very existence represents for Sutpen the scandal of an irreducible *otherness:* Bon is the reminder of the other race as well as of the other sex (he is "black" like his mother); he is a rem(a)inder, too, of another time, of a past which Sutpen, the indefatigable rebeginner, the "self-made" man forever in the making, has vainly sought to erase from his life. To Sutpen "blackness," first encountered in the face of the liveried "monkey nigger" who stood at the forbidden door of the planter's mansion, is not so much a matter of a race as a private symbol of outrage and frustration; it means to him what "whiteness" meant to Captain Ahab: the inscrutable blankness of reality and its stubborn resistance to man's conquering will.[79] In denying recognition to Bon—and so repeating in reverse the rejection he had himself suffered as a boy—Sutpen refuses once again to acknowledge that the world is not, and cannot be made into, the imperium of his megalomaniac self.

As for Henry, the younger son, he never breaks out of the iron circle of paternal rule. His extravagant triangular fantasies about Bon, Judith, and himself may no doubt be interpreted as a circuitous counterplot, an unconscious attempt to thwart his father's design. It is with Sutpen's will, however, that he identifies in the end, for in killing his half-brother he acts as the father's appointed avenger. Henry thus becomes Sutpen's instrument of retaliation against his first-born. Whether he has ever been more to him than an instrument we do not know for sure, but as there is no hint whatever of a personal feeling on Sutpen's part after Henry's disappearance, it seems safe to assume that Sutpen is just as indifferent to the loss of his second son as to the death of the first.

In the last resort, then, neither son is properly acknowledged.[80] The father-son relationship, exemplified by Sutpen and his male offspring, is of such a nature as to preclude the very possibility of an act of recognition. In a sense it is no relationship at all: the son is doomed either to be *absorbed* (like Henry, who spends the rest of his life as a recluse in the father's house) or to be *expelled* (like Bon, his masochistic son, or Bond, his idiot grandson: the rejected residues of Sutpen's scheme); either he becomes the father's double or dissolves into noth-ingness. As in all unmediated dual relationships, twoness finally re-verts to oneness.[81]

In Sutpen's world there is indeed only room for *one*—one desire, one will, one power, one "imperial self."[82] Sutpen is the absolute father, an arresting reincarnation of the archaic paternal figure pos-tulated in Freud's anthropological speculations, the *Urvater* who "was lord and father to the entire horde and unrestricted in his power,"[83] and who "loved no one but himself, or other people only in so far as they served his needs."[84] According to Freud, the ferocious and jealous father of prehistoric times was eventually killed, dis-membered, and devoured by his sons, and out of their sense of guilt and need for atonement arose the systems of totems and taboos, of substitutions and prohibitions which govern the symbolic order of all human societies. Before being murdered, the "father of the primal horde" *was* the law, absolutely; in death, he came to *represent* the law, metaphorically, thus allowing the unrestricted violence of primi-tive paternal power to be replaced by the rules of patriarchal author-ity. In *Absalom, Absalom!* there are a number of striking parallels to Freud's "scientific myth," yet the differences are perhaps even more significant. Patricide here is preceded by fratricide: "[Sutpen's] sons destroyed one another and then him."[85] And since he was the instiga-tor of fratricide, the "original sin" is his. In this novel as in all of Faulk-ner's works, the primal crime is not patricide;[86] the first figure of guilt, the originator of evil is never the son. Filial guilt is always inherited guilt, and the curse that afflicts generation after generation always begins with the misdeeds of a "primal father."

Faulkner's fiction thus seems to reverse the Freudian pattern, since what it places at the origin is not the murder of the father but the father's sin. It seems to, yet it does not, for, as *Absalom, Absalom!* reveals, before Sutpen, the arrogant, ruthless father, there was Sutpen, the weak, affronted son. The son is always father to the man, and the father's sins are the son's revenge. In the novel, Sutpen appears no doubt as a beginner and begetter (and he thinks of himself precisely in these terms); he strikes us as a demiurgic figure of tremendous power, but as such he is largely a retroactive creation of the narrators' (es-pecially Rosa's) myth-making. Sutpen is not (at) the origin or, rather, he is a false origin, a *proton pseudos*, an origin (re)constructed from its traces and effects. What he stands for is the quintessential *phallacy:* the omnipotence of infantile desire as projected onto the father. In contradistinction to the powerless living fathers of the present, Sutpen and his analogues in Faulkner's novels apparently possess the preroga- tives of the strong father, but if they refer us back to the dreaded and envied rival of the primary Oedipal relation, they never come to func- tion as the symbolic agencies of its dissolution. To put the matter into Lacanian terms, they never come to act the role of the "dead father" who guarantees the law. Faulkner's great ancestral figures, we might say, are essentially "ghostly fathers."[87] The trouble with them is that they are dead, but not dead enough to allow their descendants to live.

Absalom, Absalom! is Faulkner's most sustained invocation of the father, conjuring up his spectral presence with a power and intensity unmatched in Faulkner's other novels. Yet the novelist's involvement with fathers and sons hardly diminished in his later works, and in this respect two at least would deserve close scrutiny: *Go Down, Moses* and *A Fable.*

In *Go Down, Moses,* the theme is again dramatized through the enmeshed fates of the descendants, white and black, of a Southern dynasty founder.[88] But the scope of vision here is even broader than in *Absalom, Absalom!,* for through the introduction of the wilderness motif and the story of Ike McCaslin's initiation into the secrets of the ritual hunt, the patriarchal system of white society is brought into sig- nificant contrast with the totemic fraternity of the vanishing Indian culture.[89] Faulkner's subtle counterpointing of cultural patterns in *Go Down, Moses* almost suggests an anthropologist's approach. In *A Fable,* on the other hand, he writes more overtly than ever in the mythic mode and offers a displaced and extremely elaborate transcrip- tion of Christ's Passion. It is revealing, however, that each novel includes a lengthy debate between a son and a father (or father sub- stitute): that between Ike and Cass Edmonds in *Go, Down Moses;* that between the Corporal and the old General in *A Fable.* And in each novel, too, the son comes to reject his paternal heritage—Ike am- biguously, through the relinquishment of the McCaslin property; the heroic, Christlike Corporal through the willed sacrifice of his life.

So the father-son struggle still figures prominently in Faulkner's later fiction. Something is lost, though, of the tragic urgency with which it was presented in the earlier novels. In *A Fable*, for example, the confrontation is primarily an ideological debate in which father and son stand for antithetical philosophical positions; it lacks the bitter pathos of Quentin's dialogue with Mr. Compson in *The Sound and the Fury,* and if it echoes Ike's conversation with Cass in *Go Down, Moses,* it has little of the latter's emotional charge. Remarkable, too, is the emergence, in Faulkner's later novels, of interceding spiritual fathers and of young heroes whose initiation into manhood no longer fails.[90] And apart from Lucius Carothers McCaslin, there is no successor to Thomas Sutpen. The General in *A Fable* is no doubt a powerful father figure, but he is also a very ambiguous character and, strangely enough, it is he—not the meek Corporal—who voices Faulkner's humanistic belief that man will not only "endure" but "prevail."[91]

Should we infer from this shift in outlook and tonality that the ghosts were ultimately laid to rest? At this point, let me return briefly to the autobiographical implications of Faulkner's writing. It is now common knowledge that Colonel Sartoris, the first mythicized ancestor, was at least partly patterned on Colonel William Clark Falkner, the author's legendary great-grandfather,[92] and we also know that identification with the latter was perhaps one of the very germs of Faulkner's literary vocation.[93] The model he had not found in his prosaic father he found in his glamorous forefather, and if there was no opportunity for Faulkner to equal his heroic exploits,[94] he could at least attempt to emulate the successful author of *The White Rose of Memphis.* And perhaps, if he showed enough daring and perseverance, he might even be able to best him.

This comparison should not suggest that Faulkner was a special case, but simply to indicate the autobiographical relevance of the ancestral/paternal theme in his fiction. And "autobiography" here is to be understood not in its trivial anecdotical sense, as the record of a life already lived, but quite literally as the writing (the production through written words) of a self, its inscription in the space of a text. The implication is that fatherhood and sonship are not to be seen merely as themes on the level of mimetic representation, but that they are deeply involved in the *writer's* venture and relate back to his maddest desire: the desire to seize the authority of an original *author* —the authority, that is, of an origin, a founder, a father.[95] In this respect, as in so many others, *Absalom, Absalom!* appears again as the key text, for its narrative scheme, its fabric as well as its fable, points emphatically to what is perhaps the ultimate stake of the writing game: mastery. Quentin and Sutpen are, as we have seen, the novel's polar figures. In their common bid for mastery, they turn out to be strangely alike. Sutpen is a man of deeds, Quentin a man of words; one attempts to father a world, the other tries to tell a tale. But both strive to create order out of chaos, to gain control over time, and to master "the maelstrom of unbearable reality."[96] And Faulkner, the writer, is at once in Quentin the fumbling narrator and interpreter, and in Sutpen the faltering founder—in son and in father. Their "design" is his and so is their failure.

The desire to foreclose the father's name and to establish a name for *one's self* has been one of the mainsprings of Western art and literature ever since the Renaissance. With the Romantics, it developed into a burning, all-consuming obsession.[97] Faulkner is their heir, and for him too literature was a way to singularize himself, to make himself unique and unforgettable, to prove and proclaim his difference. No sooner did he begin to publish than he changed his patronym from "Falkner" to "Faulkner," thus inscribing the difference, prophetically, in his very name.[98] His was indeed the romantic dream of autogenesis, the fantasy of giving birth to an *oeuvre* and being reborn in it—son and father to his work. And in a sense his dream came true. Yet one might argue as well that the experience of writing dispelled the dream, for its agonies and ecstasies taught him humility rather than pride. The experience led him to the sobering realization that writing is a process of dispossession and dismemberment rather than self-creation, and that instead of nourishing the self, the *oeuvre* feeds on it, vampirelike. The experience made him discover that the artist is not the father or god of his creation but only one of its conditions, and that the name with which he signs his work is a kind of imposture. For in the last resort it is the work that, through an ironical reversal, comes to sign his name, a name no longer his, referring as it does to a series of books rather than to a person. However "great" they may be, writers are fated to be eventually effaced by their writing. That fate Faulkner not only acknowledged as a necessity but subscribed to as a desirable return to anonymity: "It is my ambition to be, as a private individual, abolished and voided from history, leaving it markless, no refuse save the printed books; I wish I had had enough sense to see ahead thirty years ago and, like some of the Elizabethans, not signed them. It is my aim, and every effort bent, that the sum and history of my life, which in the same sentence is my obit and epitaph too, shall be them both: He made the books and died."[99]

The Dead Father in Faulkner

JOHN T. IRWIN

Father Time is an ancient conflation, based in part on a similarity of names, of two figures—Kronos, Zeus' father, and Chronos, the personification of time. As we know, that conflation ultimately led to the attachment of at least two of the major legends of Kronos to Father Time—first, that Kronos is a son who castrated his father, Ouranos, and was in turn castrated by his own son Zeus, and second, that Kronos is a father who devours his children. Discussing the evolution of the iconography of Father Time, the art historian Erwin Panofsky notes that the learned writers of the fourth and fifth centuries A.D. began to provide the old figure of Kronos/Saturn with new attributes and "reinterpreted the original features of his image as symbols of time. His sickle, traditionally explained either as an agricultural symbol or as the instrument of castration, came to be interpreted as a symbol of *tempora quae sicut falx in se recurrent;* and the mythical tale that he had devoured his children was said to signify that Time, who had already been termed 'sharp-toothed' by Simonides and *edax rerum* by Ovid, devours whatever he has created."[1]

In discussing the nature of time, Nietzsche alludes to both the legends of Kronos that became associated with Father Time. In the passage from *Zarathustra* in which he talks about the revenge against time, he mentions "this law of time that it must devour its children" (252), and in *Philosophy in the Tragic Age of the Greeks* he says, "As Heraclitus sees time, so does Schopenhauer. He repeatedly said of it that every moment in it exists only insofar as it has just consumed the preceding one, its father, and then is immediately consumed likewise."[2] One might say that the struggle between the father and the son

inevitably turns into a dispute about the nature of time, not just because the authority of the father is based on priority in time, but
because the essence of time is that in the discontinuous, passing
moment it is experienced as a problem of the endless displacement of
the generator by the generated, while in the continuity of the memory
trace it is experienced as a problem of the endless destruction of the
generated by the generator. In this last sense, we refer not just to the
experience that what is generated in and by time is as well consumed in
and by time, but also to the experience that the price which the generative moment exacts for its displacement into the past is a castration of
the present through memory. In tropes such as "the golden age," "the
lost world," "the good old days," the past convicts the present of in-
adequacy through lack of priority, lack of originality, since to be a
copy is to be a diminution, because the running on of time is a running
down, because to come after is to be fated to repeat the life of another
rather than to live one's own.

In *The Sound and the Fury,* the struggle between Quentin and his
father that runs through the stream-of-consciousness narrative of
Quentin's last day is primarily a dispute about time. The narrative begins with Quentin's waking in the morning ("I was in time again")[3] to
the ticking of his grandfather's watch, the watch that his father had
presented to him, saying, "I give it to you not that you may remember
time, but that you may forget it now and then for a moment and not
spend all your breath trying to conquer it" (95). Quentin twists the
hands off his grandfather's watch on the morning of the day when he
forever frees himself and his posterity from the cycles of time and generation. When Quentin is out walking that morning, he passes the
shopwindow of a watch store and turns away so as not to see what
time it is, but there is a clock on a building and Quentin sees the time in
spite of himself: he says, "I thought about how, when you dont want
to do a thing, your body will try to trick you into doing it, sort of un-
awares" (102). And that, of course, is precisely Quentin's sense of time
—that it is a compulsion, a fate. For his father has told him that a man
is the sum of his misfortunes and that time is his misfortune like "a gull
on an invisible wire attached through space dragged" (123). In his
struggle against his father and thus against time, Quentin must confront the same problem that he faces in the story of Sutpen and his sons

—whether a man's father is his fate. In *Absalom, Absalom!* when Shreve begins to sound like Quentin's father, Quentin thinks, *"Am I going to have to have to hear it all again.* . . . *I am going to have to hear it all over again I am already hearing it all over again I am listening to it all over again I shall have to never listen to anything else but this again forever so apparently not only a man never outlives his father but not even his friends and acquaintances do."*[4]

When Quentin demands that his father act against the seducer Dalton Ames, Quentin, by taking this initiative, is in effect trying to supplant his father, to seize his authority. But Quentin's father refuses to act, and the sense of Mr. Compson's refusal is that Quentin cannot seize his father's authority because there is no authority to seize. Quentin's alcoholic, nihilistic father presents himself as an emasculated son, ruined by General Compson's failure. Mr. Compson psychologically castrates Quentin by confronting him with a father figure, a model for manhood, who is himself a castrated son. Mr. Compson possesses no authority that Quentin could seize because what Mr. Compson inherited from the General was not power but impotence. If Quentin is a son struggling in the grip of Father Time, so is his father. And it is exactly that argument that Mr. Compson uses against Quentin. When Quentin demands that they act against the seducer, Mr. Compson answers in essence, "Do you realize how many times this has happened before and how many times it will happen again? You are seeking a once-and-for-all solution to this problem, but there are no once-and-for-all solutions. One has no force, no authority to act in this matter because one has no originality. The very repetitive nature of time precludes the existence of originality within its cycles. You cannot be the father because I am not the father—only Time is the father." When Quentin demands that they avenge Candace's virginity, his father replies, "Women are never virgins. Purity is a negative state and therefore contrary to nature. It's nature is hurting you not Caddy and I said That's just words and he said So is virginity and I said you dont know. You cant know and he said Yes. On the instant when we come to realise that tragedy is second-hand" (135). In essence Quentin's father says, "We cannot act because there exists no virginity to avenge and because there exists no authority by which we could avenge since we have no originality. We are second-hand.

You are a copy of a copy. To you, a son who has only been a son, it might seem that a father has authority because he comes first, but to one who has been both a father and a son, it is clear that to come before is not necessarily to come first, that priority is not necessarily originality. My fate was determined by my father as your fate is determined by yours." Quentin's attempt to avenge his sister's lost virginity (proving thereby that it had once existed) and maintain the family honor is an attempt to maintain the possibility of "virginity" in a larger sense, the possibility of the existence of a virgin space within which one can still be first, within which one can have authority through originality, a virgin space like that Mississippi wilderness into which the first Compson (Jason Lycurgus I) rode in 1811 to seize the land later known as the Compson Domain, the land "fit to breed princes, statesmen and generals and bishops, to avenge the dispossessed Compsons from Culloden and Carolina and Kentucky" (7), just as Sutpen came to Mississippi to get land and found a dynasty that would avenge the dispossessed Sutpens of West Virginia. In a letter to Malcolm Cowley, Faulkner said that Quentin regarded Sutpen as "originless."[5] Which is to say that, being without origin, Sutpen tries to become his own origin, his own father, an attempt implicit in the very act of choosing a father figure to replace his real father. When Quentin tells the story of the Sutpens in *Absalom, Absalom!*, he is not just telling his own personal story, he is telling the story of the Compson family as well.

The event that destroyed Sutpen's attempt to found a dynasty is the same event that began the decline of the Compson family—the Civil War closed off the virgin space and the time of origins, so that the antebellum South became in the minds of postwar Southerners that debilitating "golden age and lost world" in comparison with which the present is inadequate. The decline of the Compsons began with General Compson "who failed at Shiloh in '62 and failed again though not so badly at Resaca in '64, who put the first mortgage on the still intact square mile to a New England carpetbagger in '66, after the old town had been burned by the Federal General Smith and the new little town, in time to be populated mainly by the descendants not of Compsons but of Snopeses, had begun to encroach and then nibble at and into it as the failed brigadier spent the next forty years selling fragments of it off to keep up the mortgage on the remainder" (7). The last of the Compson Domain is sold by Quentin's father to send Quentin to Harvard.

Mr. Compson's denial of the existence of an authority by which he could act necessarily entails his denial of virginity, for there is no possiblity of that originality from which authority springs if there is no virgin space within which one can be first. And for the same reason Quentin's obsession with Candace's loss of virginity is necessarily an obsession with his own impotence, since the absence of the virgin space renders him powerless. When Mr. Compson refuses to act against Dalton Ames, Quentin tries to force him to take some action by claiming that he and Candace have committed incest—that primal affront to the authority of the father. But where there is no authority there can be no affront, and where the father feels his own inherited impotence, he cannot believe that his son has power. Mr. Compson tells Quentin that he doesn't believe that he and Candace committed incest, and Quentin says, "If we could have just done something so dreadful and Father said That's sad too, people cannot do anything that dreadful they cannot do anything very dreadful at all they cannot even remember tomorrow what seemed dreadful today and I said, You can shirk all things and he said, Ah can you" (99). Since Mr. Compson believes that man is helpless in the grip of time, that everything is fated, there is no question of shirking or not shirking, for there is no question of willing. In discussing the revenge against time, Nietzsche speaks of those preachers of despair who say, "Alas, the stone *It was* cannot be moved" (252), and Mr. Compson's last words in Quentin's narrative are "was the saddest word of all there is nothing else in the world its not despair until time its not even time until it was" (197).

Is there no virgin space in which one can be first, in which one can have authority through originality? This is the question that Quentin must face in trying to decide whether his father is right, whether he is doomed to be an impotent failure like his father and grandfather. And it is in light of this question that we can gain an insight into Quentin's act of narration in *Absalom, Absalom!,* for what is at work in Quentin's struggle to bring the story of the Sutpens under control is the question of whether narration itself constitutes a space in which one can be original, whether an "author" possesses "authority," whether that repetition which in life Quentin has experienced as a compulsive fate can be transformed in narration, through an act of the will, into a power, a mastery of time. Indeed, Rosa Coldfield suggests to Quentin when she first involves him in the story of the Sutpens that becoming an author represents an alternative to repeating his father's life in the decayed world of the postwar South: " 'Because you are going away to attend the college at Harvard they tell me,' Miss Coldfield said. 'So I dont imagine you will ever come back here and settle down as a country lawyer in a little town like Jefferson, since Northern people have already seen to it that there is little left in the South for a young man. So maybe you will enter the literary profession as so many Southern gentlemen and gentlewomen too are doing now and maybe some day you will remember this and write about it' " (9–10). We noted earlier that the dialogue between Quentin and his father about virginity that runs through the first part of *Absalom, Absalom!* appears to be a continuation of their discussions of Candace's loss of virginity and Quentin's inability to lose his virginity contained in Quentin's section of *The Sound and the Fury*. Thus, the struggle between father and son that marked their dialogue in *The Sound and the Fury* is continued in their narration of *Absalom, Absalom!*. For Quentin, the act of narrating Sutpen's story, of bringing that story under authorial control, becomes a struggle in which he tries to best his father, a struggle to seize "authority" by achieving temporal priority to his father in the narrative act. At the beginning of the novel, Quentin is a passive narrator. The story seems to choose him. Rosa involves him in the narrative against his will, and he spends the first half of the book listening to Rosa and his father tell what they know or surmise. But in the second half, when he and Shreve begin their imaginative reconstruction of the story, Quentin seems to move from a passive role to an active role in the narrative repetition of the past.

So far I have mainly discussed the experience of repetition as a compulsion, as a fate, using Freud's analysis of the mechanism of the repetition compulsion in *Beyond the Pleasure Principle* as the basis for my remarks. But in that same text, Freud also examines the experience of repetition as a power—repetition as a means of achieving mastery. He points out that in children's play an event that the child originally experienced as something unpleasant will be repeated and now experienced as a source of pleasure, as a game. He describes the game of *fort/da* that he had observed being played by a little boy of one and a half. The infant would throw away a toy and as he did, utter a sound that Freud took to be the German word *fort*—"gone." The child would then recover the toy and say the word *da*—"there." Freud surmised that the child had created a game by which he had mastered the traumatic event of seeing his mother leave him and into which he had incorporated the joyful event of her return. Freud points out that the mechanism of this game in which one actively repeats an unpleasant occurrence as a source of pleasure can be interpreted in various ways. First of all, he remarks that at the outset the child "was in a *passive* situation—he was overpowered by the experience; but, by repeating it, unpleasurable though it was, as a game, he took on an *active* part. These efforts might be put down to an instinct for mastery that was acting independently of whether the memory was in itself pleasurable or not. But still another interpretation may be attempted. Throwing away the object so that it was 'gone' might satisfy an impulse of the child's, which was suppressed in his actual life, to revenge himself on his mother for going away from him. In that case it would have a defiant meaning: 'All right, then, go away! I don't need you. I'm sending you away myself' " (*SE*, 18:16).

Freud makes a further point about the nature of children's games that has a direct bearing on our interest in the son's effort to become his father: ". . . it is obvious that all their play is influenced by a wish that dominates them the whole time—the wish to be grown-up and to be able to do what grown-up people do. It can also be observed that the unpleasurable nature of an experience does not always unsuit it for play. If the doctor looks down a child's throat or carries out some small operation on him, we may be quite sure that these frightening experiences will be the subject of the next game; but we must not in that connection overlook the fact that there is a yield of pleasure from another source. As the child passes over from the passivity of the experience to the activity of the game, he hands on the disagreeable experience to one of his playmates and in this way revenges himself on a substitute" (*SE*, 18:17). Significantly, Freud refers to this mastery through repetition as "revenge," and his remarks suggest that this revenge has two major elements—repetition and reversal. In the game of *fort/da* the child repeats the traumatic situation but reverses the roles. Instead of passively suffering rejection when his mother leaves, he actively rejects her by symbolically sending her away. And in the other case, the child repeats the unpleasant incident that he experienced but now inflicts on a playmate, on a substitute, what was formerly inflicted on him.

In this mechanism of a repetition in which the active and passive roles are reversed, we have the very essence of revenge. But we must distinguish between two different situations: in the ideal situation, the revenge is inflicted on the same person who originally delivered the affront—the person who was originally active is now forced to assume the passive role in the same scenario; in the other situation, the revenge is inflicted on a substitute. This second situation sheds light on Sutpen's attempt to master the traumatic affront that he suffered as a boy from the man who became his surrogate father, to master it by repeating that affront in reverse, inflicting it on his own son Charles Bon. This scenario of revenge on a substitute sheds light as well on the connection between repetition and the fantasy of the reversal of generations and on the psychological mechanism of generation itself. The primal affront that the son suffers at the hands of the father and for which the son seeks revenge throughout his life is the very fact of being a son—of being the generated in relation to the generator, the passive in relation to the active, the effect in relation to the cause. He seeks revenge on his father for the generation of an existence which the son, in relation to the father, must always experience as a dependency. But if revenge involves a repetition in which the active and passive roles are reversed, then the very nature of time precludes the son's taking revenge on his father, for since time is irreversible, the son can never really effect that reversal by which he would become his father's father. The son's only alternative is to take revenge on a substitute— that is, to become a father himself and thus repeat the generative situation as a reversal in which he now inflicts on his own son, who is a substitute for the grandfather, the affront of being a son, that affront that the father had previously suffered from his own father. We can see now why Nietzsche, in connecting the revenge against time with the "envy of your fathers" (that envy which the son feels for his father and which the son has inherited from his father, who was himself a son), says, "What was silent in the father speaks in the son; and often I found the son the unveiled secret of the father."

When Sutpen takes revenge on a substitute for the affront that he received as a boy, he takes revenge not just on Charles Bon but on Henry as well. For if the primal affront is the very fact of being a son, then acknowledgment and rejection, inheritance and disinheritance are simply the positive and negative modes of delivering the affront of the son's dependency on the father. Further, we can see the centrality of the notion of revenge on a substitute to the figure of the double. The brother avenger and the brother seducer are, as I have pointed out, substitutes for the father and the son in the Oedipal triangle, but if the revenge which the father inflicts on the son is a substitute for the revenge that the father wishes to inflict on his own father, then the brother avenger's killing of the brother seducer becomes a double action: the avenger's murder of the seducer (son) is a symbolic substitute for the seducer's murder of the avenger (father). This adds another dimension to Henry's murder of Bon: Henry is the younger brother and Bon the older, and the killing of the older brother by the younger is a common substitute for the murder of the father by the son. Thus, when Henry kills Bon, he is the father-surrogate killing the son, but since Henry, like Bon, is also in love with their sister Judith, he is as well the younger brother (son) killing the older brother who symbolizes the father, the father who is the rival for the mother and who punishes the incest between brother and sister, son and mother. The multiple, reversible character of these relationships is only what we would expect in a closed system like the Oedipal triangle, and it is precisely this multiple, reversible character that gives the Oedipal triangle a charge of emotional energy that becomes overpowering as it cycles and builds. The very mechanism of doubling is an embodiment of that revenge on a substitute which we find in generation, for it is the threat from the father in the castration fear that fixes the son in that secondary narcissism from which the figure of the double as ambivalent Other springs. When the bright self (the ego influenced by the superego) kills the dark self (the ego influenced by the unconscious), we have in this murder of the son as related to his mother by the son as related to his father the reversed repetition of that repressed desire which the son felt when he first desired his mother and was faced with the threat of castration—the desire of the son to murder his father. For the psychologically impotent son who cannot have a child, the act of generating a double is his equivalent of that revenge on the father through a substitute which the potent son seeks by the act of generating a son.

Keeping in mind this notion of revenge on a substitute, we can now understand how Quentin's act of narration in *Absalom, Absalom!* is an attempt to seize his father's authority by gaining temporal priority. In the struggle with his father, Quentin will prove that he is a better man by being a better narrator—he will assume the authority of an author because his father does not know the whole story, does not know the true reason for Bon's murder, while Quentin does. Instead of listening passively while his father talks, Quentin will assume the active role, and his father will listen while Quentin talks. And the basis of Quentin's authority to tell the story to his father is that Quentin, by a journey into the dark, womblike Sutpen mansion, a journey back into the past, has learned more about events that occurred before he was born than either his father or grandfather knew:

"Your father," Shreve said. "He seems to have got an awful lot of delayed information awful quick, after having waited forty-five years. If he knew all this, what was his reason for telling you that the trouble between Henry and Bon was the octoroon woman?"

"He didn't know it then. Grandfather didn't tell him all of it either, like Sutpen never told Grandfather quite all of it."

"Then who did tell him?"

"I did." Quentin did not move, did not look up while Shreve watched him. "The day after we—after that night when we—"

"Oh," Shreve said. "After you and the old aunt. I see. Go on. . . ." (266)

In terms of the narrative act, Quentin achieves temporal priority over his father, and within the narrative Quentin takes revenge against his father, against time, through a substitute—his roommate Shreve. As Quentin had to listen to his father tell the story in the first half of the novel, so in the second half Shreve must listen while Quentin tells the story. But what begins as Shreve listening to Quentin talk soon turns into a struggle between them for control of the narration with Shreve frequently interrupting Quentin to say, "Let me tell it now."

That struggle, which is a repetition in reverse of the struggle between Mr. Compson and Quentin, makes Quentin realize the truth of his father's argument in *The Sound and the Fury*—that priority is not necessarily originality, that to come before is not necessarily to come first. For Quentin realizes that by taking revenge against his father through a substitute, by assuming the role of active teller (father) and making Sheve be the passive listener (son), he thereby passes on to Shreve the affront of sonship, the affront of dependency, and thus ensures that Shreve will try to take revenge on him by seizing "authority," by taking control of the narrative. What Quentin realizes is that generation as revenge on a substitute is an endless cycle of reversibility in which revenge only means passing on the affront to another who, seeking revenge in turn, passes on the affront, so that the affront and the revenge are self-perpetuating. Indeed, the word "revenge," as opposed to the word "vengeance," suggests this self-perpetuating quality—*re-*, again + *venger*, to take vengeance—to take vengeance again and again and again, because the very taking of revenge is the passing on of an affront that must be revenged. We might note in this regard that the repetition compulsion is itself a form of revenge through a substitute. If, as Freud says, the act of repression always results in the return of the repressed, that is, if repression endows the repressed material with the repetition compulsion, and if the repressed can return only by a displacement, can slip through the ego's defenses only by a substitution in which the same is reconstituted as different, then the repetition compulsion is a revenge through substitution, wherein the repressed takes revenge on the ego for that act of will by which the repressed material was rejected, takes revenge by a repetition in reverse, by a return of the repressed that is experienced as a compulsive overruling of the will, a rendering passive of the will by the unwilled return of that very material which the will had previously tried to render passive by repressing it. As revenge on a substitute is a self-perpetuating cycle of affront and revenge, so too repression, return of the repressed, re-repression, and re-return are self-perpetuating. In his work on compulsion neurosis, the psychoanalyst Wilhelm Stekel discusses the case of a patient who reenacted the Oedipal struggle with his father through the scenario of an incestuous attachment to his sister and a struggle with his brother. Stekel notes that the patient's compulsive-repetitive acts were a "correction of the past," and he links this impulse to correct the past to that "unquenchable thirst for revenge so characteristic of compulsion neurotics."[6] At one point in the analysis, the patient describes his illness as an "originality neurosis" (449).

In his narrative struggle with Shreve, Quentin directly experiences the cyclic reversibility involved in revenge on a substitute—he experiences the maddening paradox of generation in time. At the beginning of their narrative, Quentin talks and Shreve listens, and in their imaginative reenactment of the story of the Sutpens, Quentin identifies with Henry, the father-surrogate, and Shreve identifies with Charles Bon, the son, the outsider. But as the roles of brother avenger and brother seducer are reversible (precisely because the roles for which they are substitutes—father and son—are reversible through substitution), so Quentin and Shreve begin to alternate in their identifications with Henry and Bon, and Quentin finds that Shreve is narrating and that he (Quentin) is listening and that Shreve sounds like Quentin's father. Quentin not only learns that *"a man never outlives his father"* and that he is going to have to listen to this same story over and over again for the rest of his life, but he realizes as well that in their narration he and Shreve *"are both Father"*—*"Maybe nothing every happens once and is finished. . . . Yes, we are both Father. Or maybe Father and I are both Shreve, maybe it took Father and me both to make Shreve or Shreve and me both to make Father or maybe Thomas Sutpen to make all of us."* In terms of a generative sequence of narrators, Mr. Compson, Quentin, and Shreve are father, son, and grandson (reincarnation of the father). Confronting that cyclic reversibility, Quentin realizes that if sons seek revenge on their fathers for the affront of sonship by a repetition in reverse, if they seek to supplant their fathers, then the very fathers whom the sons wish to become are themselves nothing but sons who had sons in order to take that same revenge on their own fathers. Generation as revenge against the father, as revenge against time, is a circular labyrinth; it only establishes time's mastery all the more, for generation establishes the rule that a man never outlives his father, simply because a man's son will be the reincarnation of that father. And if for Quentin the act of narration is an analogue of this revenge on a substitute, then narration does not achieve mastery over time; rather, it traps the narrator more surely within the coils of time. What Quentin realizes is that the solution he seeks must be one that frees him alike from time and generation, from fate and revenge: he must die childless, he must free himself from time without having passed on the self-perpetuating affront of sonship. What Quentin seeks is a once-and-for-all solution, a non-temporal, an eternal solution. When Mr. Compson refuses to believe that Quentin and Candace have committed incest and simply says, "we must just stay awake and see evil done for a little while its not always," Quentin replies, "it doesnt have to be even that long for a man of courage":

and he do you consider that courage and i yes sir dont you and he every man is the arbiter of his own virtues whether or not you consider it courageous is of more importance than the act itself than any act otherwise you could not be in earnest. . . . but you are still blind to what is in yourself to that part of general truth the sequence of natural events and their causes which shadows every mans brow even benjys you are not thinking of finitude you are contemplating an apotheosis in which a temporary state of mind will become symmetrical above the flesh and aware both of itself and of the flesh it will not quite discard you will not even be dead and i temporary. . . . (196)

Of Quentin's search for an eternal solution Faulkner says, in the appendix to *The Sound and the Fury,* that as Quentin "loved not his sister's body but some concept of Compson honor precariously and (he knew well) only temporarily supported by the minute fragile membrane of her maidenhead," so he "loved not the idea of incest which he would not commit, but some presbyterian concept of its eternal punishment: he, not God, could by that means cast himself and his sister both into hell, where he could guard her forever and keep her forevermore intact amid the eternal fires" (9).

From Mr. Compson's statement and from Faulkner's, we can abstract the elements of the solution that Quentin seeks. First, it will be an action that transforms the temporal into the eternal: "a temporary state of mind will become symmetrical above the flesh"; a temporary virginity will, by an eternal punishment, be rendered "forevermore intact." Second, the action, a death, will be a punishment in which the one who punishes and the one punished will be the same, it will be self-inflicted—a suicide. Quentin, not God, will cast himself and his sister into the eternal fires, cast not just himself but Candace as well, so that

Quentin's suicide will also be a symbolic incest (a return to the waters of birth, to the womb) that maintains not just Candace's virginity but Quentin's too. Third, this action, this death, will be an "apotheosis," a deification. And finally, in this death whereby "a temporary state of mind will become symmetrical above the flesh and aware both of itself and of the flesh it will not quite discard," Quentin "will not even be dead." Considering these elements, we can see who the model is for Quentin's solution and why Faulkner places Quentin's suicide in the context of Christ's passion—that self-sacrifice of the son to satisfy the justice of the father, that active willing of passivity as a self-inflicted revenge. When Quentin tries to clean the blood off his clothes from the fight with Gerald Bland, he thinks, "Maybe a pattern of blood he could call that the one Christ was wearing" (190).

As the central enigmatic event in *Absalom, Absalom!* is Henry's murder of Bon, so its equivalent in *The Sound and the Fury* is Quentin's suicide, and the structures of both books, with their multiple perspectives in narration, point up the fact that the significance of these events is irreducibly ambiguous. Thus, Henry's murder of Bon can be seen as the killing of the son by the father, but it can also be seen as the killing of the father by the son. And what of Quentin's suicide—is it finally an act of nihilistic despair, or a last desperate effort of the will to assert its mastery over time, or is it an active willing of passivity that, as a distorted image of Christ's death, is meant to be "redemptive" of Quentin's unborn, and now never to be born, progeny, who have been freed once and for all from mortality and from the spirit of revenge that is generation? Certainly, by putting Quentin's suicide in the context of Christ's death, Faulkner makes the significance of Quentin's act more ambiguous, but this strategy works in two directions, for it also points up the irreducible ambiguities in the significance of Christ's death itself. With characters like Quentin and Joe Christmas, Faulkner uses the context of Christ's death to raise questions about the actions of these characters, and he uses their actions to question the meaning of the Christ role. His most explicit questioning of the ambiguous significance of Christ's redemptive act occurs in *A Fable* (1954), where Christ's Passion and death are reenacted during World War I in that struggle between the old general and the corporal, between the father who has supreme authority and the illegitimate son who is under a sentence of death.

Viewing Quentin's suicide in the context of Christ's willing sacrifice of his own life, we find in the very concept of sacrifice a link that joins those two triadic structures whose interplay shapes *The Sound and the Fury* and *Absalom, Absalom!*—the Oedipal triangle (father, mother, son) and the three generations of patrilinearity (grandfather, father, son, or father, son, grandson). The psychoanalyst Guy Rosolato has discussed the way in which the fantasy of the murder of the father sustains the movement from the closed Oedipal triangle to the indefinite linearity of generation (three generations of men) within the religious structure of sacrifice. Rosolato argues that all sacrifice is a putting to death of the father through the victim, and he discusses the sacrifices of Isaac and Jesus as structures in which the lethal confrontation between the father and the son in the Oedipal triangle is transformed into an alliance between the father and the son by the substitution of another male figure for the female figure in the triad. This transformation involves a mutation in the image of the father. What Rosolato calls the "idealized father" (the father of prehistoric times, "ferocious, jealous, all-powerful, whose control over others and over his sons is unlimited, a protector in exchange for total submission, and absolute master of the laws of which he is the sole origin")[7] is a figure whose relationship with the son follows the rule of two, that is, there exist only two alternatives in the son's relationship with his father—all or nothing, victory or defeat. The relationship of the son to the idealized father is a fight to the death in which, from the son's point of view, the idealized father must become the "murdered father." Sacrifice transforms this situation by means of the rule of three, the rule of mediation. Through the use of a substitute, the murder of the father can be accomplished in an indirect, in a symbolic manner, so that the figure of the "dead father" takes the place of the figure of the murdered father. Through the symbolic substitution inherent in the mediating sacrifice, the Oedipal situation is surmounted, and one passes into the patrilineal situation.

Discussing the sacrifice of Isaac, Rosolato points out that in that covenent between God and Abraham which is to become the covenant between the father and the son, there exist two different times. First, a time of preparation (Gen. 17), in which the marks of that covenant are established, so that it is as if the law were imposed in anteriority without the knowledge of either Abraham or Isaac. Thus, the father, Abra-

ham, is not the origin of the law but must submit to it just like his son
Isaac. There are three marks of the covenant between God and Abraham: in the name, in the flesh, and in the future promise. First, God
changes Abram's name to Abraham as a sign of his nomination;
second, God establishes circumcision as a visible sign of the agreement
between God, Abraham, and his posterity; and finally, God promises
Abraham and Sara a son in their old age. With the birth of Isaac, who
bears the name designated by God and who is circumcised eight days
after his birth according to God's command, the third masculine person is now present and the alliance between the father and the son can
now supplant their conflict in the Oedipal triangle, an alliance between God and Abraham that the sacrifice of Isaac will "definitively
confirm" (65). In that sacrifice, God, Abraham, and Isaac are related
as grandfather, father, and son, so that when Abraham raises the knife
over Isaac it is the father threatening the son, but since the son is the re-
incorporation of the grandfather, it is also the son threatening the
father, and at that moment Abraham realizes the principle on which
the alliance is based—that the death wish against one's father means
the death of one's son. When God suspends the sacrifice of Isaac, God,
the idealized father, is transformed into the dead father, for God takes
upon himself the death that would have been meted out to the son. The
angel that stops Abraham from killing Isaac shows him the ram that
will take the place of the son in the sacrifice—a substitution indicative
of the fact that Isaac is himself a substitute. The ram will now take the
place of God in the sacrifice, and by accepting this death, God, the
idealized father (the sole origin of the law, the one to whom the law is
responsible and who can abrogate it at will), is transformed into the
dead father (one who is responsible *to* the law, one who is bound by
a covenant).

When Abraham suspends the threat against his son, "he opts for a
law: precisely that of an order, of a succession of generations in death"
(68). The law that Abraham accepts is that in time fathers die before
their sons—as opposed to the law of the idealized father in the Oedipal
triangle whereby sons die before their fathers. Abraham "accepts this
succession, and refuses, what was possible for him, to destroy Isaac;
he admits this new generation which he could have destroyed, re-
pulsed or denied. He recognizes Isaac" (68). And the mark of that

recognition is circumcision, the mark that the father has accepted his own death, has accepted his displacement, his succession by his son—the mark on the son's phallus that is a sign of the surmounting of the Oedipal castration threat. Isaac carries this mark of recognition as an "assurance that he (Isaac) will have in turn to experience a similar mutation and recognition" (68). Abraham "accepts the fact that Isaac could harbor toward him the same death wish; he assumes that danger: circumcision is still there to testify to the surmounting; it is an assurance of his confidence in the identical progression by Isaac" (68). Rosolato points out that the ram, Isaac's substitute in the sacrifice, is an animal with seminal connotations, and that in the sacrifice the ram represents a "partial object"—the penis. The destruction of the ram represents the father's renunciation of the phallic power in favor of his successor, his son, renunciation that has its reward in the son's progeny. Thus, when Abaham returns from the sacrifice, he learns that children have been born in his absence, one of whom, Rebecca, will be Isaac's future wife.

Circumcision as a mark of recognition that the father confers on the son points up the fact that, in the alliance, paternity involves two acts: generation and acknowledgment. The very nature of birth makes it clear who the son's mother is, but the establishment of who the son's father is requires an act of acknowledgment—the father must "recognize" the child as his son. The substitutive, sacrificial ram considered as a partial object, as the penis, emphasizes the fact that the whole basis of the sacrificial structure is the intermediary third term, the substitute, the link. Like God's recognition of Abraham, Abraham's recognition of Isaac involves three marks of identification: circumcision (the visible marking of the penis), the conferring of a name, and the promise that Isaac will now have sons in turn. Thus there is an equivalence established between the grandson, the penis, and the name as intermediary third terms linking the grandfather and the father (i.e., the father and the son), for the law of succession that Abraham accepts is also a law of transmission. The father's acceptance of his own death, of his succession by his son, his renunciation of the phallic power, is a transmission of that phallic power to his son, a transmission that requires identifying marks precisely because what is transmitted is not just the power to generate, but the power to generate *in a line descend-*

ing from the father. And that is why the religion that is established by God's covenant with Abraham (a covenant confirmed by Isaac's sacrifice) is a religion of patriarchs, a religion of genealogy. Rosolato points out that in the one, two, three order of succession of grandfather, father, son, the zero point is the death of the father, and he notes that the succession, the transmission in which the father dies while the name identified with the generative power is passed on and the phallic, linking power is reborn "corresponds to the act of symbolization where the thing 'dies' in order to be reborn with renewed vigor in the network of the laws of language" (70).

Comparing the sacrifice of Isaac with that of Jesus, Rosolato notes that in the latter case the two triadic structures linked by the death of the father are apparent: the Oedipal triangle (the Holy Family) and the three masculine persons (the Trinity). Rosolato contends that though the elements of the Oedipal triangle are present in the Holy Family, the corresponding desires do not appear. Yet one must point out that the fecundation of Mary by God is a supplanting of Joseph in that triangle, and since Jesus, the son, is himself that God, then it is, in a sense, the son who has impregnated his own mother, and Jesus' birth, as befits the birth of a god, is incestuous. By an incestuous birth that somehow preserves the virginity of his mother, Jesus is born in order to sacrifice himself, thereby redeeming man from time and mortality by giving him eternal life. One thinks of Quentin's distorted solution in which a suicide, a putting to death of oneself, as a symbolic incest (the return to the womb) is meant to preserve eternally intact the temporary virginity of his sister and himself as well as free his descendants from time and death by freeing them from generation.

The numerous differences that exist between the sacrifices of Isaac and Jesus pertain to a shift in the concept of genealogy. The first and most notable difference is that in the sacrifice of Isaac the son is spared, while in the sacrifice of Jesus the son dies. With Isaac, the ram is substituted for the son, but with Jesus, the son is substituted for the paschal lamb (the male lamb that was killed so that the firstborn would be spared). In the sacrifice of Jesus, the son offers himself up (Jesus is both the priest and the victim) as an atonement for man's offense against God. Thus, the son is put to death to satisfy the guilt that man feels for the Oedipal death wish against the father, but since the son is the father ("I and the Father are one," John 10:30), then "this sacrifice allows beneath the cover of the Son the representation of the Oedipal wishes (the death of the Father, or of God)" (78). In the sacrifice of Jesus, the sovereignty of a single God is put to death: the death of the supreme authority of the idealized father. As in the sacrifice of Isaac where the idealized father, who is the origin of the law and who can abrogate the law at will, is transformed, by God's taking death upon himself, into the dead father, who is responsible to the law (the covenant between God and Abraham—the old law), so in the sacrifice of Jesus, the unlimited authority of the idealized father is slain by God's taking death upon himself, and the dead father is now responsible to the new law. The old law is a law of genealogical succession and transmission: the father accepts the law that fathers die before their sons. Thus, Isaac is spared, and the covenant is transmitted to and by his progeny. But in the sacrifice of Jesus, the only son dies, and here we find that shift in the concept of genealogy that is the principal difference between the sacrifices of Isaac and Jesus, for the sacrifice of the childless only son marks an "interruption of genealogy" (82). Judaism is a religion of progeniture, a religion of continuity according to the blood, of physical descent from the fathers. Christianity, on the other hand, is a religion not of physical genealogy but of conversion. That interruption of genealogy represented by the sacrifice of Jesus is, in fact, a substitution of a spiritual genealogy for a physical genealogy. In the sacrifice of Isaac, the promise of the phallic power to generate new physical life in the face of death is transmitted by a line of physical descent from father to son, but with the sacrifice of Jesus, the promise is no longer one of a new physical life but of a new spiritual life. No longer is it a question of that physical immortality which one achieves through one's children; it is, rather, a question of personal immortality in an afterlife. And that future promise is transmitted not according to a physical genealogy but according to a spiritual one, and thus it is open through conversion to any man who accepts the sacrifice of Jesus. The priests who renew that sacrifice in the Mass are, like Jesus, celibate, partly as a sign that they have to do not with the generation of new physical life, a physical life that must always be in bondage to death, but with the generation of a new spiritual life—they are ghostly fathers.

This shift in the concept of genealogy between the sacrifices of Isaac and Jesus takes the form of a shift within the triadic structures pertaining to each sacrifice. In the triad of God, Abraham, and Isaac, the person who is to be sacrificed is the third member, Isaac, while in the triad of the Father, the Son, and the Holy Spirit it is the second member, Jesus, who is sacrificed. By the substitution of the sacrificial ram for Isaac, the father can renounce the phallic power by the *physical* destruction of the ram and then have that power restored to *physical* life in Isaac and his progeny. But with the sacrifice of Jesus, we have the destruction of *physical* life in the Crucifixion and the restoration of *spiritual* life in the Resurrection. When Jesus, the second member of the triad, offers himself up, it is as if, in the earlier triad, Abraham had turned the sacrificial knife on himself, as if Abraham had become the sacrificial ram. And indeed, one of the titles of Jesus is the "lamb of god." In the Christian triad, that phallic, intermediary term whereby the power to generate spiritual life is transmitted is not the Son, who after his sacrifice returns to the Father, but the Holy Spirit, whom the Son asks the Father to send into the world: "And I will ask the Father, and he shall give you another Paraclete, that he may abide with you forever" (John 14:16). The very name "Paraclete"—advocate, pleader, intercessor, comforter—indicates the mediatory role of the third person, and his phallic power is shown in the spiritual fecundation that takes place at Pentecost, and in the phallic representation of the third person as a dove (Rosolato, 79–80).

The procession of the persons within the Trinity sheds further light on the shift that takes place between the sacrifices of Isaac and Jesus. In terms of Christian dogma, the relationship between the Father and the Son is called *generation:* active on the part of the Father as *paternity;* passive on the part of the Son as *filiation*. The Father is without antecedents; he is his own origin. The procession of the Son is a procession of knowledge. The Father comprehends himself, that is, he knows himself insofar as he is knowable; he puts himself so wholly into that idea of himself that that idea constitutes a separate person— the Son. We noted earlier that fatherhood involved not just generation but acknowledgment as well—the father's recognition of himself in the son. In the Trinity, the Father's act of self-knowledge, of self-recognition, *is* the generation of the Son—the Logos, the knowledge of the Father. The procession of the Holy Spirit differs from that of the Son, for the Holy Spirit proceeds from both the Father *and* the Son by an act known as *spiration:* "active on the part of the Father and the Son, and passive on the part of the Holy Spirit" (79). As the procession of the second person was an act of knowledge, so that of the third person is an act of will, an act of love between the Father and the Son. The Father and the Son look at each other and seeing that each is perfect, they love each other completely, putting themselves so wholly into that love that that love constitutes a separate person—the Holy Spirit. We should note that the processions of the Son and the Holy Spirit represent a kind of narcissistic doubling in which God makes himself, first, the sole object of his own knowledge, and then the sole object of his own love. Further, the generative relationship of the Son to the Father—filiation—is a passive relationship, and the climax of that sacrifice, whose denouement is the Crucifixion, is Jesus' active willing of his own passivity in the hands of the Father: "My Father, if it be possible, let this chalice pass from me. Nevertheless, not as I will, but as thou wilt" (Matt. 26:39). The climax of the sacrifice is the total submission of the Son's will to the Father's will, so that the Son's will becomes one with, is wed to, that of the Father. In this connection, we should also note that in some heterodox Christian traditions a feminine element is reintroduced into the masculine triad, thus reproducing the Oedipal triangle. Sometimes it is the Son who is feminized, as with the medieval mystic Julian of Norwich, who, discussing the "motherhood of God" in *The Revelations of Divine Love,* speaks of "Mother Jesus."[8] Sometimes it is the Holy Spirit, as with certain early Christian sects for whom the Paraclete was a feminine principle (Rosolato, 87). Yeats refers to these traditions of a feminine element in the Trinity in his series of poems called "Supernatural Songs." One need only add that there is an obvious movement from the Son's passivity in relation to the Father and their generation of a third person between them to a concept of the second person as feminine. Indeed, the imagery of the climactic moment when Jesus accepts his Father's will suggests the feminization of the Son. Referring to his approaching death, Jesus does not say, "Let this sword pass from me," but, "Let this chalice pass from me." The image of the cup, with its feminine connotations, accords with that death in which, by an active willing of his own passivity, Jesus will have his hands and feet pierced by nails and his side pierced by a lance. Indeed, one could view that death as a *liebestod,* a sexual act that, because Jesus is both the priest and the victim, is incestuous.

Rosolato points out that there exists, on the margins of Christianity, the aim of "a sort of revenge against God" by means of the sacrifice itself (82). Since Jesus' sacrifice is an atonement for an offense of man against God, justice requires that the sacrificial victim be both man and God. In that sacrifice, man puts God to death in an action symbolic of man's attempt to supplant God (the son to supplant the father, i.e., the doctrine of equality) within the context of religion as evolving humanism. In Christianity, not only does God become man, and man put God to death, but as a result of that death, man now enjoys a privilege that formerly belonged only to the gods—immortality. The structure of atonement by means of a sacrificial victim is, of course, that of revenge on a substitute. The collective guilt that the sons feel for the death wish against the father is discharged by putting that guilt on a scapegoat who will represent the son in relation to the communal priest (the father), but that sacrifice of a substitute allows a further unconscious substitution in which the victim represents the father, and the community (the band of brothers) is able to act out the death wish against him.

6   Post-Modern Paternity:

Donald Barthelme's *The Dead Father*

ROBERT CON DAVIS

Among late twentieth-century American novels, the one that most seriously attempts to define the father in recent, or post-modern, fiction, and possibly the most important "father" novel since *Ulysses* and *Absalom, Absalom!*, is Donald Barthelme's *The Dead Father* (1975). This complex and brilliant work accomplishes nothing less than a major redefinition of what the father in fiction is, and it does this as it forces novelistic attention to range back over the structure of the father in English fiction. Difficult to approach—as are many other post-modern novels—Barthelme's novel forces one to rediscover how to read a novel, as the first lines, presenting a view of paternity that verges on patent absurdity, show this novel's resistance to any simple interpretation:

The Dead Father's head. The main thing is, his eyes are open. Staring up into the sky. The eyes a two-valued blue, the blues of the Gitanes cigarette pack. The head never moves. Decades of staring. The brow is noble, good Christ, what else: Broad and noble. And serene, of course, he's dead, what else if not serene. . . . He is not perfect, thank God for that. . . . No one can remember when he was not here in our city positioned like a sleeper in troubled sleep.[1]

Barthelme's portrait of the fictional father, for all of its detail, presents a cryptic caricature that teeters between profundity and nonsense. If one moves in for a close-up of the head, a shift that breaks up its continuous lines, then, as the noble brow and blue eyes dissolve, a rogues' gallery of many fathers takes shape in place of the single face. At the right end of this gallery stand Squire Allworthy, John Jarndyce, Edward Overton, and others who are stern but ultimately benevolent toward their children. To the extreme right of Jarndyce and the gallery's other saintly figures emanates the paternal white light that John Bunyan's Christian found in the Celestial City. At the gallery's left end stand Mr. Murdstone, Mr. M'Choakumchild, Sir Austen Feverel, Huck Finn's Pap, and Thomas Sutpen, and, to the extreme left of these child haters, a grim reaper (like Wash Jones or Percy Grimm) who, as the polar opposite of the celestial light, mindlessly sweeps a scythe through young limbs. But, with a shift back, this close-up of the rogues' gallery's many fathers dissolves and, once again, from a distance appears the single, sphinxlike head. Like a blank-eyed Greek statue who gazes at the world and flinches at nothing, his head turns toward an ultimate and elusive point that only he sees. How he can be dead, though "only in a sense" (14), suggests portentously a grasp of the paternal tradition in Anglo-American fiction.

A fiction that taps this tradition by daring to seize the father as a whole stands in peril of some presumption, as does the attempt to understand that fiction. Such a fiction, flirting with the absurd, invests everything in an attempt to leap out of and then to turn to embrace its tradition, in this case the paternal tradition and that of the novel itself. If the fiction cannot make the leap, then, like Herman Melville's *The Confidence-Man*, it breaks into pieces. From the perspective of a purely thematic criticism, it can be shown that the rogues' gallery figures exist separately and without meaningful relationship in a tradition: literary symbol and structure simply do not exist. But against such fragmentation and reduction literature brings symbols into existence by taking enormous chances with our understanding of tradition that become authentic fiction when they succeed.

The Dead Father begins in a description of the father's great body half-buried in the middle of a French city. Sitting motionless, "staring up into the sky," he appears to be dead, but the narrator cautions that he is not, not entirely. The details of his features soon make it apparent that his different parts are emblems of paternity and that this character is to be taken as a complex symbol. His noble brow stands for mental power and concentration. His rugged jawline indicates formidable will and endurance. His blue eyes and gray hair show his attractive and even dashing appearance. His "full red lips [are] drawn back in a slight rictus . . . disclosing a bit of mackerel salad lodged between two of the stained four," as absurd evidence of great appetite and desire. Although held in place by chains, like Prometheus, the figure in this audacious attempt to capture a literary symbol is easily recognizable as a father: authority, aloofness, great appetite—it is all here in a sketch. This being so, and granting what seems like true veneration in this description, it must be wondered why the narrator is quick to add that the father, though admirable, "is not perfect, thank God for that." In fact, he adds, "we want the Dead Father to be dead." And further, in a strident tone, "we sit with tears in our eyes wanting the Dead Father to be dead—meanwhile doing amazing things with our hands" (2–5). That the father is dead and that his children should want his death are facts, in Barthelme's words, "Endshrouded in endigmas" (172).

The fact to be dealt with here, as in much other post-modern fiction, is that literary paternity is not linked inextricably with "fathers" as figures in stories. Even though the relationship of children, mothers, and fathers at the thematic level of narrative constitutes the family material from which fictions are made, at the structural level of the text the meaning of that relationship takes shape as a "symbolic father," ultimately a function in narrative structure. This function floats freely, to a considerable extent, without mooring in images of the father, either social or personal, because it is a structural aspect of narrative: it prohibits mere repetition and mere sequentiality, lapses into narcissism, in effect forbidding an untold story, either in the form of silence or in the mechanical repetition that imitates silence. Specifically, it is the essential "no" expressed as a dilemma (a riddle to be solved, a family member to be found, an injustice to be surmounted, etc.) that, as Vladimir Propp notes, comes at the beginning of every narrative to generate its structure. The problem of Barthelme's post-modern fiction is this: how does a novel, part of an English tradition of fiction (*Robinson Crusoe, The Ordeal of Richard Feverel,* etc.) that explicitly articulates the function of paternity both thematically and structurally, exist within its tradition without being overcome by it?

For, although in one way free of the tyranny of father figures, the post-modern novel still must deal with the residue of father images, mostly social and economic in origin, that belong to the English tradition of realistic fiction; indelibly inscribed in that tradition is the portrait of a mature gentleman in a suit with vest, with graying hair and glasses and perhaps a watch chain slung across his middle. He is Squire Allworthy, Sir Austen Feverel, Edward Overton, or Jason Lycurgus Compson, III—a composite of the rogues' gallery figures. His exclusive power to signify the paternal metaphor has been rescinded since James Joyce's *Ulysses,* but he and his special privilege are still there as a living memory in the English literary tradition. No longer recognizing that privilege, the post-modern novel, nonetheless, must continue to deal with it, since how it deals with tradition gives post-modern fiction its identity.

The Dead Father, for example, manifests wholly traditional structures. Primarily, there is the quest: the Dead Father seeks renewal in a search for the Golden Fleece, and on this journey he performs heroic deeds in combat and tells of past conquests in love. The fact of this mythic journey alone links Barthelme's novel to *Robinson Crusoe, Huckleberry Finn, Moby Dick, Ulysses* and many others. Also in line with quest conventions, as the journey's end nears a female (her name is "Mother") is liberated, her entrance into the action obviously connected with the consummation of the journey. Further, the Dead Father has a helper on the quest in his son, who enlists nineteen men to tow his father toward his goal. Additionally, the son recounts undertaking an initiation directly connected with his ability to aid his father and to be on the quest. Along with the quest, there is the highly traditional novelistic device of the book-within-a-book. The novel's "A Manual for Sons" gives practical guidance, in the manner of a field manual, for identifying and dealing with what it calls the important nineteen of the twenty-two possible kinds of fathers. Both of these conventional literary devices, the quest and the book-within-a-book, create a picture, and an accurate one, of a novel solidly ensconced in the English tradition.

On closer examination, however, these aspects of the novel reveal profound irony in its traditionalism. First, although the novel contains a quest, it is one that casts suspicion on the status of its quester: he is at times comatose and at other times frenetic. To begin with, the Dead Father is being towed by nineteen men who pull a cable attached by a titanium band to his waist. Still, he does perform heroic deeds: when he is not being pulled along, the Dead Father goes "slaying" through the countryside with an enormous sword, slicing up exotic animals and men. After leveling one grove of musicians, the destroyer stands pleased with himself:

The Dead Father resting with his two hands on the hilt of his sword, which was planted in the red and steaming earth.

My anger, he said proudly.

Then the Dead Father sheathing his sword pulled from his trousers his ancient prick and pissed upon the dead artists, severally and together, to the best of his ability—four minutes, or one pint. (12)

He would like to go out of control in the use of his "ancient prick," but he can find no women to participate, and he is restrained constantly in his sexual advances by Thomas, son and helper. When the Dead Father misbehaves, sexually or otherwise, Thomas raps his father squarely on the forehead in a rebuke to his authority and to the seriousness of the journey. Thus, the "aid" Thomas gives him is double-edged, as Thomas compels his father to remain, in effect, a prisoner on the quest. In doing so, Thomas is "killing me" (158), as the Dead Father complains. "Not we," Thomas answers. "Processes are killing you, not we. Inexorable processes" (158).

In the second major irony of the novel, Mother's appearance at the end reflects a pattern of feminine experience that does not belong in the traditional masculine cast of the quest. Mother, in fact, travels with the Dead Father's retinue, not as a participant, but as "a horse-man on the hill" (32) following and observing its progress from a distance. When she does join the group, she does so to make a grocery list for her children. The Dead Father states, rather pointedly, as the mysterious figure on a horse rides away: "I don't remember her very well . . . what was her name?" (170).

And not only is Mother foreign to him; his daughters Julie and Emma he sees only as possibilities for sexual conquest and is virtually unable to communicate with them. Were the Dead Father to attempt to talk to them, he would find that they, while speaking English, have a language of their own. Instead of the Germanic assertion-question-response pattern of English conversation, Julie and Emma speak a language of free association mixed with guardedly private connota-

tions—a language of the oppressed. In the first such conversation,
Julie addresses Emma:

Whose little girl are you?
I get by, I get by.
Time to go.
Hoping this will reach you at a favorable moment.
Bad things can happen to people.
Is that a threat?
Dragged him all this distance without any rootytoottoot.
Is that a threat?
Take it any way you like it. (23)

The large margin of indirection in their talk, like Mother's erratic participation in the Dead Father's journey, veers away perversely from
the predictable path of formal discourse. As if not dependent on the
stringencies of verbal exchange, they communicate through what is
unstated but recognized as mutual experience. They do reach a desti-
nation in their conversation, but the route they take cannot be known
in advance. In sum, their oblique communication and Mother's
roundabout way of traveling suggest an a-linear model of behavior
foreign to the rational economies associated with paternal authority.

In a third major irony of the novel, Thomas' status on the quest as
helper and apparent heir to the Dead Father's pre-eminence is shown
to be suspect. For example, in response to the Dead Father's command, "explain yourself. It is always interesting to hear someone explaining himself" (56), Thomas responds with a stutter, "I was
bbbbbbborn twice-twenty-less one years ago in a great city" (57).
Finally, after a period of poaching from government fish hatcheries
and spending several years in a monastery, Thomas began reading
philosophy, only to discover "that I had no talent for philosophy"
(58). Two salient aspects of Thomas' explanation of himself are that
he has so little success in his endeavors, and that he can sustain himself
with very limited successes. Thomas implies that his strength is to be
found in his failures, as the first requirement of one who would become the father is that he is willing to undergo preparation, that is, to
be a son, who by definition is in a passive or subservient position.

The hidden strength in Thomas' passivity is revealed in the initiation story he tells the Dead Father. He relates that he was kidnaped

and tortured by a group of men who claimed simply that he "was wrong and had always been wrong and would always be wrong" (40) and that he would be held until he "accommodated" (41). After some time Thomas was brought to see the Great Father Serpent, who "would if I answered the riddle correctly grant me a boon . . . [but] I would never answer the riddle correctly so my hopes they said, should not be got up" (43). Standing before Thomas, the "serpent of huge bigness which held in its mouth a sheet of tin on which something was written" continually calls out "for the foreskins of the uninitiated" (44). As the Great Father Serpent makes preparation for riddling, Thomas slips beneath the tin sheet and finds the answer to the riddle that was "the most arcane item in the arcana," according to the serpent. Then, the riddling begins: "*What do you really feel?*" asks the serpent. Having seen the correct answer, Thomas responds immediately, with a stutter, "Like murderinging." Shocked by receiving the right answer, the serpent has no choice but to award Thomas the ability "to carry out this foulness," but rushes to caution that "having the power [to murder] is often enough. You don't have to actually do it." Thomas, too, is stunned, for even though he steals the riddle's answer, he is struck by what *murderinging* calls up in himself: "what I was wondering and marveling at was the closeness with which what I had answered accorded with my feelings, my lost feelings that I had never found before." Underneath the facade of an obedient son, Thomas finds that he is a murderer. Then, having submitted to the Great Father Serpent's riddling, the transformed Thomas is set free by the kidnapers to be, as he says, "abroad in the city with murderinging in mind—the dream of a stutterer" (46).

In the initiation rite, an exercise in creative passivity, Thomas taps the "lost feelings that I had never found before" and acknowledges guilt for a primal crime that he has no distinct memory of committing. Yet the admission of a murderous desire makes it unnecessary for him to murder: by accepting guilt for a crime that has already taken place, Thomas need not perform the act he has acknowledged responsibility for. In effect, because Thomas identifies the source of his aggressivity, he need not play out aggression by killing fathers. This admission, and the ability to accept guilt and limitation that it implies, place him in line for the Dead Father's authority.

The psychology of his initiation is enlarged upon in "A Manual for Sons"—a document that mysteriously falls into Thomas' hands. Here the initiate's confrontation with paternal opposition is described in psychological terms: "They [fathers] block your path. They cannot be climbed over, neither can they be slithered past. They are the 'past,' and very likely the slither, if the slither is thought of as that accommodating maneuver you make to escape notice, or get by unscathed. If you attempt to go around one, you will find that another (winking at the first) has mysteriously appeared athwart the trail. Or maybe it is the same one, moving with the speed of paternity" (129). Whether a single entity or a multiple projection, the father is a principle of opposition. He is always the past, as finding is necessarily an experience of refinding, just as Thomas "refinds" the desire for murder in his confrontation with the Great Father Serpent. The meaning of the father-as-obstacle is elaborated by Julie when she explains, in a crucial passage, that after "the fucked mother conceives" and "the whelping . . . [is] whelped . . . then the dialogue begins. The father speaks to it. The 'it' whirling as in a centrifuge. Looking for something to tie to. Like a boat in a storm. What is there? The father . . . the postlike quality of the father" (77). According to the metapsychology of Julie and "A Manual for Sons," the father's dual function is to be the one who intrudes in the child's free state and also to be the primary object in relation to which the child is established in the world. That is, as the child's first intruder who blocks continuance in the "storm," the father presents a solution to a dilemma he himself creates for the child.

This metapsychological account of the rise of mind can be organized as follows: (1) the first catastrophic encounter with the father-as-object is a confusing centrifugal experience both of being spoken to and of speaking, since in the first state there is no separation between agent and receiver of an action; (2) a horizon of object relations comes up at the moment when the child finds the father as a primary object in the world and in so doing separates him- or herself from that world; (3) then, a mooring in the father-as-object lays a basis for a relationship with that world, which in turn is the matrix for all that is humanly intelligible. This world, as Julie suggests, establishes itself on the ruins of the pre-world where the father first intrudes, and her calling the father the post that orients the "it" that becomes human is a recognition of the father as a primary principle of function in the mind's structure.

This recognition of the paternal function takes shape as the awareness of a dead father, as Thomas' discovery of an archaic (and latent) desire to murder a father suggests. Likewise, "A Manual for Sons" recounts the origin of the father's power in an initial patricide, after which

you must deal with the memory of a father. Often that memory is more potent than the living presence of a father, is an inner voice commanding, haranguing, yesing and noing—a binary code, yes no yes no yes no yes no, governing your every, your slightest movement, mental or physical. At what point do you become yourself? Never, wholly, you are always partly him. (144)

This is, in fact, Freud's dead father, a representation of the process of internalizing symbolic authority as conscience. As Jacques Lacan puts it, "the symbolic Father is, in so far as he signifies" the law of this process, "the dead Father."[2] The passage shows that Thomas' memory of his fantasized desire for murder is the archaic expression for the father as the source of opposition, the principle of the "binary code." And the manual clearly describes a theory of mind consonant with Julie's. From this point of view, the Dead Father's old prerogatives—to love all women, to go slaying, to have his own way—are vestiges of an imaginary show of power that has less import as he gets closer to the end of the quest, his symbolic function then appearing as the true legacy to the mental life of his children.

Thus, the several traditional elements of *The Dead Father*, while anchoring the novel in the English tradition of fiction, have an underside of meaning that subverts the significance they would have in realistic fiction. First, the quest is undertaken by one whose power to act is not commensurate with the romantic (in Northrop Frye's terminology) nature of the quest, since the Dead Father must be towed along. Second, the stature of a father figure is drastically diminished by Thomas' seizure and destruction of his prerogatives. Third, women, usually goals to be accomplished and treasures to be discovered on the quest, are found here in a sphere, outside of the paternal domain, that the Dead Father has no access to. Fourth, Thomas' initiation experience reveals a great antipathy toward the father, one that leads him to imprison the Dead Father on an ambiguous journey. Last, "A Manual for Sons" tells plainly what the rest of the novel suggests all along: the father's authority is not a social force—expressed by privileged males who perform particular acts in the world—but a function within the structure of the mind that can be depicted only symbolically. The primary "endigma," then, that this novel points to, is the meaning of the Dead Father—a figure the novel presents simultaneously as a character in a fiction and as a symbolic function.

Another look at the figure of the Dead Father is in order. He is like a god who has been brought down from a great height for ritual dismemberment on earth. In his lowly state, he is being towed, cable to waist, by nineteen men to a trench where he will be buried by waiting bulldozers. Still, he has "authority," as Julie says, "fragile, yet present. He is like a bubble you do not want to burst" (67). At the same time, she states bluntly, "The father is a motherfucker" (76). The divided response of his children reflects, in a general way, the creative and destructive aspects of the Dead Father's nature. For the first part, when he copulates he is a tremendous engine of culture. With his fertile "ancient prick" he creates objects in the world, various things like the poker chip, the punching bag, both light and heavy, the midget Bible, the slot-machine chip, the Savings & Loan Association, "Six and three quarters per cent compounded momentarily . . . I guarantee it," and people, "some thousands of children of the ordinary sort" (36–38). In his destructive phase, he turns around to plow under his creations with the same glee he took in making them. This rapaciousness, represented by his "ancient prick" and swinging sword, knows no restraint, only its own desire and expression. For instance, after he has given a speech of ponderous gobbledygook to the retinue pulling him and is asked what the speech meant, he answers, "Thank you . . . it meant I made a speech" (51). He believes that all utterance expresses himself. He says: "All lines [are] my lines. All figure and all ground mine, out of my head. All colors mine" (19). His is a primary encounter with the world by which he knows no bounds and strikes nothing to check his progress. Or, rather, he finds a way of discounting obstacles so that he appears to remain unencumbered. "Having it both ways," he says truthfully, "is a thing I like" (15).

This comic characterization is a rough but accurate representation of the paternal function, a self-contained opposition contingent on nothing outside of itself. Still, as one who swaggeringly copulates and slays, a variation of the composite authoritarian figure with glasses and suit and vest, he is only one image of opposition, one not precisely equivalent to the symbolic father. Suggesting more of the symbolic function (in a theory of mind) described by Julie and "A Manual for Sons" is the operation that goes on in the Dead Father's left leg. Inside it is a mechanism that works "ceaselessly night and day through all the hours for the good of all." The leg contains "small booths with sliding doors" in which people confess their sin and guilt. "The confessions are taped, scrambled, recomposed, dramatized, and then appear in the city's theaters, a new feature-length film every Friday. One can recognize moments of one's own, sometimes" (4). Thus, into the left leg's process of transformation goes the raw material of guilt and pain, and out of it come the articulations of being human and the connections with a deeper self, the products of culture. To be sure, the Dead Father as a character is a megalomaniacal, narcissistic sacker of reality, that is, a hard-edged caricature of the father, but his children need what he makes possible—culture.

It is curious that the paternal symbolic function is lodged casually in the Dead Father's left leg; but then he only took on this function, as he explains to his son, because "mechanical experience was a part of experience there was room for, in my vastness. I wanted to know what machines know." And what do they know? "Machines are sober, uncomplaining, endlessly efficient, and work ceaselessly through all the hours for the good of all" (13). The Dead Father manifests the symbolic process—the metapsychology Julie describes, the creation of conscience "A Manual for Sons" explains, and the cultural production derived from guilt, "a new feature-length film every Friday"—in the innocuous left leg, a member of his body not connected with his particular swaggering personality (the leg, in fact, is detachable!). This tenuous link emphasizes that the symbolic process, though based on paternal opposition, is not synonymous with this image of the father, this paternal image being an imperfect indicator of that process.

It is essential to the concept of the symbolic father that any one image fall short of encompassing the symbol; in fact, an image of the father must fail so that the place it leaves empty can indicate the symbolic function and not the particularity of the agent of that function.[3] The Dead Father, for instance, is classified by his children as "an old fart" (10), one whose time has passed and who, therefore, is no longer needed: to ease him out, Thomas systematically denies him privileges and, at last, any participation with his children. The Dead Father even comes to view himself as inadequate, reflecting in a Molly-Bloom-like interior monologue on what he as a father did not know: "There were things I never knew[:] . . . what made the leaves fibrillate on the trees . . . what made the heart stop and how unicorns got trapped in tapestries. . . . But AndI dealt out 1,856,700 slaps with the open hand and 22,009,800 boxes on the ear." In short, he was busy dominating others and "never figured out figured out wot sort of animal AndI was. Endshrouded in endigmas. Never knew wot's wot" (172). At the end of the quest, as the Dead Father is bulldozed into the trench, the symbolic authority of his left leg is taken up, internalized, by his children; he dies, in effect, so that his function can be reborn in those who have relations with him. The narrator's relief that the Dead Father "is not perfect, thank God for that" alludes to the necessity of paternal failure—death or absence—so that the symbol may be signified— somewhat as the death of an ancestor makes a totem possible. "We *want* the Dead Father to be dead," the narrator proclaims, so that the *father* may belong to his children.

This novel's manner of signifying the father structurally belongs to tradition: like the fathers in *Robinson Crusoe, Tom Jones,* and *Huckleberry Finn* the father must be lost so that, in his absence, his function can be known. From the structural point of view, in fact, it is father absence, not presence, that signifies the father: the father is lost so that his meaning can be found symbolically. At the same time, the manner in which the father is presented here is not a mere repetition. Barthelme draws his paternal material from the rogues' gallery of traditional images, compresses it into a single image of the father, then allows that image to fall like a straw man, leaving the locus of the father in its place. In this way, Barthelme's novel uses the material of the realistic novel to advance beyond the realistic novel and is at once thoroughly traditional and post-modern. Not truly satiric or parodic, possibilities that would orient *The Dead Father* toward a merely traditional depiction of the father, this fiction employs irony to undermine its own materials in order to signify the father anew.

So, simultaneously a representation of the rogues' gallery of fathers (the whole of the paternal tradition) and a denial of paternity, the

Dead Father's character comprises a fiction at a high level of abstraction. A fiction dealing in these cerebral strokes—the whole of the paternal tradition in fiction is evoked and then desiccated—verges on defining itself more as criticism than as fiction. For one thing, to posit fiction at this level of abstraction is to gamble reader engagement on very thin odds: character, plot, theme, setting, and symbolism—all are tossed into a sea of abstraction that only specialized knowledge (a critical awareness) of the English tradition and its underlying structures can navigate. The danger of avant garde fiction has been voiced before, about *Ulysses* and *Finnegans Wake,* about Faulkner's novels, and about many others; with Joyce and Faulkner, readers have come into being because their novels needed reading—they were too important to be left unread. The special boldness (and danger) of Barthelme's fiction is that it flirts with surface nonsense, as does much fiction by William Gass, Thomas Pynchon, John Barth, Hunter Thompson, and Tom Robbins. This flirtation creates the appearance of peripatetic elements (the name "Oedipa Maas" in *The Crying of Lot 49* is a good example) that are methodically drained of their significance, so that the father—as a principle of order—is continually promised, but his articulation is deferred, sometimes indefinitely. This narrative technique, an apparent abnegation of the father, can be deciphered as fictional sense only at another level very far removed from the play of images and from what is commonly known as texture—elements that traditionally convey the pleasure of the text for readers.

Of course, in the structural consideration of a text, the novel that can be comprehended never lacks an indication of the father. "Every narrative," as Roland Barthes says, "is a staging of the (absent, hidden, or hypostatized) father,"[4] and the loss of that staging "would deprive literature of many of its pleasures."[5] And it must be admitted that one alternative to the father in fiction could be to abandon pleasure and to strive for a blissful state of unintelligible rapture, a lyric gesture. It is here, then, between two fictional possibilities that Barthelme's novel is to be understood. On one side of it is what Barthes calls "pleasure"—*jouir,* the state of recognition and comprehension—and on the other is what he calls "bliss"—*jouissance,* the ecstasy of being transported. Within these coordinates, nearly abjuring comprehension, *The Dead Father* hurtles toward blissful transport.

In this search for bliss, *The Dead Father* wagers the ancient bet that the father may be seized in his totality, directly: it tries to grasp his essential shape—in effect, to break through his pasteboard mask. This ambitious striving, a strike against tradition, necessarily requires a sacrifice of pleasure, one that Barthelme boldly makes. That the bet is lost and the father not seized are foregone conclusions; that loss is as much a part of the ritual of fiction-making as is the need to take such risks. Paradoxically, it is in that necessary "failure" at the level of narrative structure, wherein the father is not seized in his totality, that the novel signifies most directly the paternal symbol it cannot possess.

Epilogue:

The Discourse of Jacques Lacan

ROBERT CON DAVIS

In the retrospective moment of an epilogue one often re-maps a book's journey and then speculates on the unmapped territory beyond the book. However, in this Age of the Reader (following hard on the Age of the Critic) it seems fitting to speculate not on the ideal perspective of the book's vision (and, thus, on the multiple visions of the six critics in this book), but rather on the object of the book's atten-tion, that is, on the always elusive but necessary ideal reader that the book must speak to in order to exist. Such a reader Nathaniel Haw-thorne describes in the "Custom-House" preface to *The Scarlet Letter* as one who possesses "the one heart and mind of perfect sympathy" with the book, "as if the printed book, thrown at large on the wide world, were certain to find out the divided segment of the writer's own nature." Such an ideal reader of Lacanian criticism about the father in fiction, to many minds, may be of a rather contentious and specialized sort. Rather harmlessly, this reader possesses interest in the literature treated in this book and is curious about Lacan's underlying methodo-logical and ideological assumptions. And already familiar with previ-ous experiments in Freudian criticism, the reader knows enough about Jacques Lacan to be curious about how a hermeneutics might be built on his seemingly oracular but provocative theoretical assertions. As for being contentious, this reader (certainly not *my* ideal reader) per-haps is familiar with feminist reassessments of current critical theory and practice and is unimpressed by the feminist reinterpretation of lit-erature along the lines of sexual ideology. And he knows (the reader is likely a "he") of criticism based on Marxist assumptions, but anxious-ly fears the reductionism of Marxist approaches to literature—the in-

evitable destruction by politics of the "literariness" of literature. Tired
of feminism, wary of Marxism, this slightly anxious male reader turns
to the secure shelter of phallocentricism and bourgeois idealism as he
comfortably peruses the critical verities of the patriarchal/bourgeois
tradition embodied in Lacan's work—reassured by the undemocratic
thought that if Jacques Lacan is not always clear and helpful, he is at
least always difficult to read and is, thus, not for everyone.

Such a reader is a fiction, and a dangerous one, as it is certain that
his assumptions—if "he" in fact exists—belie the context of current
criticism on which Lacan has an influence and certainly distort Lacan's work and the motive from which this book rises. On the contrary, the ideal reader of the present book is likely to be an avid reader
of Marxist, feminist, Freudian, or deconstructive criticism (probably
all of them), especially as they can be understood through post-struc-
turalist theories of language. Such a reader is well aware that the
"problem of the subject" (what is called traditionally "truth value" or
the "meaning of meaning") is a critical concern that consistently runs
through schools of contemporary criticism, as the work, in particular,
of Jacques Lacan and Jacques Derrida has made it virtually impossible
for post-modern interpreters to adopt critical stances in total ignorance of the theoretical problems involved in all systems of analysis
(self-contradiction, unwarranted historical assumptions, class biases,
etc.). Our ideal reader is likely to be not a strict factionalist at all, but is
interested in seeking out the hidden and underlying motives in critical
systems and in understanding narrative function as a strategy in relation to those motives. In short, our ideal reader of Lacanian criticism
is one who has taken seriously Lacan's and Derrida's analysis of the
metaphysics of presence and is interested in unveiling assumptions
concerning ideology and standards of "truth" and in "placing under
erasure" that which is specious theoretically.

Our ideal reader, in fact, comes to Lacanian thought for an important perspective on how to dismantle standard presences in literature,
such as father figures, mother substitutes, Christ figures, neurotics,
and outsiders, and to find, instead, functions and transformations in
fiction that can be examined critically in the context of their real environment—within narrative structure. To that end, a Lacanian question regarding narrative (the question of this book) can be asked of

The Odyssey, of *Bleak House*, or of any text: what does it mean for the father to be the subject of a narrative? The answer is not a taxonomy of inferiority complexes, Oedipal complexes, and mother attachments—as the essays in this book show—but a sophisticated confrontation with narrative structure as a complex of (ultimately) indeterminate elements constituted on many levels of textuality. In its answer, the Lacanian elaboration of the psychoanalytical subject is an Einsteinian advance over the Newtonian desexualized (and taxonomic) psychoanalysis that often, especially in the United States, passes for Freudian thought. The Lacanian subject is a subject alive and in motion that never can be known directly, but can be known only in its absence, in the traces it leaves behind: in the presence of an absence that is language.

The principal motive for seeing in Lacanian thought (erroneously) a position held against feminist and Marxist approaches to literature has two parts. The first, as Juliet Mitchell has shown at length in *Psychoanalysis and Feminism*,[1] results from a misunderstanding of analysis that is predicated on the existence of the unconscious. Lacan's analysis of the discourse of the Other (which is unconscious) appears to many radical feminists simply as another incarnation of patriarchal idealism and yet another refusal to confront women's real, oppressed condition as it can be reflected in literature. Similarly, Marxist critics have seen in Lacan's work a failure to face—even a betrayal of—the essentially materialist struggle of the class system. Lacan's fixation on the unconscious, according to this position, fails to recognize the ideological character of literature, the same ideological content that gives meaning to other human "production." However, neither the feminist nor the Marxist critique has been able to see through to the meaning of Lacan's elaboration of the subject as the process of signification, wherein Lacan actually deconstructs the phallocentric cast of personal identity and finds, in its place, a chain of always partial objects empowered to operate as a system of signification (for two notable exceptions to this generality, see Juliet Mitchell's important work, especially *Psychoanalysis and Feminism*, and Frederic Jameson's "Imaginary and Symbolic in Lacan: Marxism, Psychoanalytic Criticism, and the Problem of the Subject").[2] As Rosalind Coward and John Ellis hold, "the extreme and justifiable hostility from Marxists and, especially, [from] feminists" is not a reaction at all to the reality of Lacanian thought, but to the true defects of bourgeois ideology. The ultimate effect of Lacan's analysis, as they show, "is a complete undermining of the notion of a unified subject, the assumption on which all bourgeois ideology is founded."[3] Coward and Ellis elaborate Lacan's position in relation to ideology as follows:

Lacan demonstrates the construction of the subject in language, through a process in which the imaginary identification of self as a unified whole in a mirror is an essential part. This puts in place the subject (hitherto uncoordinated) in relation to a predicatable outside. But this is no simple process, because the imaginary wholeness which is identified in the mirror is an identification which is retained as the prototype for all identifications as the child enters cultural and specific social formations as a language-using subject. Lacan's concept of the imaginary provides a route for understanding how the positioning of a subject in relation to langauge and, therefore, [to] social relations is always accomplished in specific ideological formations. The identifications made by the infant in the process by which it produces itself in discourse are always already in ideology.[4]

Lacan's elaboration of the subject, as Coward and Ellis here explain, is as well an elaboration of ideology and of materiality, of the "predicatable outside."

The ideal reader also would be aware of the limits of Lacanian interpretation. For example, in her trenchant assessment of the Lacanian wager in literary criticism, Gayatri Chakravorty Spivak points out its inevitable reductionist tendency—what every system of interpretation ultimately falls prey to. What I am calling the psychoanalytic confrontation with narrative structure, Spivak deftly deflates as "the tropological or narratological crosshatching of a text" in which a "psychoanalytic scenario" (particularly the scene that depicts "access to law through the interdict of the father—the passage into the semiotic triangle of Oedipus") is unfolded, much as any allegorical system of reference is unfolded and revealed through narrative.[5] Spivak's deconstruction makes of Lacanian criticism a rather simple impulse to allegorize. The Lacanian interpretation, then, unable completely to escape the allegorizing tendency, is one that, in rewriting its texts, creates its own texts for analysis (as do other interpretive systems) and then elaborates itself through its own creations in what constitutes a critical act of doubling. Text and hermeneutics, while separate, are mirror images of each other. Yet the privilege that Lacanian interpretation grants to itself, while theoretically reversible, is not a naive one, either. It represents a subtle strategy implemented precariously in support of intelligibility and intended, as Spivak has it, to give "us a little more turning room to play in" (226) than we would have with a criticism based solely on Derridian deconstruction. In the age of Lacan and Derrida the only alternative to granting this critical "turning room" is to efface the difference between literary text and interpretation and to risk "a perpetual deconstruction . . . of the distinction between the two" (225)—in effect, to lock the door on all commentary and explanation. Theoretical sophistication, and a measure of special privilege, make of Lacanian criticism "so abject a thing as an instrument of intelligibility" (226)—not a single dimension of truth, but a process of knowing: not the stasis of revealed knowledge, but the activity of imperfect analysis.

When Lacanian criticism is thrown into such doubt theoretically, however, it emerges still useful as a mode of critical thought. Lacanian criticism elaborates what Lacan calls the imaginary relations within a text, formal oppositions and unconscious operations that comprise the structure of narrative. It does so toward the end of demonstrating a text's particular articulation of the symbolic father, an articulation that is never a presence within the text, but is always a virtual (never-to-be-accomplished) aim of narrative. Hence, all narratives must in some sense fail. And of course the interpretive system that attempts to inspect its double in the "dilatory space" (Peter Brooks' phrase) of the text is itself dilatory: the never-to-be-realized symbolic father is analyzed within the never-to-be-concluded relations of the imaginary. However, we can bring our own privileged deconstruction to this indeterminate critical activity, and we find a familiar theme of psychoanalysis—the drive of the pleasure principle and its modulation by the reality principle. The "desire" of Lacanian interpretation, like that in any text, seeks complete satisfaction in its object (the mother). But because it meets the resistance of imaginary relations, it must seek satisfaction in segments, according to a paternal formula, and in time. The attempt to work through such obstacles is not critical dawdling, but the process of negotiating the gap between need and demand and

of binding desire to the law, to the father. Historically, the great alternative to such binding is the spectre of the unchecked death wish in
the ultimate merger of subject and object, desire and law, self and the
natural world. In contemporary criticism this quintessential romantic
tendency (the great theme of romantic poetry) can be seen in Gilles
Deleuze and Felix Guattari's *Anti-Oedipus: Capitalism and Schizophrenia*, wherein the unveiling of a Dionysian "flux" and "flow"
supplants the activity of analysis. The historical moment, according to
this view, has arrived in which the authority of repression has been
rescinded, and we all may be liberated as the figure of the father topples over, and the fallen regime of hegemony no longer blocks the flux
and flow of revealed truth.[6]

However, in the Western tradition, and for most contemporary
commentators, the dilatory space is generally valorized in the term
"love." Juliet Flower MacCannell uses the word in this sense when she
describes the narrative subject as existing "by virtue of love's lending it
the imaginary space, the temporal extension that desire would otherwise usurp."[7] In the consideration of narrative structure, it must
follow that love exists within the subjectivity the father makes possible
and, hence, comes ultimately from the father (I asked earlier, "What
does it mean for the father to be the subject of a narrative?"). Love
(and desire) seeks the mother through the rule of its own operation.
Our ideal reader, I think, would see this set of relationships and the
operation of repression not as sexist and hegemonic, but as one statement of the conditions under which narrative and discourse exist.

And finally, the ideal reader of this book is not (necessarily) a Lacanian at all, but a reader who sees that a discussion of the father
useful to literary criticism must find a way to escape the prison-house
of particularity by moving from an image of the father to his meaning
in symbolism, that is to say, from fathers to the Father. The critical
gaze that encompasses the fathers and the Father is, strictly speaking,
an apocalyptic view of beginnings and ends and of the complete identity of the Father. Who can know him? And yet meaning does exist in a
world of signification and discourse. Father figures may seem to
march along discretely in time, but desire for the father's function
transcends every order of succession. And though we grant the limitations of knowledge about the father (and of Lacanian criticism as a

hermeneutics), we can see that the separation of image and symbol (of Lacan's imaginary and symbolic) is a condition of narrative, and of experience in time, whereby the father must be known imperfectly. Each manifestation is simultaneously a repetition and a new orientation to him. The means for breaking out of the prison of particular knowledge about the father must be found in the textual relationship that tunnels between Lacan's imaginary and symbolic orders. Homer's dictum, for example, "It's a wise child that knows its own father," indicates a passage between the imaginary and the symbolic, for implicit in the statement is the assumption that to be in the parent-child relationship by being a child is to be in a relationship where one has knowledge of the father. The child does not have to go a step further by becoming the father to gain knowledge. But, rather, by remaining in childhood and respecting castration (perpetually), the child gains knowledge of another whom he or she cannot and need not supplant in order to know. The child *is* an orientation to knowledge, and the child's only fulfillment rests in that essentially narrative relationship—according to a "bond," as Cordelia said of her tie to Lear— that the father makes possible. The son remains a son even as he repeats his father's sonship when he has a child of his own.

Psychoanalysis shows that to know the father means taking the position of the child, in fact being the dependent child that one is in relation to the text. One comes to literary texts to find and take hold of the father. One soon discovers that his symbolic function cannot be possessed, but it can be accepted as a gift, one to be received as an orientation from the text and toward the symbol, and for which one assumes a castration debt in relationship. In narration (relationship) as one reads (lives), one can pay the debt of being in discourse only by thereafter assuming more debt, and ever more debt in order continually to replay the drama of "passage into the semiotic triangle of Oedipus." In this activity direct (what Lacan calls "real") knowledge of the father, like knowledge of the mother, is outside of articulation and impossible, as signification begins with absence. In the imaginary relations of the text, where absence, opposition, and discourse converge, the paternal gift makes narration an ever present possibility.

Notes

Introduction

1 Anthony Wilden, *The Language of the Self: The Function of Language in Psycho-analysis* (Baltimore: The Johns Hopkins Press, 1968).

2 John T. Irwin, *Doubling and Incest/Repetition and Revenge: A Speculative Reading of Faulkner* (Baltimore: The Johns Hopkins Press, 1975).

3 See my "Post-Modern Paternity: Donald Barthelme's *The Dead Father,*" *Delta* (Montpellier) 8 (May 1979):127–140; "*Other Voices, Other Rooms* and the Ocularity of American Fiction," *Delta* 11 (forthcoming); "The Symbolic Father in Yoknapatawpha County," *The Journal of Narrative Technique* 10, 1 (Winter 1980):39–55, and the soon-to-be-completed *The Paternal Romance: The Father in Fiction.* See, also, my "Critical Introduction: The Family in Literature," *Arizona Quarterly* 36 (Spring 1980):5–19 for a Freudian interpretation of the father and the family as structures in literature.

4 "Postscript" in *The Odyssey: Homer,* trans. Robert Fitzgerald (Garden City: Anchor Books, 1963), p. 494.

5 *Homer: The Odyssey,* trans. Robert Fitzgerald (Garden City: Doubleday, 1961), p. 20. Subsequent references to the epic (except for the one reference to the E. V. Rieu translation) will be to this edition and will be noted in the text.

6 *Homer: The Odyssey,* trans. E. V. Rieu (Baltimore: Penguin Books, 1946), p. 30.

7 H. J. Rose, *A Handbook of Greek Mythology* (London: Methuen, 1965), p. 238.

8 Jacques Lacan, *The Four Fundamental Concepts of Psycho-analysis,* ed. Jacques-Alain Miller and trans. Alan Sheridan (New York: W. W. Norton, 1978), p. 29.

9 Irwin, *Doubling and Incest/Repetition and Revenge,* p. 133.

10 Lacan, *The Four Fundamental Concepts of Psycho-analysis,* p. 191.

11 J. Laplanche and J.-B. Pontalis, *The Language of Psycho-analysis,* trans. Donald Nicholson-Smith (New York: W. W. Norton, 1973), p. 407.

12 Laplanche and Pontalis, *The Language of Psycho-analysis,* p. 286.

13 Jacques Lacan, "Desire and the Interpretation of Desire in *Hamlet,*" *Yale French Studies* 55/56 (1977): 42.

14 Lacan quoted in Anika Lemaire, *Jacques Lacan,* trans. David Macey (London and Boston: Routledge and Kegan Paul, 1977), p. 85.

15   Peter Brooks, "Freud's Masterplot: Questions of Narrative," *Yale French Studies*
     55/56 (1977): 295.

16   Lacan, "Desire and the Interpretation of Desire in *Hamlet*," p. 44.

17   John Burnaby, *Augustine: Later Works* (Philadelphia: Westminster Press, 1955),
     p. 20.

18   Burnaby, *Augustine: Later Works*, p. 20.

19   For the theory of zero in relation to integers, see Anthony Wilden's discussion of
     Frege in *System and Structure: Essays in Communication and Exchange* (London:
     Tavistock Publications, 1972), pp. 178–88.

20   Jacques Lacan, "Of Structure as an Inmixing of an Otherness Prerequisite to Any
     Subject Whatever," *The Language of Criticism and the Sciences of Man: The
     Structuralist Controversy*, ed. Richard Macksey and Eugenio Donato (Baltimore
     and London: The Johns Hopkins Press, 1970), p. 190.

21   Laplanche and Pontalis, *The Language of Psycho-analysis*, p. 8.

22   For a clear explanation of the distinction between need, demand, and desire, see
     Alan Sheridan's note in Lacan, *The Four Fundamental Concepts of Psycho-analy-
     sis*, pp. 278–79.

23   Wilden, *The Language of the Self*, p. 187.

1   Paternity and the Subject in *Bleak House*

1   Lacan's work is available to readers of English in *Écrits: A Selection*, trans. Alan
    Sheridan (New York: W. W. Norton, 1977). *Écrits* was published in French by
    Éditions du Seuil in 1966. There is also *The Four Fundamental Concepts of
    Psycho-analysis*, ed. Jacques-Alain Miller and trans. Alan Sheridan (New York:
    W. W. Norton, 1978). Useful commentaries in English are the following: Anthony
    Wilden, *The Language of the Self* (Baltimore: The Johns Hopkins Press, 1968);
    Anika Lemaire, *Jacques Lacan*, trans. David Macey (London: Routledge and
    Kegan Paul, 1977); Rosalind Coward and John Ellis, "On the Subject of Lacan," in
    *Language and Materialism: Developments in Semiology and the Theory of the
    Subject* (London: Routledge and Kegan Paul, 1977), chapter 6.

2   For most readers of the novel, the two narratives are separated by a "gulf . . .
    greater than can be bridged by any connection" (G. Armour Craig, "The Unpoetic
    Compromise," *Twentieth Century Interpretations of* Bleak House, ed. Jacob Korg
    [Englewood Cliffs, N.J.: Prentice-Hall, 1968], p. 60). And most readers too have
    objected to what one calls Esther's "coy self-consciousness" (Leonard W. Deen,
    "Style and Unity in *Bleak House*," [in Korg, p. 54], although Deen sees a unifying
    power in the "theme and satiric intention" of the novel [Korg, p. 55]). Robert A.
    Donovan argues that Esther provides a unifying "system of moral values" (Korg,
    p. 44).

3   Reading *Bleak House* in the light of some Lacanian interpretations of Freud has
    left me with some cautions to issue. I am not attempting to systematize Lacan's
    thought or even to explicate it. I have imported into my understanding of the novel
    certain Lacanian-Freudian concepts that seem relevant and explanatory. How true

this conjunction of ideas may remain to psychoanalytic theory, and particularly to its Lacanian development, I leave to others to judge. To English-speaking readers, Lacan's thought and style, even in the translated forms that most will rely on, seem at times obscure, at times elliptical, and at all times difficult.

4   The passages quoted are from Coward and Ellis, *Language and Materialism*, p. 111. I want to acknowledge here my particular debt to these writers.

5   The paternal metaphor has for so long served to designate the means whereby the individual enters culture that it seems to be necessary to human culture as Western thought understands it. Perhaps the metaphor will continue to serve and the familial source of individuality continue to be valued, though a critical awareness of the adoption of sexual roles no doubt will modify these judgments.

2   "The Captive King": The Absent Father in Melville's Text

1   References will be made to the following editions: *Redburn: His First Voyage* (New York: Russell and Russell, 1963), hereafter referred to as *R*. *White Jacket: or The World in a Man-of-War* (New York: Russell and Russell, 1963), hereafter referred to as *WJ*. *Moby Dick*, ed. H. Hayford and Hershel Parker (New York: W. W. Norton, 1978), hereafter referred to as *MD*. *Pierre: or, The Ambiguities*, ed. Henry A. Murray (1949; New York: Hendricks House, 1957), hereafter referred to as *P*. *The Confidence-Man*, ed. Hershel Parker (New York: W.W. Norton, 1971), hereafter referred to as *CM*.

2   The question of the metaphor is expanded in my book, *Melville, Signes et Métaphores* (Lausanne: L'Age d'Homme, 1980).

3   I am referring here to Jacques Lacan's *Écrits* (Paris: Editions du Seuil, 1966), and especially to "The Signification of the Phallus" and to "On a possible treatment of psychosis," and also to the article by J. Laplanche and M. Leclaire, "The Unconscious: A Psychoanalytic Study," *Yale French Studies* 48 (1973).

4   Reference should be made here to Michel Serres' seminal work, and in the present instance to *La Naissance de la Physique dans le texte de Lucrèce, Fleuves et Turbulences* (Paris: Editions de Minuit, 1977). This chapter owes much to him. For a mention of his work and a related study of the concept of "cataract," see Jeffrey Mehlman, "Cataract: Diderot's Discursive Politics, 1749–1751," *Glyph* 2 (Baltimore: The Johns Hopkins Press, 1978).

5   The fragment was first published by Elizabeth Foster in her edition of *The Confidence-Man*. Bruce Franklin's reading, slightly different, is used here (New York: Bobbs-Merrill, 1967).

6   Gilles Deleuze, *Difference et Repetition* (Paris: Presses Universitaires de France, 1969), p. 147.

7   Most notably by Edgar Dryden, *Melville's Thematics of Form: The Great Art of Telling the Truth* (Baltimore: The Johns Hopkins Press, 1968).

8   Deleuze, *Difference et Repetition*, pp. 151–52.

9   For this, see John Irwin's excellent essay on Faulkner, *Doubling and Incest/Repetition and Revenge* (Baltimore: The Johns Hopkins Press, 1975). And of course,

René Girard's fundamental studies, most recently *Des choses cachées depuis la fondation du monde* (Paris: Grasset, 1978).

10 Thematically, *Billy Budd* would appear to belong to a study of the absent father in Melville. However, my view is that structurally and fictionally it does not and that it invites quite different considerations. To demonstrate this here would have required too much space. See my book *Melville, Signes et Métaphores* (Lausanne: L'Age d'Homme, 1980), in particular: "Deuxiéme partie: Jeux de l'imaginaire et du symbolique, 2—'Le scandale de la totalité perdue: *Billy Budd.*' "

3 A Clown's Inquest into Paternity: Fathers, Dead or Alive, in *Ulysses* and *Finnegans Wake*

1 From Robert Georgin, foreword to *Lacan*, Cahiers Cistre No. 3 (Lausanne: L'Age d'Homme, 1977), pp. 15–16.

2 James Joyce, *Finnegans Wake* (London: Faber and Faber, 1939, 1968), p. 135, line 26.

3 James Joyce, *Ulysses* (London: The Bodley Head, reprinted 1949), p. 16. Hereafter, this text is referred to as *U*.

4 Joyce wrote "Fusione di Bloom e Stephen" in the scheme he sent to Linati; see Richard Ellmann, *Ulysses on the Liffey* (London: Faber and Faber, 1972), who reproduces it in the appendix, n. pag.

5 For Jacques Lacan, "the real is impossible" and I use the term "impossible" in the same way; see Jacques Lacan, *Écrits: A Selection*, trans. Alan Sheridan (London: Tavistock Publications, 1977), passim.

6 James Joyce, *Letters, Volume Two*, ed. Richard Ellmann (London: Faber and Faber, 1966), p. 101, letter dated 29 July 1905.

7 See the excellent article by Jane Ford, "Why Is Milly in Mullingar?" *James Joyce Quarterly* 14, 4 (Summer 1977): 436–49.

8 Don Gifford and Robert J. Seidman quote that song in *Notes for Joyce: An Annotation of James Joyce's Ulysses* (New York: Dutton, 1974), p. 248.

9 See Ellmann, *Ulysses on the Liffey*: "Notte Alta" refers to "Ulisse (Bloom)" and "Alba (dawn)" to "Telemaco (Stephen)."

10 James Joyce, *A Portrait of the Artist as a Young Man: Text, Criticism and Notes*, ed. Chester G. Anderson (1916; New York: Viking Critical Library, 1968). Hereafter, this text is referred to as *P*.

11 Jacques Lacan, *Écrits*, pp. 20–25, 66–68, and 81–87.

12 James Joyce, *Letters: Volume Two*, pp. 107–08. This letter is dated 18 (September) 1905, thus posterior to the fragment referred to in note 6. According to the letter, after the "mystical" identification, without a name all resemblance vanishes. But Joyce had to be made aware of the fictive nature of paternity before choosing a name. For Lucia's name the situation will be quite different.

13 Jacques Lacan, *Écrits*, p. 149.

14 The nationalistic Citizen had thrown at Bloom such a tin of Jacob's biscuits, from the Dublin biscuit manufactory owned by W. and R. Jacobs.

15 I developed that point in "Lapsus ex machina," *Poetique* 26 (1976): 152–72. See also "L'infini et la castration" in *Scilicet* 4 (1973): 75–133, and more generally the texts of Daniel Sibony, particularly *L'Autre incastrable* (Paris: Seuil, 1978).

16 Freud published his paper on family romances as part of Otto Rank's *Der Mythus von der Geburt des Helden*, 1909, translated into English in 1914.

17 For Lacan, "L'Inconscient est le discours de l'Autre," the big or capitalized Other being first the silent place of the analyst. See *Écrits* pp. 312–15, and also *Écrits* (Paris: Seuil, 1966); especially the Schema L, p. 53.

18 Lacan distinguishes between the phallus, as symbol of the lack or of castration, and the anatomical reality of the penis; see *Écrits*, pp. 281–91.

19 The *Portrait* already plays on this theme: "—So we must distinguish between elliptical and ellipsoidal. . . . What price ellipsoidal balls! Chase me, ladies, I'm in the cavalry!" (*P*, pp. 191–92).

20 Stanislaus Joyce, *My Brother's Keeper: James Joyce's Early Years*, ed. R. Ellmann (New York: Viking Press, 1958), p. 69, my italics.

21 Sigmund Freud, *Jokes and their Relation to the Unconscious* (1905), trans. James Strachey (London: Routledge and Kegan Paul, 1966), p. 37.

22 "Pool the begg" alludes to Poolbeg, from Poll Beag, "little hole," the lighthouse at the bar of Dublin Harbour.

23 Jacques Lacan, *Écrits*, p. 199.

24 See P. W. Joyce, *A Short History of Ireland from the Earliest Times to 1608* (London: Longmans, Green and Co., 1893), chapter 7, "The laws of compensation and distress," pp. 47–55, and chapter 8, "Grades and Groups of Society," pp. 55–60.

25 See also 316.08.

26 Giambattista Vico, *Opere*, ed. Fausto Nicolini (Milano: Napoli Ricciardi Editore, 1953); I use his *Principi di Scienza Nuova*, pp. 365–905, hereafter *SN*, which I quote by the number of the paragraph to allow for easy identification.

27 Giambattista Vico, *Opere*, section 5, "Politica Poetica," chapter 1, pp. 622–35, chapter 2, pp. 635–47 (§582–618).

28 See Richard Ellmann, *James Joyce* (London: Oxford University Press, 1966), p. 411, for a clear summary.

29 Ibid.

30 I am indebted to Petr Skrabanek's list of Slavonic words in the *Wake:* "Slavansky Slavar," in *A Wake Newslitter* 9, 4 (August 1972): 51–68. I also thank my brothers, whose fluency in Russian proved a great help in the deciphering of several obscure passages.

31 According to Richard Ellmann's "Joyce's Library in 1920," in *The Consciousness of Joyce* (London: Faber and Faber, 1977), appendix, p. 131.

32 Brendan O Hehir, *A Gaelic Lexicon for Finnegans Wake and Glossary for Joyce's Other Works* (Berkeley and Los Angeles: University of California Press, 1967), p. 182.

33 This is the theory of "early bisectualism" which *Finnegans Wake* develops on

pp. 523–24 and which has never been fully commented upon. The most obvious reference is to Freud, *Three Essays on the Theory of Sexuality* (London: The Hogarth Press, 1966), volume 7, p. 125.

34 See Franklin Walton, "Wilde at the Wake," *James Joyce Quarterly* 14, 3 (Spring 1977):300–12.

35 John T. Noonan, Jr., *Contraception: A History of Its Treatment by the Catholic Theologians and Canonists* (Cambridge: Harvard University Press, 1966), p. 91.

36 See Margot Norris, *The Decentered Universe of Finnegans Wake: A Structuralist Analysis* (Baltimore: The Johns Hopkins Press, 1976), p. 104 and passim.

37 Joyce plays on the famous misspelling of the word "hesitancy" as "hesitency" by Pigott, one of Parnell's accusers; see James S. Atherton, *The Books at the Wake* (London: Faber and Faber, 1959), pp. 102–03.

38 "It is also the defence and indictment of the book itself," *Letters: Volume One*, ed. Stuart Gilbert (London: Faber and Faber, 1957), p. 406.

39 Stanislaus Joyce, *The Complete Dublin Diary*, ed. George H. Healey (Ithaca: Cornell University Press, 1971), hereafter *DD*.

40 These terms are borrowed from Otto Rank, though with quite a different emphasis; see Jean Kimball, "James Joyce and Otto Rank: the Incest Motif in *Ulysses*," *James Joyce Quarterly* 13, 3 (Spring 1976):366–79.

41 Jacques Mercanton, *Les Heures de James Joyce* (Lausanne: L'Age d'Homme, 1967), p. 36.

42 James Joyce, *Letters: Volume One*, p. 237.

43 Stanislaus Joyce, *My Brother's Keeper*, p. 224.

44 Atherton, *The Books at the Wake*, p. 31.

45 See Lacan's various interpretations of that expression in *Écrits*, pp. 128, 171, 299, 313–14.

46 James Atherton lists the references to the meeting of Moses with God: *The Books at the Wake*, pp. 179–80.

47 Freud's source is Ernst Sellin, *Mose und seine Bedeutung fur die israelitisch-judische Religionsgeschechte* (Werner Scholl: Leipzig Erlangen, 1922), p. 16 and passim. His main arguments in *Moses and Monotheism: Three Essays* (London: The Hogarth Press, 1966), volume 23, pp. 7–137, are based on Sellin's book.

48 I would like to qualify in this way the many relevant suggestions to be found in Helmut Bonheim's analysis of the father in *Finnegans Wake*, in *Joyce's Benefictions* (Berkeley and Los Angeles: University of California Press, 1964).

49 Ellmann, *James Joyce*, p. 737.

50 Ibid., p. 180. John Joyce agreed reluctantly and once only!

51 Ibid., p. 755.

4 Fathers in Faulkner

1 *Mosquitoes* (New York: Boni and Liveright, 1927), p. 320.

2 *Soldiers' Pay* (New York: Liveright, 1926), p. 230.

3 "Appendix: Compson 1699–1945," in *The Sound and the Fury* (New York: Vin-

tage Books, 1967), p. 424. The Compson Appendix was first published in the Viking *Portable Faulkner* edited by Malcolm Cowley in 1946.

4   *As I Lay Dying* (New York: Random House, 1964), p. 202.

5   *Pylon* (New York: Smith and Haas, 1935), p. 20.

6   *Go Down, Moses* (New York: Random House, 1942), p. 308.

7   *Light in August* (New York: Smith and Haas, 1932), p. 450.

8   John T. Irwin, *Doubling and Incest/Repetition and Revenge: A Speculative Reading of Faulkner* (Baltimore and London: The Johns Hopkins Press, 1976), p. 103. Though it deals almost exclusively with *The Sound and the Fury* and *Absalom, Absalom!*, Irwin's is beyond doubt the most provocative essay on the question of fatherhood in Faulkner's fiction.

9   From Medieval Latin *patronus*, patron, patron saint; from Latin, defender, advocate; from *pater*, chief, father.

10 "Group Psychology and the Analysis of the Ego," in *The Standard Edition of the Complete Psychological Works of Sigmund Freud*, ed. and trans. James Strachey (London: The Hogarth Press, 1955), chapter 18 (p. 105). All further references to Freud are to this edition, hereafter cited as *SE*.

11 In "The Ego and the Id," Freud argues that identification with the father "takes place earlier than any object cathexis" (*SE*, chapter 19 [p. 31]); in "Group Psychology and the Analysis of the Ego," he points out that it "helps to prepare the way" for the Oedipus complex (*SE*, chapter 18 [p. 105]). In "The Dissolution of the Oedipus Complex," however, the emphasis falls on the identification with the father, or rather with the father's authority that *follows* the Oedipal crisis (*SE*, chapter 19 [pp. 176–77]). A distinction should no doubt be made between the global, undifferentiated pre-Oedipal identification and the later, partial identification which leads to the formation of the superego. Yet Freud's statements on the subject are obviously not quite consistent. For a full discussion of the problem of identification, see "Freud et le complexe d'Oedipe," René Girard, *La Violence et le Sacré* (Paris: Bernard Grasset, 1972), pp. 235–64.

12 See "The Ego and the Id," in *SE*, chapter 19 (p. 33).

13 Marie-Cecile and Edmond Ortigues, *Oedipe Africain* (Paris: Plon, 1973), p. 390. My translation.

14 Jacques Lacan, *Écrits* (Paris: Seuil, 1966), p. 278. For the name-of-the-father as "the signifier of the function of the father," see also "D'une question préliminaire à tout traitement possible de la psychose," *Écrits*, pp. 531–83. For the notion of the dead father, see Lacan, "Le Mythe individuel du névrosé" (Paris, 1953, mimeographed), and Guy Rosolato's two essays, "Du Père" and "Trois générations d'hommes dans le mythe religieux et la généalogie," in *Essais sur le symbolique* (Paris: Gallimard, 1969), pp. 36–58, 59–96.

15 See Eugene D. Genovese, *Roll, Jordan Roll: The World the Slaves Made* (New York: Random House, 1974), pp. 73–75, 133–49, and passim.

16 Despite the gallantry of the Southern armies, the experience of defeat could hardly fail to damage the Southern male self-image. On the other hand, the Civil War had taught Southern women to take many responsibilities which had previously been

considered outside their "sphere," and this change in social roles was bound to alter their sense of themselves in relation to their husbands and fathers. On this point, see Anne Firor Scott's fine study, *The Southern Lady: From Pedestal to Politics 1830–1930* (Chicago: University of Chicago Press, 1970).

17   *Sartoris* (New York: Harcourt, Brace and Company, 1929), pp. 1–2. The opening of *Sartoris* is unquestionably superior to that of *Flags in the Dust,* and it seems safe to assume that the improvement is due to authorial rather than editorial revision.

18   The first full discussion of myth-making in *Sartoris* was Olga W. Vickery's in *The Novels of William Faulkner* (Baton Rouge: Louisiana State University Press, 1959), pp. 15–27.

19   *Sartoris*, p. 23.

20   On the function of prestige in Faulkner's fiction, see Michel Gresset, "La Tyrannie du Regard ou la Relation Absolue: Origine, émergence et persistance d'une problématique du mal dans l'oeuvre de William Faulkner" (Diss., Paris-Sorbonne, 1976), pp. 320–44.

21   The only exception is the Colonel's son, Bayard II, in Faulkner's later Sartoris novel, *The Unvanquished* (1938).

22   On Bayard's largely unconscious relation to the Sartoris myth, see Dieter Meindl, *Bewusstsein als Schicksal: Zu Struktur und Entwicklung von William Faulkners Generationenromanen* (Stuttgart: Metzler, 1974), pp. 11–30.

23   On Bayard's ambivalent relationship to his brother, see Ralph Page, "John Sartoris: Friend or Foe," *Arizona Quarterly* 23 (Spring 1967):27–33, and Meindl, *Bewusstsein als Schicksal,* pp. 14–30.

24   *Sartoris*, p. 380.

25   Ibid.

26   Ibid., p. 375.

27   The following analysis of the father-son relationship in *The Sound and the Fury* is in part a recapitulation and reformulation of my essay, "Noces Noires, Noces Blanches: Le jeu du desir et de la mort dans le monologue de Quentin Compson," *Recherches Anglaises et Nord-Americaines* (Strasbourg) 6 (1973):142–69; rev. and trans. in *The Most Splendid Failure: Faulkner's The Sound and the Fury* (Bloomington: Indiana University Press, 1976), pp. 90–120.

28   *Faulkner in the University: Class Conferences at the University of Virginia, 1957–58,* ed. Frederick L. Gwynn and Joseph L. Blotner (Charlottesville: University of Virginia Press, 1959), p. 3.

29   Psychologically and even physically, Jason is his mother's son, and in social terms he sees himself as a Bascomb rather than as an aristocratic Compson.

30   *The Sound and the Fury* (New York: Cape and Smith, 1929), p. 93.

31   See *The Most Splendid Failure,* p. 114.

32   *Faulkner in the University,* p. 3.

33   See "Appendix," pp. 406–11.

34   See *The Sound and the Fury,* p. 93.

35   See *The Most Splendid Failure,* pp. 175–206.

36   *As I Lay Dying* and *Sanctuary,* the two novels published between *The Sound and*

the Fury and *Light in August,* are less directly concerned with fatherhood and, therefore, are not discussed in this essay. In *As I Lay Dying,* the paternal role is taken over by Addie, the phallic mother. *Sanctuary* depicts a lawless society in which fatherhood either is reduced to abject helplessness (Pap, the blind old man) or is perverted into lurid parody ("Daddy" Popeye).

37   As Cleanth Brooks does in *William Faulkner: The Yoknapatawpha Country* (New Haven and London: Yale University Press, 1963), pp. 52–55.

38   See *Light in August,* p. 331.

39   Apart from Christmas, the more memorable *pharmakos* figures in Faulkner's fiction are Benjy and Quentin Compson (*The Sound and the Fury*), Darl Bundren (*As I Lay Dying*), Goodwin (*Sanctuary*), Roger Shumann (*Pylon*), Charles Bon (*Absalom, Absalom!*), and the "crucified" corporal in *A Fable.*

40   Joel Kovel, *White Racism: A Psychohistory* (New York: Vintage Books, 1970), pp. 68–79 and passim.

41   In Freudian terms, the word "solution" is hardly appropriate in this context, for racism has never "solved" anything; "representation" seems to me to be a much better word.

42   Kovel, *White Racism,* pp. 71–72.

43   See John L. Longley, *The Tragic Mask: A Study of Faulkner's Heroes* (Chapel Hill: University of North Carolina Press, 1963), pp. 193–95.

44   See Freud, *Totem and Taboo* (1913), in *SE,* chapter 13, pp. 1–161.

45   John T. Irwin's useful distinction between the brother seducer (a surrogate of the son) and the brother avenger (a surrogate of the father) finds here another illustration. The murder of Christmas by Percy Grimm belongs to the same pattern as the murder of Charles Bon by Henry in *Absalom, Absalom!* That Christmas and Grimm are fraternal figures is suggested by the two striving and blending faces which Hightower contemplates in his final vision (see *Light in August,* pp. 465–66).

46   See *Light in August,* pp. 363–64.

47   *Light in August,* p. 414.

48   *Light in August,* pp. 437–39.

49   This negative concept of God appears as well in *Sartoris, Absalom, Absalom!, The Wild Palms, The Hamlet,* and *Go Down, Moses.* It is probably closer to the "evil God" of Greek tragedy than to the wrathful Jehovah of the Old Testament. On this point, see Paul Ricoeur, "Le Dieu méchant et la vision 'tragique' de l'existence," in *Finitude et culpabilité: La symbolique du mal* (Paris: Aubier, 1960), volume II, pp. 199–217.

50   *Light in August,* p. 191.

51   For a discussion of the patriarchal order and its degeneracy, see Franklin G. Burroughs, Jr., "God the Father and Motherless Children: *Light in August,*" *Twentieth Century Literature* 19 (July 1973): 189–202.

52   This place is a son's place, which accounts to some extent for Joanna's bisexuality. Physiologically her sex is female; in genealogical terms it is male.

53   *Light in August,* p. 465.

54 In his preoccupation with a heroic past, Hightower resembles the Sartorises, yet while young Bayard is still capable of an active identification, Hightower turns the heroic ideal into an object for aesthetic contemplation.

55 See *Light in August*, p. 57.

56 See *Light in August*, p. 452.

57 *Light in August*, p. 461.

58 In point of fact, Milly Hines is allowed by her father to die. With Joanna and Hightower's wife, she is one of the female victims of the fanatical "idealism" of men.

59 *Light in August*, pp. 236–37.

60 See *Light in August*, p. 437.

61 See Frank R. Giordano, Jr., "*Absalom, Absalom!* as a Portrait of the Artist," in *From Irving to Steinbeck: Studies of American Literature in Honor of Harry R. Warfel*, ed. Motley Deakin and Peter Lisca (Gainesville: University of Florida Press, 1972), pp. 97–107. See also François Pitavy's full and fine discussion of *Absalom, Absalom!* in "William Faulkner romançier, 1929–1939" (Diss., Paris-Sorbonne, 1978), pp. 393–639, esp. pp. 619–39.

62 As Mr. Compson notes, 'it must have been Henry who seduced Judith, not Bon" (*Absalom, Absalom!*, New York: Random House, 1936), p. 99.

63 According to Mr. Compson, Henry identifies with both Bon and Judith: "In fact, perhaps this is the pure and perfect incest: the brother realizing that the sister's virginity must be destroyed in order to have existed at all, taking that virginity in the person of the brother-in-law, the man whom he would be if he could become, metamorphose into, the lover, the husband; by whom he would be despoiled, choose for despoiler, if he could become, metamorphose into the sister, the mistress, the bride" (*Absalom, Absalom!*, p. 96).

64 See Irwin, *Doubling and Incest/Repetition and Revenge*, pp. 28–30.

65 *Faulkner in the University*, p. 275.

66 *Absalom, Absalom!*, p. 89.

67 See Freud, *SE*, chapter 9, pp. 237–41.

68 *Faulkner in the University*, p. 3.

70 The Greek verb *arkhein* means at once to begin, to rule, to command—verbs of the father.

71 *Absalom, Absalom!*, pp. 8–9.

72 *Absalom, Absalom!*, p. 262.

73 *Absalom, Absalom!*, p. 237.

74 It is worth noting that in "Family Romances" Freud illustrates his point in terms recalling Sutpen's experience at the planter's mansion: ". . . the child's imagination becomes engaged in the task of getting free from the parents of whom he now has a low opinion and of replacing them by others, who, as a rule, are of a higher social standing. He will make use in this connection of any opportune coincidences from his actual experience, such as his becoming acquainted with the Lord of the Manor or some landed proprietor if he lives in the country or with some member of the aristocracy if he lives in town" (*SE*, chapter 9 [pp. 238–39]).

75 *Absalom, Absalom!*, p. 165.

76   *Absalom, Absalom!*, p. 263.

77   *Absalom, Absalom!*, p. 23.

78   *Absalom, Absalom!*, p. 240.

79   On Ahab and Sutpen, see James Guetti, *The Limits of Metaphor: A Study of Mel-ville, Conrad, and Faulkner* (Ithaca, N.Y.: Cornell University Press, 1967), pp. 82–85, 95, 103.

80   The only evidence to the contrary is Sutpen's outcry in the scene (reconstructed by Quentin and Shreve) of his encounter with Henry during the war: "—Henry . . . —My son" (*Absalom, Absalom!*, p. 353). Sutpen's words closely echo David's in the Bible (cf. 2 Samuel 18:33); yet, contrary to David's, they do not express grief. At this point, it should be remembered, Henry still stands for the hope that Sut-pen's design will be fulfilled.

81   In this respect the father-son relationship in *Absalom, Absalom!* suggests the pre-Oedipal relationship between mother and child, which the father normally is as-sumed to transform into a triangular pattern. Sutpen might also be defined as a phallic mother, gathering in himself all parental attributes, just as Addie Bundren does in *As I Lay Dying*.

82   I borrow the phrase from Quentin Anderson's book, *The Imperial Self: An Essay in Literary and Cultural History* (N.Y.: Random House, 1971). Focusing on Emerson, Whitman, and Henry James, Anderson contends that in their over-emphasis on the claims of the individual self and their utter disregard for the needs of communal life, these writers exemplify a major trend of American culture. While Anderson's study is heavily biased, it provides a number of valid insights into the regressive and narcissistic tendencies of American romanticism and American literature at large. It fails, however, to give proper credit to those Ameri-can writers, from Hawthorne and Melville through Fitzgerald and Faulkner, who have exposed the devastating effects of self-centered "innocence." As a fictional hero, Thomas Sutpen belongs with such strong-willed men of design as Colonel Pyncheon, Hollingsworth, Ahab, and Jay Gatsby. There has been much needless discussion as to Sutpen's representative character, based on the dubious assump-tion that he had to be either a typical Southern planter or a typical non-Southern American. In fact, even though Sutpen lacks the social graces of the gentleman-planter, there can be no question that he embodies to some extent the feudal dream of the ante-bellum South. But this dream, one might argue, was itself a paradoxical version of the American dream, even as the latter was an outgrowth of the Pro-methean fantasies of post-Renaissance Western Culture.

83   Freud, *Moses and Monotheism*, in *SE*, chapter 23 (p. 81).

84   Freud, *Group Psychology and the Analysis of the Ego*, in *SE*, chapter 18 (p. 123).

85   *Faulkner in the University*, p. 35.

86   Significantly, while there are many symbolic and displaced forms of patricide in Faulkner's novels, there is no direct representation of it as in Dostoevski's *Brothers Karamazov*.

87   The paradigm of the ghostly father in Western literature is Hamlet's father, mur-dered "in the blossoms of [his] sin." In terms of sonship and fatherhood, the arche-

types of Faulkner's fiction seem to be Hamlet and his father rather than Oedipus and Laius. Oedipus had no complex: he killed his father, married his mother, and then paid the debt. Hamlet commits neither patricide nor incest, though he is obsessed by both. Contrary to that of Oedipus, his is the tragedy of unfulfilled desire and of the unpaid debt. Consider Faulkner's guilt-ridden and helpless sons: they are all Hamlets.

88 The two most prominent characters in *Go Down, Moses* are the white Isaac McCaslin and the black Lucas Beauchamp, both descended from the same ancestor. It is interesting to note that they are opposites. One repudiates his patrimony, the other claims it. And while Isaac has (too) many fathers, Lucas, Carothers McCaslin's black grandson, "who fathered himself, intact and complete, contemptuous, as old Carothers must have been, of all blood black white yellow or red, including his own" (*Go Down, Moses,* p. 118), is paradoxically the first of Faulkner's heirs to identify with the ancestor in such a way as to become his re-embodiment, i.e., his own father.

89 In every possible aspect the two cultures are shown to be opposed diametrically. The first is—or rather was—a tribal hunter culture in which man and beast and man and earth are united by mystical ties; the second has developed into an agrarian society based on private ownership and exploitation of the land. Indian religion is founded on animism; white religion centers on the otherworldly transcendence of a single God. Most important, in totemic brotherhood the bond which unites the brothers is not blood kinship, but is symbolic kinship through common veneration for the same totem, the same ancestor spirit. Contrary to vulgar assumptions, the difference between the two worlds is not the difference between "nature" and "civilization." The point is that while one society was ruled by law of *symbolic exchange*, the other is not and tends to reduce all relationships to monetary transactions. As can be seen from Ike's dealings with the descendants of his grandfather's slaves, even he is incapable of envisioning another mode of relationship. Ike indeed has missed the point: his initiation is a failure, for he has reversed its true meaning (i.e., the passage from nature to culture) and sentimentalized it into a romantic return to a pristine wilderness. Ironically enough, he shares the error with most critics of *Go Down, Moses.*

90 Bayard Sartoris in *The Unvanquished,* Charles Mallison in *Intruder in the Dust,* Lucius Priest in *The Reivers.*

91 See *A Fable* (New York: Random House, 1954), p. 354. Faulkner made the same statement in his Nobel Prize speech.

92 See Malcolm Cowley, *The Faulkner-Cowley File: Letters and Memories, 1944–1962* (New York: Viking Press, 1966), p. 66.

93 See Joseph Blotner, *Faulkner: A Biography* (New York: Random House, 1974), chapter 1 (p. 105).

94 It is worth recalling, however, that Faulkner felt extremely frustrated about missing the opportunity for heroism provided by World War I.

95 *Author* is related to the past principle *auctus,* of the Latin verb *augere,* to increase; *auctor* designates the increaser, the creator, the founder, and *auctoritas* means

foundation, production, invention (in addition to meaning a right to possession).

96   *Absalom, Absalom!, p.* 150.

97   On the myth of autogenesis in English romanticism, see Leslie Brisman, *Romantic Origins* (Ithaca and London: Cornell University Press, 1978).

98   The reference is to "L'Apres-Midi d'un Faune," Faulkner's first published poem, which appeared in *The New Republic* on August 6, 1919.

99   Cowley, *The Faulkner-Cowley File,* p. 126.

5   The Dead Father in Faulkner

1   Erwin Panofsky, *Studies in Iconology* (New York: Harper and Row, 1962), p. 74.

2   Friedrich Wilhelm Nietzsche, *Philosophy in the Tragic Age of the Greeks,* trans. Marianne Cowan (Chicago: Henry Regnery, 1962), pp. 52–53.

3   *The Sound and the Fury* (New York: Random House, 1946), p. 95. All subsequent quotations from this novel will be shown in the text.

4   *Absalom, Absalom!* (New York: Random House, 1964), Modern Library College Edition, p. 277. All subsequent references to this novel will be shown in the text.

5   Malcolm Cowley, *A Second Flowering* (New York: Viking Press, 1974), p. 143.

6   Wilhelm Stekel, *Compulsion and Doubt,* trans. Emil A. Gutheil (New York: Washington Square Press, 1967), p. 474. Subsequent references to this book will be shown in the text.

7   Guy Rosolato, *Essai sur le symbolique* (Paris: Gallimard, 1969), p. 63. All subsequent quotations from Rosolato are taken from this edition.

8   Julian of Norwich, *The Revelations of Divine Love,* trans. Clifton Wolters (Harmondsworth, Middlesex, England: Penguin Books, 1966), pp. 164–70.

6   Post-Modern Paternity: Donald Barthelme's *The Dead Father*

1   *The Dead Father* (New York: Farrar, Straus, and Giroux, 1975), pp. 3–4. Further page references to this novel will appear in the text.

2   Jacques Lacan, *Écrits: A Selection,* trans. Alan Sheridan (New York: W. W. Norton, 1977), p. 199.

3   Jacques Lacan describes this situation theoretically when he says, "the failure of the signifier in the Other, as locus of the signifier, is the significance of the Other as locus of the law." *Écrits,* p. 221.

4   Roland Barthes, *The Pleasure of the Text,* trans. Richard Miller (New York: Hill and Wang, 1975), p. 10.

5   Barthes, *The Pleasure of the Text,* p. 47.

Epilogue

1   Juliet Mitchell, *Psychoanalysis and Feminism* (New York: Pantheon Books, 1974).

2   Frederic Jameson, "Imaginary and Symbolic in Lacan: Marxism, Psychoanalytic

Criticism, and the Problem of the Subject," *Yale French Studies* 55/56 (1977): 338–95.

3   Rosalind Coward and John Ellis, *Language and Materialism: Developments in Semiology and the Theory of the Subject* (London and Boston: Routledge and Kegan Paul, 1977), p. 7.

4   Coward and Ellis, *Language and Materialism*, pp. 75–76.

5   Gayatri Chakravorty Spivak, "The Letter as Cutting Edge," *Yale French Studies* 55/56 (1977): 222. Subsequent page references will be noted in the text.

6   Gilles Deleuze and Felix Guattari, *Anti-Oedipus: Capitalism and Schizophrenia*, trans. Robert Hurley, Mark Seem, and Helen R. Lane (New York: Viking Press, 1977).

7   Juliet Flower MacCannell, "Nature and Self-Love: A Reinterpretation of Rousseau's 'Passion Primitive,' " *PMLA* 92, 5 (October 1977): 900.

Index